The Politics of

The Politics of Insects

David Cronenberg's Cinema of Confrontation

Scott Wilson

BLOOMSBURY

LONDON • NEW DELHI • NEW YORK • SYDNEY

Bloomsbury Academic
An imprint of Bloomsbury Publishing Plc

175 Fifth Avenue	50 Bedford Square
New York	London
NY 10010	WC1B 3DP
USA	UK

www.bloomsbury.com

First published 2011
Paperback edition published 2013

Library of Congress Cataloging-in-Publication Data
A catalogue record for this book is available from the Library of Congress

ISBN: HB: 978-1-4411-9155-7
PB: 978-1-6235-6339-4

Printed and bound in the United States of America

To Teresa Callaghan

Contents

Acknowledgements

This book emerges as a result of my own long fascination with the cinema of David Cronenberg, and also, in no small part, to the tireless support of my friends and family, often against their better judgement, given the kinds of conversations Cronenberg's films inevitably lead to.

First and foremost, thanks are owed to Teresa Callaghan. Her hard work and continued self-sacrifice in the face of my academic selfishness goes far beyond the bounds of expectation. Hopefully this document stands as partial repayment for her years of dedication and surplus-labor: at the very least it might indicate that we can start watching something else of an evening. No promises, though.

I am grateful to Misha Kavka for her support and encouragement while this book was gestating as a doctoral dissertation. Indeed, I thank her for salvaging this project from the dustbin of history, and for providing both encouragement and discipline, in equal measures, exactly as required.

My editor at Continuum, the entirely fabulous Katie Gallof, has been wonderfully supportive in moving this project through to completion and I am in her debt both for editorial advice and also for suggestions on what to listen to while bringing this all to a close.

I am fortunate to be surrounded by family, friends and colleagues who have all, in their way, helped keep this book alive when, in the face of yet more Body Horror, I might have lessened my resolve. A special thank you to Diana Callaghan, to Carolyn Alexander, Rudd Hughes, Lily Richards and Mark Taylor of Unity Books (New Zealand's foremost independent bookshop!), Carla Seth, Stephen Turner, Sue Lawrie, Lynley Williams, Steve Marshall and Athina Tsoulis. Thanks and much love also to my family and especially to my sister Robyn.

Chapter 1

The Filmmaker as Heretic

Introduction: The Politics of Insects

Midway through David Cronenberg's 1986 remake of *The Fly*, as Seth Brundle (Jeff Goldblum) begins to fully comprehend the accident that will eventually lead to his death, he makes the following statement:

> Have you ever heard of insect politics? Neither have I. Insects . . . don't have politics. They're very brutal. No . . . compassion. No . . . compromise. We can't trust the insect. I'd like to become the first insect politician. (Cronenberg, 1986)

Brundle has, as a result of the telepod mishap that is the film's central event, become the 'Brundlefly', a human-insect amalgam. *The Fly* illustrates Brundle's becoming, his increasing alterity, even as it functions as a discussion of this state and the implications of transformation in general. The full import of Brundle's statement will be dealt with in the next chapter; its use here lies in the way Brundle's wish to become the first insect politician demonstrates the political and philosophical concerns that exist at the centre of what Chris Rodley refers to as 'the Cronenberg Project' (Rodley, 1997, xv). This 'project', so called, is summed up by Rodley (and others) as a continued exploration of transformation as a means of renegotiating the human, both bodily and psychically. Of course, while I agree that Cronenberg's project does do these things, suffice it to say that there is more at work in the cinema of David Cronenberg, not least of which is the way such transformation functions to reveal a host of structures that surround, govern, control and, if need be, punish transformation and the transforming individual.

The distinction that may be made between Brundle's desire and Cronenberg's intentions, as evidenced by his entire filmic output, lies in how the character and the director each view and negotiate the fact of transformation. *The Fly* functions as an essay on a particular form of transformation, and most critical commentary about the film tends to focus on the superficial fact of this activity: *The Fly*, most obviously, details Seth Brundle's physical transformation from Brundle to Brundlefly and, finally, to the human-fly-telepod organism that is his final stage before death. What is often overlooked and yet hinted at by Brundle's dialogue (as scripted by Cronenberg) is the relationship between transformation (in any form) and the host of ideological structures that exist to legislate such transformation. As William Beard explains, Brundle's desire to function as the intermediary between the human and insect must fail

> . . . because insectness is so intractably and horrifyingly evil in human terms that it cannot be mediated. There may be shades of humanity, signified by various degrees of trust, compassion, compromise – but there are no shades of insectness. (Beard, 2001, 220)

Brundle's transformation removes him from the human and takes him to a place from which there can be neither return nor mediation; in so doing, it speaks volumes about both points – the point at which he begins to transform (as human) and our conceptions of the point at which he ends (as non-human). This movement towards a limit point of human experience, especially as it impacts on the ability of the film to represent such movement adequately, is pivotal to Cronenberg's cinema and will be explored in greater detail below.

Despite the pejorative associations that popularly accumulate around the notion of a specifically Cronenbergian transformation, as it occurs in his cinema, transformation qua transformation is, at its very essence, a neutral act. As Cronenberg notes, 'I think that change itself is fairly neutral, but it contains the potential to be either positive or negative' (Kermode, 1992). The act itself only becomes coloured, as it were, when it impacts with the many structures that govern our complex social constructions. Cronenberg further explains,

> It's my conceit that perhaps some diseases perceived as diseases which destroy a well-functioning machine, in fact change the machine into a machine that does something else, and we have to figure out what it is that the machine now does. Instead of having a defective machine, we have a nicely functioning machine that just has a different purpose. (Cronenberg, quoted in Newman, 1988, 116)

Thus Cronenberg's cinema is one of transformation, but – and this is essential – of transformation as it intersects with those legislative and necessarily disciplinary structures that move to limit, control or prevent outright such alterations. Cronenberg's films, therefore, utilize transformation in order to more fully examine the structures that surround the transformative being, that provide it with meaning and, when threatened, move to stop or, at its most extreme, punish it for having transformed. Regardless of any specific articulation in the context of each text, these films highlight the ways in which the beings who inhabit Cronenberg's narratives are disciplined as they attempt their various transformations and because of them.

Every transformation, in the eyes of these disciplinary structures, is a potentially dangerous act in that it offers the subject undergoing transformation possibilities that previously were unavailable – whether forbidden or simply unthinkable. Brundle demonstrates this with his continued transformation away from both the initial position of human and past the relatively stable insect-human hybrid who occupies the central third of the film. Brundle's personal transformation only becomes dangerous when it contravenes the boundaries within which humanity, as it is conceived, can operate. It is dangerous because the very act of Brundle's transformation forces us to recognize the essentially arbitrary nature of those structures that are in place to govern and prevent such changes. To conceive of an insect politics is therefore to begin to imagine a new order of consciousness; one that, for Brundle, does away with compassion and compromise. What Brundle offers is a glimpse of a new social structure and, within that, a new way of imagining the body within the body politic. Brundle's body becomes one version among many of the 'new flesh' celebrated by Cronenberg's films. It is for this reason that

> [i]t has been widely observed that what David Cronenberg 'disturbs' is the institutional: order, systems, rules. His films thematize the transgression of boundaries of all kinds – biological, psychological, emotional, sexual, social and political. (Ramsey & Wilson, 1993/4)

All of Cronenberg's films are concerned not just with transformation but with what happens when transformation becomes transgression. The particular forms these explorations take will be detailed in later chapters, but it is worth noting, even at this early stage, that Cronenberg's own views of transformation are anything but celebratory. As closer examination of the films will reveal, the Cronenbergian hero (a figure whose very existence – or, at least, whose heroism – can and will be disputed) is an ambivalent figure, often passively swept along towards a change she or he can barely comprehend and which, all too often, leads to her or his demise. Similarly, Cronenberg's cinema displays a strong current of anti-transcendentalism which emerges, first, from his continued attempts to trouble and problematize the Cartesian dialectic and, second, in his attempts to explore and critique both the perceived schism between body and mind and any orthodox favouring of the mind over, and at the expense of, the body. Regardless of this, it is an 'unshakeable belief in the unavoidable nature of change (it is neither good nor bad, it simply is) [that] lies at the centre of Cronenberg's cinema' (Kermode, 1992). What remains to be explored is the manner in which Cronenberg's examination of transformation and the disciplinary measures enacted to prevent or punish it become the site from which his continued critique of these disciplinary structures emerges. This drive to critique the actions of the disciplinary and ideological structures that surround, control, censure and punish the individual attempting transformation reveals a specific set of mechanisms at work in both the form and content of Cronenberg's films. Indeed, so comprehensive is Cronenberg's continued attention to these concerns that by charting these shifts and developments across his career it becomes possible, as Robert Koehler indicates, to detect traces of the future director in every work produced (2007). Thus we can conclude that, for Cronenberg, the drive to transform is intimately related to issues of control and claims of and for agency.

The Filmmaker as Heretic

In *On Belief* (2001) Slavoj Žižek discusses the ways in which heresy can be usefully understood in relation to the dominant structure that has outlawed it. He notes that

> . . . in order for an ideological edifice to occupy the hegemonic place and legitimize the existing power relations, it HAS to compromise its founding radical message – and the ultimate 'heretics' are simply those who reject this compromise, sticking to the original message. (Žižek, 2001c, 8)

For Žižek, the heretic's mistake (the action which, once performed, requires that it be labelled heretical) is to take the original interdiction too seriously and 'overconform' to it and thus reveal, first, the dangerous absurdity inherent within it; second, the distance that exists between the 'founding radical message' and the manner with which it is practiced by those who claim to serve and uphold it; and third, the essentially arbitrary nature of the law (as emerging from the 'founding radical message') and thus of the ideological edifice that is supported and consolidated by the law's existence. This heretical impulse reveals, therefore, a 'normal' state of affairs within which

> . . . what makes the Law workable / bearable is an ideological phantasy, a shadowy zone of illicit activities into which even the most law-abiding citizens enter on occasions when it becomes apparent that the Law makes such an ass of itself that for its own sake they must make an exception to it. (Krips, 2004)

Thus, as Žižek explains, much more subversive than actually breaking the law is to '. . . *simply* . . . *do what is allowed*, that is, what the existing order explicitly allows, although it prohibits it at the level of implicit unwritten prohibitions' (Žižek, 2000b, 147; emphasis in original). This heretical act of 'overconformity' with the letter of the law therefore reveals the absurdity inherent in its absolute application that, in turn, draws attention to the fact that the law acts not to protect its subjects but to preserve its own hegemony. Žižek's point is that demonstrating that law requires a set of 'implicit unwritten prohibitions' to supplement and, at times, supplant its regular (and regulatory) functions can only be revealed by an absolute and unwavering attention to, and extension of, the explicit instructions and that this, in turn, reveals the hidden arbitrary heart of discipline, ideology and hegemony.

Elsewhere, Žižek provides an example of such heresy that is well suited to the purpose of this examination. In *The Art of the Ridiculous Sublime: On David Lynch's Lost Highway*, Žižek discusses the figure of Mr Eddy who, along with Frank Booth (from Lynch's *Blue Velvet* [1986]), is a figure

> . . . of an excessive, exuberant assertion and enjoyment of life; they [Eddy and Booth] are somehow evil 'beyond good and evil' . . . [and yet] at the same time the enforcers of the fundamental respect for the socio-symbolic Law. (Žižek, 2000a, 19)

In this fashion, Mr Eddy, who famously pistol-whips a fellow driver for being discourteous, 'enforces the rules . . . [but] does so in such an

exaggerated, excessively violent manner that his role exposes the inherently violent and arbitrary nature of the law' (Wieczorek, 2000, x). This
example demonstrates the danger of the heretic: by vigorously enforcing
the rules and demanding that others do the same, these figures reveal
what they seek to hide (however unconsciously) – that the law is, itself,
arbitrary. It is not so much that the fundamental respect for the law is an
effect or product of the law's arbitrary nature, but that respect for the law
is used to hide the fact that the law is itself arbitrary. Moreover, it is the
excessive nature of these figures' adherence that reveals the law's arbitrary (and, for Žižek, absurd) status. To negotiate the demands of any
series of ideological edifices necessarily requires 'minor' transgressions
in order to satisfy the majority of hegemonic demands, all of which work
to elide the presence and arbitrary foundation of these structures.

What we can conclude is that heresy, such as Žižek defines it, is a tak-
ing-too-far, an excessive attention to the specific requirements of the laws
that structure, govern and discipline the actions and articulations of the
subject-in-society. The pejorative term itself indicates that the act is a
threat to the ideological edifice(s). What such excesses do is draw attention to the hegemonic structures that function most efficiently when
they are effaced in the very performance of their demands. Once attention is drawn to these structures – once they become visible to or are
made visible by the subjects who are subject to them – they can no longer
claim to be 'naturally' in place: 'overidentification suspends its [the rul-
ing ideology's] efficiency' (Žižek, 2006, 65).

As will be explored below, cinema's role and function within a hegemony sees it function as, and alongside, the ideological edifices Žižek
claims are revealed through the actions of the heretic. Cinema works to
inform, instruct and discipline its audiences through the use of specific
activities, located both at the level of film form and film content. The
particular articulations of this control will be explored in depth but, as
with any ideological edifice, the efficacy of its ideological operation
depends entirely on the invisibility of its mechanisms. To draw attention
to them suspends, as Žižek confirms, their efficiency and serves only to
reveal their absurdity. This is not to suggest, however, that Cronenberg's
films (assuming they do, as I suggest, function as heretical texts) necessarily 'fail' as cinema. Part of this document's purpose is to examine the
way which Cronenberg locates his heresy, not as the totality of his cinema
but as an effective portion of a larger, disruptive-but-acquiescent project.
This paradox is important to bear in mind as we move to consider how
Cronenberg's cinema of disruption moves from its original outsider

status to performing its own particular disciplinary function. Indeed, if one thing has typified his career, it is the ability of his works and their content to provoke and disrupt.

As is clear from the discussion above, Cronenberg's films are concerned with exploring the heretical potential for cinema, utilizing narratives that explore various mechanisms of transformation, and formal techniques that unsettle and upset the standard spectatorial expectations. Thus Brundle's desire to articulate a politics of insects becomes heretical, given Žižek's schema, because it draws attention to the arbitrary construction of the politics of the human, to which the insect is compared and found to be radically alien. Further than this, Brundle's politics of insects suggests the limits of representation or meaningfulness and, hence, of the presence of those systems maintained by the hegemonic structures that work to render signification transparent.

Cinematic Apparatus as a Disciplinary Structure

The cinematic apparatus – when considered in the terms of both its construction and operation – demonstrates all the functional hallmarks of what Louis Althusser labels an Ideological State Apparatus. Indeed, it is this status that is inherent in André Bazin's recognition that

> [t]hrough the contents of the image and the resources of montage, the cinema has at its disposal a whole arsenal of means whereby to impose its interpretation of an event on the spectator. (Bazin, 2005, 24)

However, this apparatus is not nearly as cohesive as its title, and Bazin's brief note regarding its functioning, might suggest. As has been comprehensively outlined by others,[1] the cinematic apparatus is composed of a variety of functions and sites that combine to present, in direct opposition to their fractured status, a coherent spectatorial experience. In this fashion, the term *apparatus* is taken to mean

> the totality of independent operations that make up the cinema viewing situation, including (1) the technical base (specific effects produced by the various components of the film equipment, including camera, lights, film and projector); (2) the conditions of film projection (the darkened theatre, the immobility implied by the seating, the illuminated screen in front, and the light beam projected from behind

the spectator's head); (3) the film itself, as a 'text' (involving various devices to represent visual continuity, the illusion of real space, and the creation of a believable impression of reality); and (4) that 'mental machinery' of the spectator (including conscious perceptual as well as unconscious and preconscious processes) that constitute the viewer as a subject of desire. (Stam, Burgoyne & Flitterman-Lewis, 1992, 143)

In comparison with Althusser's Repressive State Apparatus, which utilizes repressive mechanisms (the army, the police, etc.) as part of its regulatory function, the Ideological State Apparatus (ISA) utilizes ideology as a means of enacting this function yet concealing its repressive nature. For Althusser, famously, the ISAs achieve the willing interpellation of subjects into the various structures of the ISAs, so that '. . . each of them [the ISAs] contributes to this single result in the way proper to it' (Althusser, 1994, 117). This indicates the importance of the form of ideological transmission as well as the content of the various messages being transmitted[2] that combine efficiently with the hegemonic conditions that generate subjects who happily partake in the process in exchange for subjecthood. Thus each piece of ideological information must necessarily be delivered as the result of a variety of formal procedures (each procedure 'proper' to the vehicle of delivery), those formal procedures themselves working to efface their own presence and role.

What is important for the transmission of ideological content, for the maintenance of the ideological edifice (Žižek) and the continued dominance of the ISA (Althusser), is that the conditions under which the ideological message is constructed, encoded and, to some extent, delivered remain hidden in order for the message itself to appear natural and thus neutral.[3] Elsewhere Jacques Aumont confirms this by noting that, when confronted by a photographic image (be it still or moving),

> . . . we *know* that the photographic image is a print, a trace, a mechanically and physico-chemically produced version of the appearance of light at a given moment, [yet] we *believe* that it is an adequate representation and we are ready to believe that it 'tells the truth' about this reality. (Aumont, 1997, 81)

This 'wilful forgetting' of what Aumont, drawing on the work of Jean-Marie Schaeffer, refers to as the *arche* of the image[4] amounts to a collusion between the spectator and the cinematic apparatus, leading to an effacing of the form in order to maintain optimal conditions for the consumption of the content. Such elisions occur throughout the sphere of cultural production. Indeed, Aumont quotes Jean-Pierre Oudart, who notes that

> [t]he characteristic of bourgeois representation is to reproduce its figures as real for a subject which is supposed to know nothing about the relations of production in which the pictorial product is inscribed just like all other products. (Oudart, quoted in Aumont, 1997, 142)

Here the key is the way in which Oudart's comment refers both specifically to the production of pictorial images and also to the conditions of production within capitalism. What is common to both is the effacing of form, of the conditions and contexts of production, so that the objects and products that emerge as a result can be encountered without their specific histories interfering with their consumption as ideological content. Thus the effacing of the cinematic apparatus within the dominant cinematic narrative form can be viewed as occurring in the same way, and for the same reasons, as the alienation of objects and labour within capitalist production. And, as with the production of objects, the

> concealment of the technical base [of cinematic production] will also bring about an inevitable ideological effect. Its inscription, its manifestation as such, on the other hand, would produce a knowledge effect, as actualization of the work process, as denunciation of ideology, and as critique of idealism. (Baudry, 1999a, 346–7)

The effacing of cinematic form, as a fundamental part of the function of the apparatus, must occur in order to lead an audience to a point at which the visible content (i.e., the film's 'story') can be consumed without endangering what Baudry refers to as a film's 'ideological effect' – its invisible and therefore effective ideological content. The functioning of these ideological effects is upset by the reintroduction of the apparatus as a visible mechanism. This in turn renders apparent the apparatus as construction (thereby transforming the ideological effect into a 'knowledge effect') and, to return to Žižek's point, runs the risk of circumventing the hegemonic purpose of the apparatus. As was noted above, the result of any ISA activity is the interpellation of subjects qua ideological products *and* consumers. For the cinematic apparatus, as an ISA, the result is the same. What is produced by this activity is the cinematic spectator who must be considered 'as an *effect* of an irreducibly heterogeneous system of discursive, social, technological and institutional

relations' (Crary, 1992, 6; emphasis in original). The governing of interpellated subjects takes a variety of forms, as does the manner in which
ideological information is transmitted to the subjects being governed,
but what all of these edifices have in common is the fact that they are all
involved in the disciplining of their subjects. Each of them, in the way
'proper' to it, provides information regarding correct and incorrect
modes of inhabiting the ideological landscape.

Cinema has a series of particular mechanisms through which its audience is disciplined, which is to say, both ideologically instructed and constructed. Through its operation and the manner of both its construction
and consumption, cinema seems closest in operation to what Foucault,
in *Discipline and Punish: The Birth of the Prison*, refers to as 'punishment as
spectacle' (Foucault, 1995, 8). As Foucault details in the opening chapters of this book, pre-modern societies are typified by the manner in
which they enact a 'spectacular event', with the criminal body on display
before a communal gaze directed at this individual whose suffering
serves as a lesson to all who watch. The move away from 'punishment as
spectacle' towards a more horizontally enacted form of social surveillance (the birth of, as Foucault details it, 'Panopticism') leads to the rise
of a variety of differentiated social gazes, within which discipline brings
to bear both its forms of power and knowledge. Punishment as spectacle
gives ways to a social system in which the punishment meted out is 'the
most hidden part of the penal process' (Foucault, 1995, 9). Instead, with
the understanding that 'it is the certainty of being punished and not the
horrifying spectacle of public punishment' (Foucault, 1995, 9) that is the
true deterrent, a panoptic plurality settles over the now-modern population which incorporates and unifies both the willingness of these spectators to gaze at the emerging spectacle of the modern age and also at each
other in light of these new ways of looking and being seen.

Cinema therefore emerged out of a culture that had replaced the
spectacular punishment with a more efficient, and inclusive, model
wherein the mechanistic gaze of the ideological edifice is articulated
through every level of a citizen's life. Foucault's *Discipline and Punish* provides an enormously thorough exploration of the spread of the panoptic
gaze, through education, health care and the legal repositories within
which it is most visible. This is not to say, however, that contemporary
(Western) society superseded the first feudal model with a second,
recognizably modern one, as though social control and the movement of
power were subject to a teleological progression towards ever-more

efficient forms of organization. Instead, these methods of control, or orchestrating how a power moves through a society as well as how its subjects utilize and respond to it, can be seen to have gathered previous models into themselves, integrating them into a cohesive (although constantly negotiated) whole.

Cinema provides a perfect example of this kind of accretion. The public spectacle of the condemned body on display alters as public punishment disappears and is replaced by the certainty of punishment under the ever-vigilant gaze of authority. In its place rise new spectacles, new bodies under examination: the dead in the morgue, the insane in the asylums and, eventually, images upon a screen. To Foucault's Panopticism, which is a clear articulation of power/knowledge in its most disciplinary mode, can be added the concept of *flânerie*, a term used as '. . . shorthand for describing the new, mobilized gaze of the precinematic spectator' (Schwartz, 1995, 88), wherein, for example, the Parisian fin de siècle citizen could find public amusement at such institutions as the Paris morgue. Here spectatorship is not linked so obviously to the articulation of power as with Foucault's Panopticon but nevertheless functions in the same way. By legitimizing both the act of examining the most private of acts and spaces and the desire to see what previously had been unavailable, this new spectatorship demonstrates how power can be articulated as, and hidden behind, knowledge. For Schwartz, these emerging discourses of the gaze prefigure the evolution of the cinematic apparatus. Deprived of the public spectacle of punishment, the flâneur can find new pleasures in the morgue as well as in the innovative dioramas and tableaux that are emerging. The apogee of these various kinds of looking can be found in the cinema that combines the gaze of a public towards a body on display in an environment that is both public and private at the same time. This is important as a way of disrupting the possibility for sympathy that often marked public executions:

> In punishment-as-spectacle a confused horror spread from the scaffold; it enveloped both executioner and condemned; and, although it was always ready to invert the shame inflicted on the victim into pity or glory, it often turned the legal violence of the executioner into shame. (Foucault, 1995, 9)

The bodies displayed upon the screen were patently not the same bodies as those previously punished in public. In that knowledge comes a safety for the audience, for if the body on the screen is to suffer some violence, it is, after all, only a representation.

Cinema, as a means for representing power, becomes equally a mechanism for determining it. The structure of film, its form, becomes the means by which discourses of power, in all their various permutations, are socially articulated. Power is, and must be, thought of as

> a process of production, rather than as a drama of representation – an affirmative place of affects and effects, and not a series of splits and absences unfolding according to a logic of negativity. (Shaviro, 1993, 23)

Thus cinema does not simply represent discourses of power (although it does that too); cinema is active in the production and articulation of these discourses in a social setting that extends, necessarily, beyond the fact of immediate consumption. Cinema functions both as a disciplinary training ground as well as a device by which these disciplinary discourses are represented. As Shaviro makes clear,

> [f]or instance, the cinematic mechanisms that objectify and fetishize women's bodies are not *consequences* of phallocentrism; rather, it is phallocentrism – understood not as a transcendental structure, but as a historically specific way of distributing gender roles and normalizing and regulating desire – that is a consequence of particular technologies of power, among which the mechanisms of cinema must be included. (Shaviro, 1993, 21–22; emphasis in original)

The exercise of power, which Foucault understands as 'a set of actions upon other actions' (Foucault, 1983, 220), becomes demonstrated not just within the content of a film's narrative, as the characters enact, enable and embody the plot and its various concerns; instead cinematic form can be viewed as a mechanism through which the power of law (of ideology) is exercised upon the law-abiding spectators, and within which the discourses of power can be heretically made visible. What is important, as Shaviro makes clear, is that the productive machinery of power as evidenced by and through the cinematic apparatus must constantly iterate the discourses through which the cinematic spectator[5] is disciplined. The necessity for a constant iteration of the variety of discourses displayed and articulated through film therefore allows us to comment on cinema's productive effects (cinema as a site of ideological presence), as distinct from the negative formulations of other theoretical discussions (cinema as a site of lack).[6] It is through these productive instances that the hegemonic positions that are spoken by and through the cinema are able to maintain their hold over a population.

However, the image will not vanish, will not reveal itself to be vacuous, empty, ineffective. This is its dangerous power, the fact that despite our knowledge of the cinematic image as simply an interplay of light and shadow on a flat surface, literally without depth, we respond viscerally to that which we understand should not be able to affect us. It holds us fast, stuck to the seat by the power of its ability to move, to transport. There are, though, moments when we break this hold, where we are encouraged to look through the image, look beyond it or, more precisely, look beyond its ideological and disciplinary horizon and towards the very limits of the image's ability to signify. The 'Cronenberg Project' (Rodley, 1997, xv) has always involved the attempt to 'show the unshowable, to speak the unspeakable' (Rodley, 1997, 43).[7] Necessarily this project will run afoul of the very structures or edifices that permit it to occur and in this running afoul will demonstrate, in Žižekian heretical fashion, the disciplinary structures that circulate around and are threatened by it. Indeed, the sheer extent and range of criticism that has dogged Cronenberg's career makes clear the manner with which a dominant ideological edifice will respond. Thus Cronenberg has been pilloried for choosing one genre over another, for choosing the wrong genre (for a Canadian, for an auteur, for an 'independent' filmmaker), for not fulfilling genre requirements correctly[8] or leaving genre behind altogether, for 'overfilling' his films and for alienating his audience. Clearly something is at work in Cronenberg's films, some aspect of his filmmaking that both fascinates and offends and which, crucially, threatens. It is in the interplay between the utilization of specific formal techniques, the delivery of personally inflected and politically motivated content, and the manner with which an audience is situated by the apparatus that is implicated that we will see Cronenberg's heretical activity.

The Canadian Heretic

Of course, Cronenberg's work does not emerge from a vacuum; his particular historical and geographic context has deeply influenced and affected his work. It is intriguing, then, that so few critical studies of Cronenberg's work have drawn attention to the specific role of his

Canadianness (or, indeed, his Jewishness) and, while the focus of this study lies elsewhere, it is useful to locate Cronenberg as he locates himself.

As explored above, the heretic stands at odds with the dominant hegemonic edifice; his or her attempts at fulfilling the hegemonic edict fail only because they perform the role too well and, through this heretical performance, reveal the performance *as* performance. Cronenberg is highly attuned to this problematic relationship. In recognizing that the contemporary Western film landscape is dominated by Hollywood, Cronenberg notes that

> the problem is that if you come from outside that American context, the films you produce are often seen as difficult, complex and not fitting within [their] formulas. (Mendik, 2000, 182)

Yet, over the course of his career, the man originally lauded and reviled as ' "the king of venereal horror", "the Baron of Blood", Dave "Deprave" Cronenberg' (Rodley, 1997, xv) has become one of Canada's most successful artists (and productive exports). This paradox has been neatly highlighted by the career retrospective exhibition The Strange Objects of David Cronenberg's Desire at the Royal Ontario Museum, wherein, as Ramsey and Wilson note,

> a filmmaker whose work was once called 'an atrocity, a disgrace to everyone connected with it – including the taxpayers' . . . now finds himself ensconced within one of the august bastions of high culture in Canada. (Ramsey & Wilson, 1993/4)

This movement, from repulsion to celebration, is another of the strange trajectories this study will examine. The act of recuperation by a system that one is, however unconsciously, involved in critiquing (or exposing) is what Žižek notes demonstrates the successful mechanisms of late capitalism:

> . . . in the generalized perversion of late capitalism, transgression itself is solicited, we are daily bombarded by gadgets and social forms which not only enable us to live with our perversions, but even directly conjure new perversions. (Žižek, 2001c, 20)

Thus one could argue that this transformation into being a recuperated object of Canada's desire is one of the major narratives of Cronenberg's

career. Certainly a cursory examination of his first few films will demonstrate how, at even this early stage, the revulsion generated by his first
commercial film was soon assuaged by the profits this film would
generate.

Shivers (1975), written by Cronenberg, was picked up for development
by Cinepix, a Canadian production company that specialized in 'gentle
and sweet sex films' (Emery, 1999) and which was, at this stage, desper-
ate to break into the American market. Shifts in the funding landscape
in Canada saw the Canadian Film Development Corporation's (CFDC)
mandate extended '. . . to provide financing, initially through a revolving
loan fund for the production of feature films in Canada' (Adria, 2001,
236), thereby providing, at least in theory, a situation of '. . . economic
and artistic fasticulation, previously enveloped by the quagmire of legislation and capitol deficiency' (Allinson, 2002). This, it was hoped, would
'. . . widen viewing audiences, saturating the United States with palpable
feature films' (Allinson, 2002) and lead to an identifiably Canadian cinema. Somewhat ironically, it was felt that the best way to achieve penetration into the lucrative American market (and, presumably, generate
Canadian cinema in the process) was through the horror genre; hence
Shivers.

However, the CFDC's decision to fund *Shivers* led directly to a public
and governmental controversy whose ripples 'continue to eddy through
the Canadian pond even to the present time' (Beard, 2001, 26). As
Cronenberg notes, an influential Canadian film critic (Robert Fulford,
writing under the pseudonym Marshall Delaney) concluded his review
by claiming, 'If using public money to produce films like [*Shivers*] is the
only way English Canada can have a film industry, then perhaps English
Canada should not have a film industry' (Fulford, quoted in Lowenstein,
2004). Such polarizing sentiments were compounded by *Shivers*' unexpected success. For an initial investment of CD$380,000, *Shivers* would
eventually return over five million dollars. And so, despite the fact that 'it
filled the coffers . . . the attitude was that they [the CBC and the CFDC]
didn't want the public coffers filled with filth' (Rodley, 1997, 52).

Shivers nonetheless provides a uniquely Canadian slant on the specific
sub-genre of Body Horror of which Cronenberg had found himself the
unwitting champion. *Shivers* begins with an advertising slide-show for the
Starliner Island apartment complex which provides us with one of the
first recognizable Cronenbergian tropes: 'a modern corporate building
in a lonely natural setting . . . the world itself seems to have been extruded
as an icy and electric, or dishevelled, crumbling habitat' (Testa, 1995).

From *Shivers* Cronenberg would go on to film *Rabid* (1976), again produced by Cinepix and again with funding from the CFDC. Despite now
being a far riskier investment, at least so far as the funding bodies were
concerned, there could be no doubt as to its financial success based on
the performance of *Shivers*. This fact meant that *Shivers*, as 'the first film
the CFDC had financed which actually returned a profit . . . [was providing funding] that could be used for other films' (Grunberg, 2006, 41).

The casting of Marilyn Chambers (best known for her role in the hard-
core adult film *Behind the Green Door* [1973]) in *Rabid* was suggested by
Cinepix producer Ivan Reitman, a long-time friend of Cronenberg's and
producer of *Shivers*, as 'a cost effective way of solidifying box-office draw'
(Allinson, 2002). With funding from the CFDC in place, surreptitiously
hidden within a cross-collateralizing multi-film deal in order to avoid any
more *Shivers*-esque publicity, *Rabid* could be made and, despite the presence of 'Marilyn Chambers, porno queen, it didn't cause anywhere near
the same kind if stir . . . and I think it was just because society was moving
on at that point' (Grunberg, 2006, 41). Certainly this may well be the
case, but it is also clear that Cronenberg had managed to find an appre-
ciative audience despite (or, perhaps, because of) his particular situation.
With both *Shivers* and *Rabid* as perfect examples, the developing sub-
genre of Body Horror, '. . . inaugurated in 1968 with George Romero's
Night of the Living Dead, is a cinema of violation and destruction of the
body' (Rodley, 1997, 2). *Shivers* makes this very clear, fulfilling the sub-
genre's desire to 'show and not tell' the particular torments suffered by
the various victims. As well as this, both *Shivers* and *Rabid* contained
within them an intriguing commentary on Canadianness, the urban-
rural divide and what Testa, utilizing the work of Northrop Frye, identifies as Canada's 'garrison mentality'. This mentality

> is a distinct sense of the space of human habitation characterized by an
> extreme 'edge-consciousness', an anxious concern with boundaries,
> walls, thresholds, houses, and the interface between self and other.
> (Testa, 1995)

As with *Shivers*, *Rabid* returned a very healthy profit (seven million Canadian dollars) on its initial investment (production costs were kept under
CD$700, 000). Added to this is the increasingly appreciative audience
Cronenberg's early films attracted. For them, the heretical filmmaker –
whose films challenged established cinematic norms, generic conventions,
national identity and the very construction of the subject in relation to
social, cultural and moral order – made perfect sense.

With these brief examples, at least three things become clear: First is that Cronenberg's refusal of narrative restoration serves a clear political purpose. Second, the Cronenbergian protagonist functions in a different fashion (and for a different purpose) than a more conventional protagonist (even allowing for the disruptions offered by horror and Body Horror), while, third, Cronenberg's own practice as a filmmaker is implicated by this ambivalence towards normative cinematic requirements. Thus the manner with which a Cronenberg film avoids the restorative trajectory of the classic narrative film is so as to generate the conditions through which the ideological edifices (which consolidate support through the pleasures mobilized by the restorative ending) are revealed to be in operation. Further to this, the 'happy ending' of *Shivers* can only be viewed as happy if one is prepared, as Cronenberg encourages us, to assume the parasites' point of view, to see the change as simply that – a transformation as devoid of 'proper' identity as of any kind of moralizing interpretation. Thus, as Cronenberg argues,

> As humans, we try to transcend the body by transforming it. For us there's no natural. It's all a force of will. Everything that exists in the sense of ethics comes from us. . . . As we change, those things change as well. (Sirius, 1997, 184)

This focus on the individual means that, for Cronenberg, 'the body is the first fact of human existence, so my imagery tends to be very body oriented and my narratives tend to be very body oriented' (Emery, 1999). Because of this, the Cronenbergian protagonist already has a different role to perform within the narrative than, say, the protagonist at the centre of a standard restorative narrative. Cronenberg's interest in transformation is played out across the bodies of the characters that populate his films. As Frank Biocca explains,

> [t]he body is . . . an expressive communication device, a social semiotic vehicle for representing mental states (e.g.: emotions, observations, plans, etc.) to others. The body emits information to the sense of other bodies, whether intentional or not. Observers of the physical or mediated body read emotional states, intentions, and personality traits by the empathetic simulation of them. *The body transmits information to other bodies through a kind of affective contagion.* (Biocca, 1997; emphasis added)

Thus the body in a Cronenberg film serves communicative functions beyond that of expressing the character of the protagonist. Where a standard film would work to match the communicative function of the protagonist's body to the narrative function (and, hence, ideological effect), Cronenberg's bodies often exceed their protagonists. As Cronenberg notes, 'there's a growing refusal to be bound by the apparent limits of what the body is. There's an attempt to transcend it by transforming it – transmutation' (Sirius, 1997). Thus his transformation of the body-on-screen, so often as a result of infection, mutation or manipulation, reflects Sontag's conclusion that '[d]isease metaphors are used to judge society not as out of balance but as repressive' (Sontag, 2002, 74). Therefore transformation is the action that leads to the problems and conflicts that form the centre of his films, meaning that attempts to transcend the body always lead directly back to the (often violent irruptions of the) flesh, and thereby serve to reveal the mechanisms which mobilize Sontag's repressive disease metaphors. In this manner, Cronenberg's films work to combine a refusal of the narrative conventions of restoration (which would tend to suggest a specific moral tone be taken with regard to the transformation that occurs) with a continued desire to highlight transformation as it impacts upon the (disciplined) bodies of his films' protagonists.

The next point to be made is that Cronenberg's films all feature a protagonist who '. . . constructs an identity for himself [*sic*] that inevitably leads to loss' (Grunberg, 2006, 7). The key here, as Grunberg makes clear, is the inevitability involved: each film details a protagonist or protagonists who attempt to define themselves in their own terms, and who *inevitably* fail in that attempt. There is, in the films and their protagonists,

> a turning away from the immediacies of communal and social circumstance, a subversion of contour and legible order, in a paradoxical drive to what exists on the far side of humanity. (Grant, 2000, 7)

This turning away, an attempt, as Cronenberg puts it, to constitute one's own reality, places both the protagonists of the films, and the films themselves, in a difficult position. As Michael Grant comments,

> Cronenberg is attempting to oppose what is undecidable to dogmatism and rationality, and his way of doing this is to try to provoke his viewers, stimulating us to participate in his film[s] by virtue of that very undecidability. (Grant, 2000, 17)

This provides Cronenberg with the means to demonstrate that such attempts carry with them a number of inevitable outcomes. It is inevitable that the opposition, however it is played out, will place the players outside the bounds of 'dogma and the rational'. It is inevitable also that the attempt by Cronenberg to marry his particular interests with a commercial industry will generate plots and narratives that result in conflict between his protagonists-in-transformation and the various disciplinary forces that seek to restrain them. Finally, it is inevitable that his films, which, if not actually celebrating these attempts to resist the dogmatic and the rational, are at least detailing a number of attempts, will draw on versions of the same disciplinary forces that function punitively within the films' various plots. Nevertheless, Cronenberg does not consider his protagonists to be victims of their changes and transformations: 'They're actually very heroic. They're actively seeking strange solutions to some strange problems' (Sirius, 1997). This much is made clear above in the discussion of *Shivers* and will be further explored in the chapters to follow.

Finally, what is made clear is the manner with which Cronenberg's own filmmaking practice is as implicated in this ambivalence towards narrative convention as the narratives he films. Cronenberg is a self-taught filmmaker. There were no film schools in existence while he was at the University of Toronto, and his education in filmmaking occurred in a largely pragmatic fashion:

> My first approach was very much mechanical, to understand the technology. . . . I bought copies of *American Cinematographer* magazine. I couldn't understand the articles, but the ads showed pictures of stuff and I gradually began to get the idea. . . . (Rodley, 1997, 11)

Cronenberg maintains this pragmatic approach to the techniques of filmmaking:

> I'm not interested in the latest camera development. I'm very anti-techno. I've never shot in Cinemascope. . . . But I can't understand a director who doesn't really understand what different lenses do. I've got to tell my cameraman what lens I want. He can't tell me. If you don't have some technological understanding of why that looks that way, you'll never understand that it can be different. (Rodley, 1997, 12)

His attention to the specifics of the art means that any analysis of his work must necessarily pay particular attention to those same techniques. Just as Cronenberg's films are concerned with exploring matters of transformation, and the penalties faced for transforming *away* from what might be considered normal or dogmatic and rational, so too are his films concerned with enacting and making visible that transformation with their own 'textual bodies'.

A Cinema of Perversion; a Cinema for Perverts

A final point for consideration comes when we ask, does David Cronenberg make a cinema of perversion, and if so, how might a cinema of perversion function within a broader heretical context? An examination of much of the critical material surrounding his career would tend to suggest yes, in the entirely pejorative and superficial sense of 'perverted' films. The fact or possibility of Cronenberg's cinematic perversion is a mainstay of many popular responses to his texts, but it is entirely possible for this perversion, first, to be more complex than might initially appear and, second for it to serve a critical and heretical function. Here Žižek's own thoughts on the relationship between cinema and perversion prove illuminating. Žižek's utilization of Lacan's definition hinges on the structural aspect of perversion: what is perverted is the subject's identification with the gaze of an other, a moment that represents a shift in subjective position within the interplay of gazes articulated by the cinematic text. Utilizing an example from Michael Mann's *Manhunter* (1986) Žižek comments that the moment Will Graham, the FBI profiler, recognizes that the victims' home movies he is watching are the same films that provided the sadistic killer with vital information, his '. . . obsessive gaze, surveying every detail of the scenery, coincides with the gaze of the murderer' (Žižek, 1992, 108) This identification, Žižek continues, '. . . is extremely unpleasant and obscene in this experience of our gaze as already the gaze of another . . . [because] such a coincidence of gazes defines the position of the pervert' (Žižek, 1992, 108). As Will Graham examines the home movies, seeking whatever they have in common, his gaze shifts from their content to their status as home movies, thereby coinciding with the gaze of the murderer, meaning an identification of (and with) the form of the home movies he is watching. It is their very status as home movies that is the key to unravelling the mystery.

However, more than simply representing a rupture in the suturing effect of conventional narrative, perverse spectatorship is an identification both with the gaze of the other and all that that gaze might possibly contain. Since the pervert, for Lacan (and, hence, Žižek) '. . . does not pursue pleasure for his own pleasure, but for the enjoyment of the Other'

(Žižek, 1992, 109), the perversely situated spectator is forced suddenly to recognize that the drive to satisfaction ordinarily rendered possible through the standard conduit of narrative and spectatorship is actually oriented towards the service and satisfaction of an other – an other that remains forever beyond the ability of the spectator (or the film, for that matter) to conceptualize and, hence, contain. The desire of this putative other, rendered visible through the formal act of perversely situating the spectator, therefore stands as a horrifying possibility, one in which the spectator, through being rendered perverse, suddenly comes to function as the object. It is worth mentioning, however, that while for Žižek the example from *Manhunter* might offer a *representation* of structural perversion, and of a perverse spectatorial positioning, it is not in itself a perverse representation. Graham's moment of recognition – that he has assumed the same structural position qua the gaze as the murderer he seeks – is not the audiences', in the same way that our looking *at* Graham looking is not the same as looking *as* he looks. Cronenberg's films, on the other hand, to the extent that they are perverse, perform that perversion by structuring their spectatorial identification at a formal level, rather than merely representing it as part of the (always already) recuperated content.

However, before we turn to explore the films themselves, the question arises, what is the value or purpose of enforcing such a deliberately uncomfortable spectatorial position upon one's audience? What is to be gained – or achieved – from such a practice? Given that I have been arguing that Cronenberg's primary purpose within his films is to engage in a critical examination of disciplinary structures as they orchestrate the experiential reality of an audience, the answer lies in this disciplinary critique. As Judith Feher-Gurewich explains, '[p]erversion is a way of thinking or desiring, or trying to stay psychically alive' (Feher-Gurewich, 2003, 192) with the fundamental difference between the normative subject and the pervert being that the latter

> . . . can access psychic gratification only by becoming the agent of the other's fantasy (his target and/or partner), in order to expose the fundamental anxiety that such a fantasy camouflages. (Feher-Gurewich, 2003, 192)

For the pervert, any attempt at satisfaction or pleasure occurs through the positioning of one's self as the point of the Other's gaze, a process which, as Feher-Gurewich notes, '. . . explains why perverse desire

produces horror, fear, and dismay in those who witness its mode of operation' (Feher-Gurewich, 2003, 192). Within the perverse position, the
standard neurotic devices for postponing (endlessly) the satisfaction of
desire in order to keep desire alive are overcome, and the pervert is able
to achieve satisfaction only at the expense of his or her pleasure. This
means that

> [w]hile perverts see more clearly than neurotics the architectonics of
> social life, they have less space to fool themselves, and without an other
> underfoot their capacity to foment dreams and expectations is ser-
> iously undermined. (Feher-Gurewich, 2003, 192)

Thus it becomes possible to see the radical potential offered to the heretical filmmaker by the act of positioning the spectator in a perverse position, with relation to the film, its content and, crucially, its apparatus.
The standard cinematic apparatus that works towards providing spectatorial satisfaction (and, hence, ideological effects) cannot operate within
a perverse position; while aware of the gaze (and hence, desire) of an
other who both demands satisfaction and oversees symbolization, there
can be no relaxing into the regulatory mechanisms of narrative and
form. Certainly satisfaction is possible – as Feher-Gurewich indicates,
perverts do indeed achieve some measure of satisfaction – but the cost is
high indeed. The result of perverse spectatorship is a paring away of the
self-effacing mechanisms at work in the standard narrative film, and a
revealing – even if only fleetingly – of the (disciplinary and, hence, ideological) mechanisms at work underneath. Indeed, the pervert's 'project'
comes to resemble the heretic's, with a desire to find some absolute and
unequivocal law, '. . . beyond the mask of social order, that can bring
solace to their torment' (Feher-Gurewich, 2003, 192). Therefore, a perverse positioning – or forcing an audience to look *as* the protagonist
looks, instead of simply looking *at* the protagonist looking – does occur
in Cronenberg's films and is as politically motivated as all of his other
heretical techniques. Indeed, positioning the spectator as perverse is a
heretical device insofar as it reveals, brutally, the structure of desire and
endlessly deferred satisfaction that is the elided centre of the standard
(neurotic) cinematic experience. Cronenberg, therefore, does more
than just produce a cinema of perversion. He utilizes his cinema to
produce an audience of perverts who, as a result of their experience,
find themselves unable to settle back into the standard spectatorial position once their complicity with the apparatus is revealed. However, this
relationship is far from stable, as will be demonstrated below.

This project seeks to explore the cinema of David Cronenberg in all its perversely heretical activities. Each chapter groups together a series of films that have some heretical concern in common, although it should be noted that these groupings are in no way meant to be exclusive and that other, equally productive groupings are possible. Each chapter, therefore, has a heretical 'theme' and examines the manner in which the theme can be raised, utilized and mobilized (in necessarily different ways) across Cronenberg's career but always with the same aim: the disruption of disciplinary structures that codify, govern and therefore limit the experience of the spectators before the screen and, by extension, of the spectators in the world at large.

Fast Company

The story of Cronenberg's *Fast Company* (1979) is, in many ways, more interesting than the film itself – a humble genre flick that explores the nether regions of decidedly working-class drag racers in a parochial heartland that is clearly designed to be neither Canada nor America but some ubiquitous fusion of the two, the better to serve audiences of both nations (and beyond). However, this is entirely the point: for the few commentaries that exist about *Fast Company*, its absence of value lies in its very apartness, its very difference, even at this early stage in his career, from the rest of Cronenberg's oeuvre. Even the most definitive of studies claims that this 'formulaic racing film . . . is almost completely uncharacteristic and almost completely uninteresting' (Beard, 2001, xii), while it has been noted elsewhere that this film is '. . . an aberration . . . being non-horror, thematically 'apart', less personal' (Rodley, 1997, xviii). In opposition to these views, the purpose of this analysis is not to necessarily consider the value of this film as either low or high art, given that most overviews of Cronenberg's career view his developmental trajectory as running positively from one to the other, but instead to explore the ways in which this film, which is, as one review of the film's DVD release puts it, '. . . a complete aberration . . .' (Benedict, 2006), also works to reveal something fundamental about Cronenberg's films as a body of work. Thus, the starting point for this section lies in the comments Cronenberg makes in his unashamedly gleeful commentary on the DVD: to understand his career one must fully explore and understand *Fast Company*. So while the film, as Cronenberg admits, '. . . doesn't seem to fit with the rest of my work now' (Rodley, 1997: 70), it also stands as the way to comprehend the particular kind of philosophical activity Cronenberg has been engaging in for the length of his career. It is the intention of this section, then, to explore *Fast Company* more closely in order to explore the ways in which its specific details exceed either its formal demands or its generic expectations.

Fast Company emerged as a perfect example of the kinds of machinations that occurred during the heyday of Canada's tax shelter years (1978–1982), a period referred to elsewhere as 'a deeply ignoble time in Canadian history' (Vatnsdal, 2004: 121). As with many films of this period – and we should note that *Shivers* and *Rabid* both form part of this initial cycle of films – *Fast Company* was considered from the outset, at least by the funders who financed it, more an opportunity to generate a sizable tax write-off and some celebrity cachet than a chance to partake in the production of any kind of art work. Cronenberg notes that the script had not been completed by the time the funding has been raised and that the film went into production with many of its final elements still to be worked out and finalized. As with many of the tax-shelter films, guarantees of funding did not necessarily mean assurances of distribution, and after a rushed production period, the production company was declared bankrupt, meaning that *Fast Company*, as an asset, was seized during litigation with it being 'barely shown anywhere' (Rodley, 1997: 70). These circumstances demonstrate perfectly why this study of Cronenberg's work must begin with *Fast Company*, for if any film in Cronenberg's canon could least reveal the hand of its maker, it surely must be this one. And yet the very restrictions that make *Fast Company* the film that it is, be they financial, technical or generic, make it possible to observe Cronenberg's actions as he seeks to trouble cinema at its centre, in the heart of genre and mechanical production-line filmmaking. Indeed, Cronenberg's then-cinematographer Mark Irwin confirms that Cronenberg

'approached this [film] more as an exercise in genre. . . . We both approached it as something that had to be presented as an exploitation movie and had to fit between the goal posts of that' (Irwin quoted in Gregory, 2004).

So to the film itself: *Fast Company* details the brief travails of a small drag-racing team sponsored by an oil company called Fast Co. The team's manager and sponsor Phil Adamson (John Saxon) has decided that 'winning is too expensive' and so is happy to maintain the team as also-rans in order to keep the product in the public eye without having to expend too much on the team itself. The team's star Lonnie 'Lucky Man' Johnson (William Smith) is himself fading into aged complacency, and this situation, exploited by Adamson, leads the team into eventual conflict when it is discovered that Adamson has no plans to replace the damaged fuel car (whose engine Lonnie blows up during a race) and, further, has sought to shift the Fast Co. brand to the team's rivals. In a final showdown, Adamson's escape in a light aeroplane ends in disaster when it crashes into a truck, and the rival team, Gary Black's 'Blacksmiths', attempt and then suffer the consequences of sabotage. The film ends with the reunited Fast Co. team splitting and Lonnie retiring with his long-distance and long-suffering girlfriend Sammy (Claudia Jennings).

Chris Rodley, in *Cronenberg on Cronenberg*, concludes his assessment of the film with the comment that, regardless of the superficial appearances of dissimilarity that have so forcefully dissuaded many from including it in their construction of Cronenberg's canon, *Fast Company* is important for four reasons. First, it marked access to a gradually increasing budget based on the commercial success of his previous two features that, in turn, provided the impetus for Cronenberg to move from low- to medium-budget features. This, second, allowed Cronenberg to further develop his technical skills as a director and, third, provided the first opportunity for him to work with material he had not written himself. Finally, *Fast Company* introduced Cronenberg to technicians with whom he would form creative relationships that would, in some cases, continue through his career (Rodley, 1997, xviii). Rodley's comments here seem designed to include the film in his exploration of Cronenberg's development but elide the film itself with a commentary on the film's content that is perfunctory at best. However, as Cronenberg himself notes, this film forms an essential part of his development,[9] and it is clear that a more thorough exploration of this film than has previously been attempted will provide valuable insights into his work and project. While the generic constraints of *Fast Company* mean that those typical Cronenbergian moments of evasion, transformation or disruption are few, they are present nevertheless, and their presence carries as much weight here as similar examples in the rest of his films do. Indeed, it can be argued that the rigorous controls (both budgetary and generic) effected upon a film such as *Fast Company* make the presence of such moments all the more heretical and therefore all the more important for a discussion such as this.

With that said, *Fast Company* provides some very useful points for any study of Canadian national cinema during this period and, like many of the tax-shelter films, the money for the production existed before the script. It may have been 'a labour of love' (Rodley, 1997, 70) but it was also designed, from the outset, to emerge into a specific cultural circumstance, to fulfil a specific need, and then to make way for the next of its kind. Thus, like all films, *Fast Company* was born as the result of economic and cultural needs, and while it might have provided the young director with the means to further his own productive CV (curriculum vitae), it was never meant to demonstrate any kind of longevity as a work of art, however high or low it might be. This inherently evanescent status inherited by exploitation and B-movies (and Cronenberg refers to *Fast Company* as a B-movie throughout his loving commentary) was further exacerbated by the fact that the distribution company responsible for the film went bust almost immediately (see Morris, 1994, 84–86). For many years, *Fast Company* languished in the realms of video store dump bins and late-night television. Nevertheless, it is by taking this film and its content at its own word, with Cronenberg's advice as a guide, that *Fast Company* reveals a unique mechanism at the heart of every Cronenberg film.

'. . . You're a lucky man, at two hundred miles an hour . . .'

As Cronenberg notes, *Fast Company* is a B-movie, where *B* is to be understood as meaning 'budget' (Cronenberg, 1979). Yet missing from his comment is the plain fact that a B-movie is also (or is considered) to be of a lower quality, not only because of the way it implicates both the machinery of motion picture production/consumption but also because it draws forth a consideration of a film's audience and the variety of expectations it might have for the film it is about to consume. Genre is, after all, a restrictive and conservative template to which a film must conform and, to an extent, carefully deviate from with permission. This permission is given at a number of points in the productive process through which the film proper emerges and is given again by the audience who come to encounter the film and, within this viewing experience, assess the degree to which the film either conforms to and confirms the requirements of its genre or deviates from them.

Fast Company is a genre film – a drag-racing film with minor road movie overtones and a penchant for western symbolism. Thus, in a series of conscious and possibly cynical nods to this genre, the film's hero, Lonnie 'Lucky Man' Johnson, becomes '. . . the world-weary gunslinger always wondering if his next duel would be his last . . . [thereby] captur[ing] the spirit of cowboy heroism' (Burkart, 1979). This attention to the sensibilities of the western is carried through the production design (Fast Co.'s team colours are red, white and blue); characterization (Johnson's protégé is Billy 'the Kid' Brooker (Nicholas Campbell) who affects a cowboy hat throughout); and setting (Cronenberg, himself a racing car enthusiast, recognizes that the drag-racing world is primarily a rural one [Cronenberg, 1979b] – as a consequence of this attention to generic detail, what urban environments the film visits are places of suspicion and deceit). It is, further, an exploitative[10] B-movie, and this fact is given, at first glance, by the presence of its stars (John Saxon, William Smith and Claudia Jennings, all B-movie career actors) and also by the visible impact the previously discussed budgetary constraints have upon the finished product. However, it is worth pointing out that it is hard to know exactly who is being exploited in this film, regardless of the ease with which this term is used by Cronenberg in discussing *Fast Company* (cf. Cronenberg, 1979; Grunberg, 2006, 48–52). Certainly there are sequences within *Fast Company* where women are exploited by men, and the film itself deals with commercial and industrial exploitation; but it is difficult to argue that anyone but the audience was exploited by the film. Indeed, if anything, the film's release and possibility for success suffered because of a consummate failure of commercial exploitation.

Nevertheless, *Fast Company* attempts something few other exploitation films do: the inclusion of material designed to promote a degree of authenticity to the topic beyond the construction of the film's self-contained diegesis. For example, while *Fast Company* was Cronenberg's first film not to have been exclusively written by him, he did enough rewriting and additional writing to gain a writing credit.[11] As he explains on the DVD's commentary track, he would incorporate into each day's shooting snatches of dialogue and context-specific phrases overheard the previous day.[12] Cronenberg's own impetus for this film is, as he has discussed, divided into two imperatives: the desire to document,[13] within the permissible framework of a genre film, a world he was personally involved in and remains dedicated to, while at the same time satisfying the requirements of this film and exploiting the access to increased production funding.

Further proof of Cronenberg's overattendance to the accuracy of the film's diegesis (and not, necessarily, to the narrative that occurs *within* this diegesis) comes with a consideration of *Fast Company*'s various racing sequences. Watching *Fast Company* is, to all intents, like watching two distinct films. Indeed, *Fast Company* is something of a nested film, with two distinct openings into its two distinct worlds and two very different styles for each of these. The first diegesis, that of the genre film, is introduced in the opening shots of the film and is quantified by the film's contemporary rock music score. This is the world of big rigs, decked out in Fast Co. signage and powering towards the Rockies. This first generic section lasts for ten shots and is controlled, measured and slow despite the song's invitation to consider ourselves part of a 'fast company'. This section's final shot is a pan from right to left[14] as the Fast Co. trucks move towards their next race meet and, as they exit the frame, the camera holds still with the highway in the foreground and, beyond it, a sliver of green pastureland, some farmhouses in the distance and a very blue sky filling the top three-quarters of the frame. This image is held while the director's name is superimposed over the clouds and sky. Given that this is a dragracing film and that the previous shots have announced a visible and audible concern with machines and masculinity, this shot offers an unusually contemplative moment as both the score and the sound of the trucks die away. This, in itself, is not unusual; many films end their title sequence with a brief pause before beginning the narrative proper. What is unusual is that a film which announces itself so thoroughly as a masculinized[15] drag-racing film should, after such a formulaic introduction, shift its diegetic concerns so thoroughly. Nothing in the film's opening sequence prepares us for the next sequence which, as noted above, functions almost as a film-within-the-film.

Thus the tenth shot of the opening sequence passes us over to the second world of *Fast Company*, wherein the film becomes a documentary of the world of hot rods, fuel and funny cars. This world is visually distinct from the diegesis of the previously established drag-racing genre film. While the film's narrative isn't entirely discarded in these sections, it is no longer the motivation for the film's technique as it was in the previous title sequence. The relationship of the shots in this sequence to each other has more to do with an accretion of detail, a grounding of the film in a kind of reality (or realism) that is, given the previous sequence, unexpected. This first documentary section of *Fast Company* is marked by a shift from the static or measured cinematography of the preceding sequence (even when panning from the top of the speeding Fast Co. truck, the camera is evenly controlled) and is typified by the use of a markedly active hand-held camera (which takes great pains to demonstrate that it is not a Steadicam).[16] There appears to be little or no artificial lighting, no obvious motivation for the transition from one shot to the next and no attempt to separate dialogue (such as one presumes to occur) from the cacophony of noise that seems to be one of the attractions of these events. Here the emphasis is on the cars themselves, and while, in this first documentary section, we do get two shots of the Fast Co. support crew, Elder (Don Francks) and P. J. (Robert Haley), the shots seem more concerned with demonstrating that their function is in the service of these vehicles than alerting us to any narrative importance and, to be perfectly fair, Elder and P. J. have little narrative value beyond their service to the machines. In this manner, Elder and P. J. become simply two more figures who circle the machines that are the central concern of these sections. The purpose of these techniques, then, appears to be the desire to capture (or be seen to be appearing to capture) reality unmediated by the distractions of narrative.

The use of documentary technique in *Fast Company*, however, should not be mistaken for an attempt to slip a documentary about hot rods into commercial circulation, hidden inside the broader form of a genre film. The point here is not that Cronenberg wanted to make a documentary and utilized *Fast Company* as the means to achieve this goal. Instead, we must consider the fact that these documentary moments in *Fast Company* have a clear purpose towards the narrative even if they themselves do not contain the forward momentum of narrative. As noted above, these sections allow for the accretion of verisimilitude, a grounding of the film's diegesis within, and indeed upon, another diegetic world. Thus Cronenberg's inclusion of these documentary moments points to two mutually implicated conclusions. First, they mark the concerns of a director who, in fulfilling the demands of the genre (a drag-racing film must include drag racing), exacts an excessive compliance with the rules he is subject to (through including documentary footage of actual drag racing). Second, this excessive compliance serves to demonstrate that the rules of these now-competing genres are indeed present. This demonstrates quite clearly Žižek's point, regarding the manner with which an overly attentive compliance to the edicts of any hegemonic structure serves only to render visible its very constructedness.

What Cronenberg does is take the constraints of the genre seriously enough to follow them through to their inevitably ludicrous conclusions. When faced with a project set in the world of drag racing, Cronenberg decides to ground the film's spurious narrative in authenticity with the utilization of documentary footage that, regardless of staging, is filmed so as to announce, with its technique, the fact of its realism. Similarly, those sections of the film that are concerned with narrative are, as we shall see, constructed so as to draw attention to their very artificiality – not at every point, to be sure, but often enough to unsettle the viewer and make the transition from one diegetic world to the next (drag-racing genre film to hot-rod documentary) more visible, more marked by the fact of transition. This collision of diegeses, without some kind of tertiary transitioning, serves to reveal to the spectators the fact that the apparatus of film exists as a structuring element and that they are being positioned by it, even as they consume what emerges from it.

This revelation occurs because of the way the two diegeses are shot and, more importantly, in the order in which we encounter them. *Fast Company*'s opening title sequence looks like any other film's; that is exactly the point. The construction of this introduction serves to provide the audience with all the tools it might need to interpret the rest of the film. In this fashion, the film announces itself as 'real' and as constructed from the same kinds of techniques that demonstrate filmic 'reality' as the majority of conventional western films. However to establish this opening sequence as grounded in conventional filmic realism and then to shift, without warning, to documentary-style footage is to invite comparison between two indices of realism: the fictional realism of narrative film, and the seemingly unmediated realism of documentary. Thus the comparison becomes one between realism and 'realer-than realism'. In this manner, the apparatus of film, normally hidden by the self-effacing conventions of conventional narrative, are revealed by an overzealous adherence to the demands of those conventions.

Exceeding the B

However, the apparatus inherent in film is revealed in *Fast Company* at other moments as well, all to the same end result: a rendering visible of the various structures that are most effective when the mechanisms of their delivery are effaced by the content they are delivering. In comparison, the following examples demonstrate the way Cronenberg's particular attention to form also serves to trouble the conventional narrative requirement for self-effacement. The first of these occurs at the end of the film's first drag race. By this stage (some three and a half minutes into the film) we have already had the introductory title sequence, the first documentary montage and then the first race. The racers, after their mad dash up the quarter mile, come to a desultory stop, and as we watch, their respective support crews, in pickup trucks, drive alongside them. This low-angle crane shot[17] works to re-establish the film's grounding in the 'prairie realism' (Cronenberg, 1979) that is so much a part of the drag-racing culture, reminding us also that, since the race has finished, the narrative can recommence. Due to the framing of this shot, we see both the track and the countryside stretching out to either side of the tarmac due to the fact that Cronenberg has chosen to shoot almost exclusively with a wide-angle lens. The fact that there seems to be a relationship between the thematic concern of the film and the shot being utilized means that the choice of lens, should it be noticed at all, seems the most appropriate, the most natural.

With this shot (see Figure 1.1) and this first post-race section, we are alerted to a shift in tone with the comparative quiet of the soundtrack. Previously the aural dimension of the film has been filled with both the title sequence's score and the various diegetic sounds required to place us within the frame or to situate us within this film's version(s) of realism. This includes the enormously loud crackle of the funny car engines, crowd noises and the diegetic narration of the track commentator, including information about the cars and, once the race is completed, the various post-race statistics we might otherwise care about and whose inclusion is required to confirm the degree of authenticity offered by the documentary footage. The requirements of cinematic and narrative realism are firmly adhered to, including the shifting concern with aural fidelity that forms a major part of the narrative text. To this end, as Cronenberg notes, enormous care is taken to replicate and deliver the engine noise of the cars as they roar off, but this is never so overwhelming as to obscure other important diegetic sounds.[18] Thus, even though

FIGURE 1.1 *Fast Company*'s 'prairie realism'.

we are closer to the cars as they roar off than the audience in the stands (it is important for this film that the racegoers are a distinct, yet indistinguishable, mass; we are never included with them or encouraged to think of ourselves as them), we are still some distance from the cars by the time they finish the race and begin to decelerate.[19] Despite this distance and the noise generated, we are still able to hear the relatively soft sound of the drag chutes as they open and flap behind the cars. The inclusion of this sound, even though it runs against diegetic fidelity, serves to explain the function of the chutes and serves to bridge both the decreasing volume of the cars as they continue up the track away from our second camera position and the reintroduction of the track commentator's voice. Yet at the moment we cut from the shot of the crowd's reaction (shot, as we might by now expect, long and wide), combined with the voice of the commentator as a diegetic summary of the events we have just seen, to the shot of the now stationary cars at the track's end, the entire diegetic soundscape dies away. Clearly the construction of cinematic realism (in whatever form) necessarily involves the inclusion of such details in this manner; but diegetic realism is not the same as a lived reality, and so aural fidelity is a shifting plane of relationships. In this manner, again, *Fast Company* is adhering to its fictional and generic requirements, placing the construction of a diegetic narrative reality over documentary actuality. We should be very aware, then, of those moments when the inclusion and manipulation of this detail is interrupted, for it is in this interruption that a break in the film's construction of continuity occurs.

What we are left with is this post-race shot, filmed from a crane and functioning as a moment of stillness after the fury of the race and the amount of information delivered in the previous shots. The insistent soundtrack of the race is emptied out, and all we hear are the sounds of the approaching support vehicles and the noises of the two drivers exiting their race cars. Again, this is consistent both with the diegesis we see and the position of the camera as a site of spectatorial positioning (i.e., for the duration of the shot we are both above and behind the cars as they sit, motionless). The sounds of the support vehicles increase as they approach our position, indicating an adherence to aural fidelity, and yet the preceding cacophony of the racing environment is erased. For the duration of these post-race shots, there is neither crowd, nor commentator, nor even race meet. Just these isolated figures and their machines.

Stranger still is the shot itself. Certainly what typifies this shot is its near-absolute stillness – the cars have stopped, and it is some seconds before the support vehicles arrive, at which point the camera tilts up slightly to reframe the support trucks in line with the hot rods. Yet the framing of this shot is unusual, almost painterly, and certainly not the kind of shot one would have expected in a film that, given the title sequence, the title itself, and the lyrical content of the theme song, seems to be concerned mainly with '[m]anly, beer-drinking, gristle-chewing, oil changing drag racing' (Pinsky, 2005). The frame is itself still. As noted above, the centre of the frame is filled with the track itself and with the two competing cars stalled in the mid-left and higher right of the frame, their drag chutes spread out behind them. To the left and right of the track are the grass tracksides, with a line of dark green trees running parallel with the track on the left and another stand of trees marking the horizon on the right. However the strangeness of the shot comes with an acknowledgement of the manner with which these compositional decisions are manipulating the way we encounter the image. Despite the presence of the cars in the foreground,[20] the structure of this shot, with the racetrack in the centre, means that the receding lines of the track continually draw our eyes up and away from the very things we should be (for narrative's sake) concentrating upon. The movement of the lines in the frame towards the vanishing point means that we, too, follow that movement. We are given something to look at – the cars and their drivers, the arrival of the support crew in balletic unison – and are yet, at the same time, told by the composition of the frame not to look, to look away, to direct our eyes up (the screen) and away (from the objects in the foreground).

This sense of both looking and not looking is further enhanced with the observation that, as the horizon line is quite high in the frame and the cars are lower in the foreground, the centre of the frame constitutes a negative space, a space of waiting and anticipation which, in a more conventional film, exists in order to be filled. Our anticipation is rewarded with the arrival of the support team, but the negative space, constituted by the lines of the track and landscape that lead us towards the vanishing point, means that even though we see the vehicles arrive, we are nevertheless encouraged to explore a space that waits to be filled and which never is.

Finally it is clear that in order to balance the relative light levels in the frame, a neutral density filter has been applied to the top half of the image. This means that the natural light from the sun is evened out over the top half of the image, leaving the unfiltered bottom half of the frame almost overexposed by comparison. This provides another motivation for our eyes, meaning that our gaze is lifted up the frame by the receding lines of the track, by the negative space that occupies so much of the frame and by a foreground that is almost too bright to look at – at least, brighter than the middle and top half of the frame. This is a frame that announces 'anywhere but here'.

Overattention to the demands of the frame might seem like paltry evidence, but similar moments abound in *Fast Company*, sequences where, like the one discussed above, there is simply too much adept activity to deliver the requirements of a generic narrative that would be equally served by far less attention to detail. Thus *Fast Company* demonstrates clearly the manner with which Cronenberg's filmmaking serves to problematize the very ideological structures it occurs within. Even with a film as superficially innocuous as an exploitative drag-racing B-movie, he is able to offer a criticism of the cinematic apparatus through the act of rendering it visible. Genre, as noted above, is a restrictive and conservative template from which a film emerges and to which it must constantly refer. Indeed, the instances provided above demonstrate that this template can be extended to the entirety of Cronenberg's works: they emerge as a result of historical, cultural and economic processes, each one of these inscribed with a multiplicity of ideological traces. Thus while the generic restrictions that govern *Fast Company* provide little room to develop a narrative of transformation (as might otherwise be recognizably Cronenbergian), Cronenberg is able to provide a heretical overdetermination at a formal level, providing, among other things, '. . . a level of detail in this movie that is disproportionate to what the screenplay actually requires' (Benedict, 2006). Further, we should be alert to the fact that despite the generic restrictions and formulaic content, Brundle's politics of insects haunts the periphery of this film. Brundle's statement suggests more than merely an attempt to bridge the transformational possibilities offered within the Cronenbergian universe. The politics of insects, as noted above, hints at the limits of discursive intelligibility, a point Beard continues when he comments on the very 'insectness' of the insect. This limit of intelligibility – which extends to include the spectator as much as the diegetic inhabitants – sits then at the horizon of *Fast Company*'s oddly composed and generically disruptive post-race shots. Therefore where these films differ from what might otherwise be referred to as a more normal/normative tradition is that these films reveal, through their overattendance to the various requirements they are subject to, that a series of structuring forces exist. These films make visible the movements and requirements of a hegemonic position that would otherwise efface its presence even as narrative cinema functions on the effacing of form. The manner with which these films accomplish this heretical overattention to, and subsequent revelation of, the apparatus of (and original impetus for) cinema will form the greater part of this project.

Chapter 2

The Body Explodes

Cartesian Difficulties

As discussed in the previous chapter, Cronenberg utilizes the body onscreen as a means of revealing previously effaced disciplinary structures that govern not just the body but, through what Sontag identifies as 'disease metaphors', the subject constituted by the body. The Cartesian mind/body dialectic is obviously called into question and Cronenberg's bringing forward of the body, usually ignored in favour of the mind-as-subject, works to reveal the elided tension inherent in this dialectic. A more considered examination of the way this tension plays out in Cronenberg's films reveals not just an exploration of these terms ('mind', 'body') as stable referents, but also a desire to destabilize these terms and undermine their unquestioned discursive validity. Hence while the body might ordinarily and conventionally serve (at least on screen) as the unquestioned vehicle for the mind, for Cronenberg there exists the distinct possibility of an alternative bodily agency, or the possibility that a bodily agency might form some kind of visceral opposition to the disciplinary forces of culture and society through which the subject itself is articulated. In this manner Cronenberg's 'body on the screen' can be seen to function as a third term mediating between the subjectivity that emerges as a result of these forces of culture and the forces of culture themselves, be they ideological or disciplinary or any combination of these. This bodily agency is a problematizing force designed to disrupt the activities of the unquestioned, hence hegemonic, articulations of the Cartesian binary, unseating post-Enlightenment rationalism and demonstrating, through a series of ultimately destructive vignettes, that the bar that separates the mind from the body is far more permeable than we might otherwise like to think.

What this means, specifically for the films in this chapter but also more broadly for all of Cronenberg's films, is that while the body contains and exhibits the agency of the subject who inhabits it, the body comes to display some kind of agency of its own, an 'agency of the flesh' with its own desires and its own (often massively disruptive) ways of achieving those ends. This bodily agency works to remind the subject, often in the most forceful and tragic ways, that the body is

> . . . mortal and open to diseases and will one day die, taking the self along with it – the mere possibility of disease reminds the self that he does not control his body . . . and [that] it represents the hidden perversions the self tries to repress. (Roche, 2004)

What David Roche reveals are the ways in which Cronenberg's films will push to the very limits the protagonists' bodies, utilizing sex and disease as the means to disturb normal – hence normalizing – conceptions of both sides of the Cartesian dialectic and, particularly, to disturb the rigorous disciplinary structures that work to keep them apart.

Shivers is, in many ways, a remarkable film. Of course, it is Cronenberg's first commercial feature and comes after the moderate success (critical though certainly not financial) of his previous two independent features, *Stereo* (1967) and *Crimes of the Future* (1969). Nevertheless, *Shivers* does not mark a complete acquiescence to the form and structure of the mainstream feature and its general reception demonstrates how unprepared the critical community (though not the public) were for a film such as this. For much of its narrative it is without a central protagonist, concentrating instead on the parallel stories of a group of people. What protagonists the film does feature do not behave in any predictable fashion, either in generic terms or broader conventional terms; further, the film does not play favourites – everyone the film touches upon is equally available to its violence and no one (literally) is spared the fate that Cronenberg ambiguously offers as the film's conclusion.

Shivers

Shivers details the events that occur at the isolated and upmarket Starliner Towers apartment complex located, according to the introductory sales pitch that begins the film, some distance from the urban sprawl of Montreal. One of the complex's inhabitants, Dr. Hobbes (Fred Doederlein) has been involved in attempts to develop a benign parasite that, when introduced to an ailing body, would consume and thereafter replace diseased organs with its own. As Hobbes' colleague, Rollo Linsky (Joe Silver), explains,

> Why not breed a parasite capable of taking over the function of any one of a bunch of human organs? Why not, for example, a parasite living in the human abdominal cavity that plugs into the circulatory system and filters the blood like a kidney? If it takes a little blood for itself, so what? Be generous. You can afford it. (Cronenberg, 2002a, 37)

However, the good scientist Hobbes has been involved in a supplementary project, one that inevitably leads to disaster. Again it is Linsky who explains things for us:

> Hobbes thought that man is an animal that thinks too much, an animal that has lost touch with his instinct, his 'primal self' . . . in other words, too much brain and not enough guts. And what he came up with to help our guts along was a human parasite that is . . . 'a combination of aphrodisiac and venereal disease, a modern version of the satyr's tongue'. (ibid., 63)

Thus emerges the horror at the centre of *Shivers* and, for the public at large, the first concrete articulation of Cronenberg's overt concerns: the manner with which the body can transform away from what might be recognizably human towards some other state of being, all without the consent of the subjects concerned. Our developing picture of Hobbes, as the narrative progresses, is retrospectively constructed along the familiar lines of the mad scientist, a man compelled by a combination of scientific hubris and unfulfilled (and only broadly hinted at) 'dangerous' desires to move beyond the bounds of Cartesian rationality. During the course of his experiments he infects his young lover[1] Annabelle (Cathy Graham) with the parasites only to discover that his experiment has been too successful, beyond his ability to control its outcome. Once infected (although, perhaps, infested is the correct word to use) Annabelle utterly succumbs to the venereal drive of the parasites, going on to infect other inhabitants of Starliner Towers. The remainder of the film details the collapse of the strictly Apollonian order of the apartment complex into a Dionysian frenzy that manages to rupture most taboos concerning permissible sexual relations as each newly infected participant joins the growing army of 'sex zombies'. *Shivers* finishes with the complex's population departing in a long line of automobiles towards the bright lights of Montreal's ordered suburbs while a radio commentary details growing reports of unprovoked and unconfirmed sexual attacks.

Shivers does not feature a conventional or central protagonist. Rather, the film focuses its attention on a small number of the apartment complex's inhabitants, in order to offer us variations on the theme of infection and response to infection, and by and large there is no all-conquering hero to save the day. Indeed, in its thorough dispensation of the major tropes of the horror genre, *Shivers*, along with a handful of other films, marks the development of a new subgenre of horror: Body Horror. Michael Grant typifies Body Horror as 'a cinema of the violation and destruction of the body . . . [a] mode of showing the horror rather than telling it' (Grant, 2000, 2), which originates with George Romero's *Night of the Living Dead* (1968). Graphic exhibition, then, is one of the most obvious tropes of Body Horror – an extreme attention paid to the various sufferings of the body-on-screen – and in this Cronenberg certainly excels. Here the body functions metaphorically, with Romero's shuffling zombies a representation of an increasingly consumption-driven middle America. Similarly Starliner Towers, 'a self-sufficient high-rise complex with the infrastructure of a small community' (Caldwell, 2002), stands in for North America as a whole. In this manner '*Shivers*' real protagonist is collective – the inhabitants of the complex [represent] modern urban North Americans in general' (Beard, 2001, 27–8).

However, it would be a mistake to read *Shivers* as just a critique of middle-class North America; it is, I contend, much more complicated than this. As noted above, the body in *Shivers* is both a point of mediation between sociocultural demands and the subjectivity that emerges as a result, as well as being an interstitial node, a nexus point at which the disciplinary activities of society intersect and are played out. The body thus functions as both the site of subjectivity (and hence agency, which, as *Shivers* begins, is presumed to reside with and in subjectivity) as well as the representative of the various successful social mechanisms that surround it, while the venereal parasite disrupts all of these categories, introducing a new disciplinary mechanism into the articulation of subjectivity. Thus, any interference with the body will result in the disruption of both of the poles (subjectivity and society) it stands between.

Further to this, Cronenberg's particular innovations within the subgenre of Body Horror mark an increased fascination with, and horror of, the body itself. This closeness of attention marks *Shivers* as a much more political film that its subgenre stablemates. The zombies in *Night of the Living Dead* are clearly part of a polemic regarding larger groups of people;

an entire class system is critiqued in Romero's films and what comes to typify the later developments in the Body Horror subgenre is the manner with which it pits classes of people against each other (and often themselves). *Shivers* is different as it recognizes that a systematic critique that begins at the level of class consciousness is already too cumbersome (and too late) to be of any real use in revealing inequitable or arbitrary structures at work. Instead, *Shivers* takes literally the notion of Body Horror – here understood not just as horror at the trauma the body suffers, but horror of the body in and of itself. The Body Horror available in *Shivers* is certainly located at the level of the viscera, meaning that the various travails of the parasites provide plenty of opportunity for spectatorial upset. But, more than this, the baseline of horror here lies in the manner with which *Shivers* reveals the instability of our most intimate structures: identity and agency.

What Cronenberg does in *Shivers* is render the body alien to subjective identity, an exercise that results in questions regarding agency that the film does not trouble itself to answer. In this manner, *Shivers* uses the disruption of the body to multiple ends. First the disruption, which occurs as a result of parasitic infestation, provides an opportunity to explore the location and function of subjective agency. So while the inhabitants of Starliner Towers behave as good bourgeois citizens prior to their infection, their actions after infestation raise questions regarding their motivations. Given the specifically venereal nature of the parasites, are their actions their own (i.e., originating within them and suppressed by the disciplinary mechanisms of culture) but facilitated and realized by the presence and influence of the parasites, or are they now essentially empty vessels inhabited solely by the procreative impulses of the parasites? *Shivers* is suitably ambiguous about resolving this problem, preferring to leave open the question of agency and, therefore, of responsibility. Second, as the body functions as the visible representation of the social disciplinary order of which Starliner Towers is a microcosm, the movement from orderly to transgressive body plays out as social disruption at the level of the increasingly poorly disciplined individual. We see this disruption of discipline occur at all levels, from the solipsistic relationship of the individual to his or her own body through to the interpersonal and broadly social. Thus the cross section of inhabitants of the apartment complex provides the means for *Shivers* to illustrate a near-total overthrow of society's most deeply held taboos and restrictions. Finally, Cronenberg is eager, through *Shivers*, to illustrate the arbitrary nature of these disciplinary controls and restrictions. As he notes,

We are part of a culture, we are part of an ethical and moral system, but all we have to do is take one step outside it and we see that none of it is absolute. Nothing is true.[2] . . . It's only a human construct, very definitely able to change and susceptible to change and rethinking. (Cronenberg, quoted in Breskin, 1992)

Thus, for Cronenberg, all of our culture's various 'ethical and moral systems' are available for scrutiny: nothing need be spared this film's acerbic gaze.

De-Eroticizing Sex

Starliner Towers represents, for the film's diegesis, an apogee of social and cultural order and an '. . . antiseptic bulwark against urban life' (Bokamper, 2000). The film's introductory sequence, delivered as a deadpan sales pitch slide-show by the building's administrator Merrick (Ronald Mlodzik), promises that we will be 'secure in the knowledge that it [Starliner Towers] belongs to you and your fellow passengers alone' (Cronenberg, 1976). Through a series of oddly composed photographs, the opening demonstrates that this apartment complex is a 'microcosm of the modernist urban aesthetics of middle-class materialism' (Beard, 2001, 30) within which one can 'sail through life in quiet and comfort' (Cronenberg, 1976). However, the life that is actually offered at Starliner Towers is not so much a sanctuary as a kind of deadening, leaving the inhabitants 'emotionally distant and socially dislocated' (Sanjek, 1996). The film constructs the inhabitants as so bereft of actual human warmth and contact as to potentially benefit from a parasitic infestation that forces them to renegotiate the social structures that have left them isolated (both from each other as inhabitants of this apartment complex and from the rest of humanity, given Starliner Towers' rural positioning). Thus Starliner Towers stands in for not only a generic North American middle-classness but also a broader state of social and cultural malaise where the very mechanisms designed to provide respite from the demands of the contemporary experience are so constraining as to reduce one's life to an inhibited rondo of dissatisfying interactions.

It is fitting, given this listless opening, that we cut from this introductory sequence and Merrick's welcoming of a prospective new couple to the apartment complex to the morning ablutions of Nicholas Tudor (Allan Migicovsky) in his bathroom. This allows for a direct comparison between the social world and the inhabitants of that world; if the advertising sequence allows us to comprehend the sterility of the place and setting of *Shivers*, cutting from here to Nicholas' obsessive self-examination in the polished surfaces of his bathroom provides for a deeper understanding of the kinds of subjects who both inhabit this place and emerge as a result of that habitation. Nicholas' morning ritual, which involves a thorough cleaning of his mouth with a dental instrument, seems obsessive and self-involved, a point further made with his dismissive tone towards his loving and attentive wife Janine (Susan Petrie). Nicholas is the first demonstration of the kind of subject who emerges as a result of the social structures exemplified by Starliner Towers, and the Tudor marriage serves as a further counterpoint to what they themselves represent. Nicholas' narcissistic self-devotion reaches a near-masturbatory climax when, as his parasites are preparing to leave his body, he lies in bed massaging the squirming lumps on his abdomen while whispering, 'C'mon boy. Here boy, here. C'mon fella. You and me. You and me are going to make good friends' (Cronenberg, 1976). However, in the general schema of social order illustrated by the inhabitants of Starliner Towers, Nicholas is somewhat atypical. All of the other inhabitants, once infected, are driven outwards (whereas Nicholas shows increased introspection) in order to further spread the parasites.

Within *Shivers* there is one other site of resistance to the parasites: the complex's resident doctor, Roger St. Luc (Paul Hampton). St. Luc, like Nicholas, is a problematic figure within the diegetic structure of *Shivers*, but for entirely different reasons. St. Luc is the closest thing to a protagonist the film has and while he is entirely passive in the narrative, neither causing nor solving the problem of infestation, his battle to remain uninfected and to do something about the infection (although quite what remains unclear) forms the bulk of the film's episodic narrative. The most thorough explication of St. Luc's character comes as he speaks with Rollo Linsky, Dr. Hobbes' former colleague and research partner, by telephone. During this conversation, his nurse, Forsythe, finishes her duties at the clinic and then changes from her uniform into a black evening gown in front of St. Luc. As Cronenberg's screenplay puts it,

> [Forsythe] begins to take off her nurse's uniform in full view of St. Luc, not being obvious about the distraction she's providing, but not taking pains to hurry dressing or be modest either. . . . In the scene that follows we cut among three basic things: Rollo in his lab, talking and eating;

St. Luc in his office, watching Forsythe get undressed and then dressed; and Hobbes's notes and scribblings. . . . (Cronenberg, 2002a, 61)

As this sequence plays out in the film, we spend a good deal of time watching Forsythe, much as one might expect. After all, she is an attractive young woman and is clearly seeking the attention and approval of St. Luc (much as the film's use of her seeks, or seems to seek, the same thing from its audience). Yet the sequence is utterly devoid of any kind of eroticism. Those points where we follow St. Luc's eyeline to Forsythe's partially naked body involve us meeting Forsythe's gaze as she looks back at St. Luc (and therefore at us) but neither of the diegetic gazes (St. Luc.'s or Forsythe's) carry any hint of arousal and so neither can ours. While Cronenberg's camera continues to fragment Forsythe's body, in the manner seemingly demanded by classical Hollywood form, the shots appear clinical and cold because those shots that frame our entry and exit from these sequences do not carry any kind of contextualizing eroticism: this is further confirmed with every reverse shot which brings us back from the object being looked at (in this instance, Forsythe and specific parts of her body) to St. Luc's utterly disinterested face. Thus the sex, by which I mean 'normal' (hetero-) sex, is rendered anything but sexy by Cronenberg's camera, which appears to deliver and yet withholds at the same time.

The closest St. Luc comes to succumbing to any kind of normal desire occurs later in the film. By this stage, the presence of the parasites is being clearly demonstrated by the increasingly extreme behaviour of Starliner's inhabitants. As St. Luc and Forsythe (who has been attacked twice) shelter in a basement, a dazed Forsythe gives the following pivotal speech:

Sometimes I have a recurrent dream. Have I ever told you about it, darling? I guess you could call it a Freudian dream, because in this dream I find myself making love to Sigmund Freud. But I'm having trouble because he's old and dying, and he smells bad and I find him repulsive. And then he tells me that everything is erotic, everything is sexual, you know what I mean? . . . He tells me that even old flesh is erotic flesh, that disease is the love of two alien kinds of creatures for each other, that dying is an act of eroticism. . . . That breathing is sexual, that talking is sexual, that just to physically exist is sexual. . . . And I believe him, and we make love beautifully. . . . (Cronenberg, 2002a, 96)

This sequence, which is delivered in a conventional shot–reverse shot alternating between high and low angle close-ups, finishes with Forsythe reaching up to hold the back of St. Luc's head as she moves to kiss him. At the point where we would expect St. Luc to respond and kiss her (finally) we cut to what can only be St. Luc's point of view as Forsythe recoils back, hissing. At the same moment, one of the parasites begins to move from her oesophagus and into her mouth (a sight that is both excremental and oddly phallic, as if Forsythe were regurgitating a penis) and St. Luc responds by punching her unconscious and then taping her mouth shut. For much of the remainder of the film, Forsythe will wear this gag, which becomes increasingly bloodstained as the parasites attempt to leave her body. St. Luc's violence towards Forsythe, and the manner with which he, literally, shuts her up, echoes Hobbes' treatment of Annabelle at the film's beginning, wherein Hobbes strangles the half-naked schoolgirl, tapes her mouth shut and eviscerates her. That both of these moments portray physically (and intellectually) superior men resorting to actual and symbolic violence in order to maintain a status quo in the face of an unfathomable threat says a great deal about Cronenberg's sophisticated critique.

At a superficial level, this moment is a clear critique of the manner with which a white, heterosexual patriarchy will assert its own desires in the face of a threat it considers aberrant, but this assessment is complicated with the realization that St. Luc's violence is normalized as the correct response when seeking to defend and maintain the interests of the patriarchal status quo. Deeper than this, though, is the realization that this moment marks a collision of desires: that of St. Luc for Forsythe (perhaps) and the spectators for the establishment of a normal – hence generically heroic and successful – couple in the face of civil disintegration as a result of the actions of the parasites. The difficulty St. Luc (and, by extension, patriarchy) faces is that the form of subjectivity that emerges as a result of parasitism is utterly unknowable and beyond our ability to comprehend. Indeed, as will be argued in ths final chapter, this new form of subjectivity is beyond our ability to represent. St. Luc's actions, then, reflect the fear of the subject as agent at losing one's agency (and, hence, one's identity) in the face of a force that can either overcome that identity or replace it entirely. Finally, St. Luc's actions (like Hobbes' and, indeed, like the actions of all authority figures in Cronenberg's films) demonstrate that when it comes to maintaining disciplinary control, violence is always a probable outcome.

Overcoming the Porn Aesthetic

At the film's climax, St. Luc finally succumbs to the shambolic horde and, '. . . after slipping away from so many of Forsythe's advances, he is nailed down at last by her parasite-passing kiss in the pool . . . amidst scenes of communal celebration; and this time he will *stay* sexualized' (Beard, 2001, 42; emphasis in original). This final point is the key one: St. Luc has denied his sexuality, his desire and his body in order to maintain the stability of his identity which, nonetheless, is overcome through the medium of sexuality – that which has been so forcefully denied. The slow-motion sequence that marks St. Luc's induction into the world of the infected, as with the film's two other slow-motion sequences, works to demonstrate the manner with which Cronenberg seeks to render visible the disciplinary structures inherent in such representations. Each of these encounters utilizes a particular kind of cinematic form in relation to its diegetic detail and it is no accident that each of these encounters is, superficially at least, erotic. A closer examination of two of these sequences reveals exactly what is at stake with Cronenberg's formalist aesthetic.

As discussed above, the sequence of Forsythe undressing for a disinterested St. Luc is de-eroticized by the absence of both formal and diegetic indicators of pleasure, or, perhaps more accurately, indicators of a permission for the spectator to take pleasure. St. Luc's disinterest frames and bookends our interpretations of Forsythe's figure exactly as the camera's overall distance and stillness keeps us from either utilizing what should have been St. Luc's engagement to construct our own fantasy of her, or utilizing the (absent) point-of-view shots to occupy St. Luc's spectatorial position. In this manner Cronenberg demonstrates Forsythe's attractiveness and yet withholds the spectatorial mechanisms conventionally utilized to generate pleasure in what would clearly be a masculinized and heterosexualized position. This moment provides our first example of the way in which a fundamental mechanism of both discipline and pleasure is manipulated by Cronenberg.

A similar aesthetic is at work with St. Luc's induction. Here we see St. Luc and Forsythe embrace in the complex's swimming pool, surrounded by scantily clad and naked complex dwellers. As the group overpowers St. Luc, Forsythe pulls him to her and, in slow motion and in close-up, delivers the kiss that passes on the parasite. Again, the same disciplinary structure is revealed in the act of denying it: the passion of Forsythe's

kiss, and the revellers' general exuberance, is undercut by the knowledge that the identities they demonstrate, and therefore the pleasures
they both experience and represent, may not actually be their own.

Two things occur with this sequence. First, the concept of Body Horror
is demonstrated to be at its most horrifying at the moment of what would
ordinarily be high pleasure. Cinematically, these people are coded as
experiencing enormous amounts of libidinal satisfaction and yet all of
this framing is undercut by the diegetic presence of the parasites that
make such pleasures a compulsion, thereby removing the pleasure from
the inhabitants as agents, and locating it in some other place. Second, as
with the scene of Forsythe undressing, this sequences serves to demonstrate that multiple structures of pleasure are being manipulated by
Cronenberg's film in order to remove the 'normal' (i.e., masculine, heterosexual and thoroughly invisible) pleasure from them. Cronenberg's
formalist approach here leads to an estrangement of some pleasures
from these sequences, which in turn become oddly cold and barren in
their absence, meaning that when the libidinal pleasure an audience
might obtain as a result of St. Luc's diegetic satisfaction is evacuated,
what remains – the spectatorial pleasures – feel hollow and unfamiliar.
This defamiliarization, in its turn, further heightens the spectatorial suspicion that something is wrong, that the object of desire (Forsythe's
body) is not permitted to be viewed as desirable. What are absent are the
mechanisms that would ordinarily grant permission for the spectator to
take pleasure from these sequences, but in their absence they become
very visible indeed.

More controversial and even more illuminating is the way *Shivers*
reveals the presence of other disciplinary structures of pleasure. These
are primarily concerned with the ways in which certain objects of desire
are or can be coded as permissible – even encouraged as ideal – while
other objects remain contraband and forbidden from such engagements. Given that the primary erotic structure, both within the film as it
begins and throughout the narrative in general, is coded as masculinist
and heterosexual, one does not need to shift the mechanisms of pleasure very far to demonstrate their presence, insofar as the clearly visible
heretonormativity which is the film's starting point only requires a slight
problematizing and the introduction of minor differences to reveal these
structures at play. However, replacng the object coded as erotic or desirable will both fundamentally alter the spectator's engagement with the
screen and reveal that structure to be utterly arbitrary in its choice of
object.

As the parasites make their way through the building, the film takes leave of the core characters to detail the chain of infection that best demonstrates both the thorough overthrow of authority at work within the film's diegesis and the manner with which these structures of representation are arbitrary in their construction and application. Beginning with Nicholas, who involuntarily vomits up one of his beloved parasites, the chain of infection moves to a large, elderly lady who is overcome while doing her laundry. She then overcomes a horrified restaurant deliveryman, whom we later see languidly smearing his face with food – a sure sign of his infection (and a canny conflation of appetites). He then stumbles into an elevator containing a middle-aged (and, to judge by her clothing, middle-class) woman and her prepubescent daughter. While we are not shown their infection, it is clear that by the time the lift arrives in the building foyer, they have both been overcome by the deliveryman. As he then assaults the complex's ineffectual security guard, the mother (now in her underwear) and the girl assist in holding the guard down to complete the infection and thereby remove the complex's remaining figure of external authority. What makes this sequence so startling is the fact that there are three avenues for the narrative to follow, each offering a different degree of transgression as it plays out. To have the parasite passed to the guard by the mother would be banal, both by the film's own particular erotic structure and also by broader extra-filmic standards. In effect, to have the mother kiss the guard would essentially render the kiss invisible as an erotic exchange, so completely would it conform to the extra-filmic structures of acceptable erotic and sexual practice. Given the context of the film's production and reception, having the deliveryman kiss the guard as deeply as the parasites seem to require would certainly be transgressive, but not nearly as much as the third option, which is the choice made by Cronenberg. With the guard restrained, it is the young girl who leans in and, again in close-up and in slow motion, kisses the guard deeply while the other two look on approvingly.

This moment is central to *Shivers'* programme of political critique for a number of reasons. First, the mere fact of utilizing the young girl as the perpetrator of what is essentially a sex crime reveals the extent of the parasites' reach. This implication, that literally everyone infected by them becomes sexually active and deliberately promiscuous, cuts to the heart of those moral and ethical structures surrounding notions of correct social and sexual behaviour. This is the manner with which the film's narrative and diegetic material intersects with the external disciplinary structures that provide an audience with its interpretive mechanisms. More importantly though, this moment reveals the collusion between any film's diegetic material and its formal mechanisms in the delivery of disciplinary material to an audience. The fact that the young girl who delivers the parasitic coup de grâce has been coded as an erotic object indicates that this coding, which results in her uncomfortable (for the audience) actions, has occurred formally and is a conclusion provided by the combination of slow motion and close-up, both of which occur end-lessly in more 'ordinary' fare in order to provide an audience with the means to concentrate on more socially acceptable erotic objects. In essence, this moment marks the intersection of two structural mech-anisms – the manner with which diegetic objects are coded as erotic, and the manner with which we may 'normally' consider children – both of which are revealed to be present at the moment they are rendered trans-gressive through their combination.

The first of these structures (formal erotic coding as a way of repre-senting parasitic infestation) requires the presence of a diegetic charac-ter to continue the chain of infection. Given the effect of infection, certain bodies would ordinarily be 'off limits' to the film's pool of poten-tial hosts, and yet to resist placing anyone in this position because of mere 'unsuitability' would undermine the narrative's own logic, which is that all of the buildings inhabitants serve equally as hosts to the parasites. Therefore, having filled the narrative position with the ordinarily contra-band figure of a young girl, the film then delivers her as an erotic object utilizing exactly the same formal techniques used as the lesbian kiss through which Betts passes the parasite to Janine, and Forsythe to St. Luc. As with Forsythe's final kiss, the presence of the parasite undermines the eroticism of the child's kiss, but because the film has accumulated more normal erotic material in relation to the parasites' functioning, it is inev-itable that the child's kiss retains this erotic overtone. Of course, *Shivers* provides many other examples of total moral upset, but it is here that we can see most clearly the relationship between any film's diegetic content, its formal choices in representing and delivering that content, and the manner with which these two ordinarily invisible mechanisms clearly articulate how an audience is meant to understand and interpret the material it encounters. Here both the formal diegetic and narrative structures require the presence of a body that, once on screen, will be coded as erotic. The fact that the body chosen is that of a pre-pubescent girl serves to reveal, through the interpretive conflict that occurs, the structures that direct our response to or away from pleasure in a disciplinary fashion.

A similar act of transgressive substitution occurs as St. Luc explores the complex, having managed to lose Forsythe in the tumult. While these journeys do have some slight narrative justification, their major purpose is to demonstrate to us the ways in which the parasites have enabled a total overthrow of the old conservative ways, represented by the building itself. As St. Luc winds his way down a service staircase, he rounds a corner to encounter two near-naked prepubescent girls on all fours, secured by collars and dog-leads to an adult figure we never quite see. St. Luc's shock (not at the sight, it must be said, but at the threat of infection) provides the motivation to cut away from this sight, but its presence and implication are clear. As with the parasitic transmission enacted by the pre-pubescent girl, these children occupy structural positions that would ordinarily be filled by other, more socially acceptable figures. It is through the filling of these positions with socially incorrect choices that these structures are made visible. Similarly, the mise-en-scène codes these two girls as sexually active and aggressive, exactly as the cinematic form had coded the elevator girl as active and aggressive.

This notion of the various structural mechanisms at work in the film explains why St. Luc must remain uninfected until the very last. While he is not the hero in any recognizable sense, he occupies a number of strategic structural places, not least of which is the last bastion of the old (diegetic) order – white, middle-class masculinity. Further to this, the overthrow of St. Luc is a generic overthrow, replacing the heroic 'last man' or survivor for the sake of the film's onslaught through another (eventually) willing participant. Finally, St. Luc's role is comparative: as the symbol of the old, normative and, hence, invisible order, he functions as a means of determining exactly how far from his moral centre these transgressions run.

Rabid

Rabid, when compared with *Shivers,* is a far more conventional film, despite the content of its narrative. As has been noted elsewhere,[3] the story contained in *Rabid* is, in many ways, a straightforward extension and elaboration of the ideas and plot of *Shivers.* What is different between them is their scale: where *Shivers* discusses the development and spread of a body-altering plague among the inhabitants of a single apartment block, *Rabid* plays out the concept of a body-altering plague within the populated cityscape (again it is Montreal that gets it, this time literally, in the neck).

Rabid details the story of Rose (Marilyn Chambers), a young motorcyclist who with her partner Hart (Frank Moore) is involved in a serious motorcycle accident. Luckily the crash is witnessed by patients at the nearby Keloid Clinic for plastic surgery, and the two are rushed there for emergency surgery. While Hart is relatively unharmed, Rose has extensive abdominal injuries and the attending surgeon, Dr Dan Keloid (Howard Ryshpan), decides to attempt an innovative new technique. This involves the grafting of 'morphogenetically neutral' tissue[4] that, while involving the possibility for the development of carcinomas, remains Rose's only hope for survival. After a month in a coma, Rose awakes to discover that the skin grafts have provided her with a new organ: located in her armpit is a puckered orifice that conceals a phallic protuberance, armed with a lethal spike at its tip. Further, she now hungers blood and begins to pursue these new appetites with disastrous consequences: every person she feeds on develops a highly virulent form of rabies that sees them awaken from their post-traumatic coma with a hunger for human flesh. Eventually Rose, who cannot face the fact that her feeding habits and the city-wide outbreak of rabid zombies are connected, decides to test the theory by feeding off a man and locking herself in a room with

FIGURE 2.1   Disposing of Rose's *Rabid* corpse.

him, to see if he falls prey to the infection. While she is on the telephone to Hart, Rose's final victim regains consciousness, frothing at the mouth, and, off camera, kills Rose. *Rabid* ends with a sequence detailing her corpse being located by a clean-up crew and dumped in the back of a garbage-compacting truck (see Figure 2.1).

Shades of Transformation

While it is clear that *Rabid* continues and develops the themes of *Shivers*, there are notable changes and alterations to the themes themselves. Most obvious of these is the fact that the transformation that occurs in *Rabid* takes two forms and has two different narrative functions, whereas the transformation in *Shivers* is the same for all participants. Clearly Rose's post-operative status as, essentially, a vampire figure is the central focus of the film's narrative and it is her story that occupies the majority of the film's screen time. Nevertheless, the secondary transformations, of her victims into rabid raving creatures,[5] are equally important and serve to demonstrate that Rose's own transformation is itself primarily generative. None of her victims develop similar supplementary organs – hers is the result of Keloid's surgery – and yet her victims emerge as a result of her transformation and, once infected, are able to themselves infect other people. Rose's victims become rabid and spread the second-stage, consciousness-destroying rabies of the film's title, whereas Rose remains virtually unaware of her status as the source of infection. This alteration of the classic vampire economy, wherein vampire begets vampire, means that, as with the parasites in *Shivers*, the rabies functions as a kind of self-directed virus interested in spreading itself regardless of the cost to the hosts. Indeed, the film makes it very clear that those infected with the rabies virus are 'beyond medical help once it [the disease] has established itself to the degree of inducing violent behaviour' (Cronenberg, 1977, 69). Thus the medical establishment's sole response to the epidemic is to execute any person infected by the virus as no cure can be found and those infected seem to die as a result of the infection regardless.

That this epidemic emerges as the result of the actions of a single individual should cause us little surprise. Keloid's role in *Rabid* is a continuation of Hobbes' in *Shivers* and the scientist figure forms a central part of most of Cronenberg's cinema. In *Shivers* Hobbes is solely responsible for the infection, indeed for the invention of the parasites in order to solve what he (alone, it would seem) perceives to be our species' primary obstacle to fulfilment: our increasing intellectualization away from our corporeal origins. For Hobbes to claim that 'man is an animal that thinks too much' is to take sides, resulting in his attempt to force the human subject more fully to one side of the Cartesian dialectic at the expense of what appears to be a hard-won and barely maintained equilibrium. The implication is that the products of 'thinking too much', be they social or cultural, are repressive and therefore somehow 'wrong' – or, at the very least, less 'natural' and Cronenberg's own filmic discourse is thus at work to assess and critique this perception. Here, the irony, reflective of Cronenberg's own position, is that Hobbes' attempt to return to a more natural condition can only be achieved through the highest degree of scientific (hence intellectual) intervention.

In *Rabid*, the intervention of science into the body is even more pronounced, primarily because the scientist figure is permitted enough screen-time to become an integral character rather than remaining, as with Cronenberg's previous scientist figures, a mere cipher.[6] What renders *Rabid* more problematic than its predecessors is the fact that, at least for the final cut of the film, there is no obvious reason for Keloid to experiment on Rose at all. In the film some covert suggestion is made as to the extent of Rose's injuries, but, as we cut from her being rolled into the operating theatre to Keloid's explanation of the surgical procedure to his attending staff, the film provides us with the 'what' of his innovative 'neutral field grafts' and none of the 'why'. Unlike Hobbes in *Shivers*, who clearly intends for his parasites to impact utterly upon the way the hosts continue their lives, there is no indication that Keloid has anything other than Rose's health and recovery as a motive. Nevertheless, regardless of Keloid's good intentions, Rose is as much a victim of his science as Annabelle and the inhabitants of Starliner Towers are victims of Hobbes'.

Keloid's actions are never questioned; diegetically, as chief surgeon he is the film's centre of authority – at least for the time being – and the narrative moves quickly to gloss over the elision of his rationale. This moment is actually central to discerning Keloid's function within Cronenberg's discourse. As with Hobbes, Keloid's role as a diegetic authority sees a conflation of his function in the public service as a surgeon with his right, as an authority figure, to proceed as he wishes. With this in mind, Keloid has no need to provide a rationale or justification for his decision to experiment on Rose: in essence, he acts as he does because he can. However this is not to say that Keloid and Hobbes function as simple examples of society's disciplinary mechanisms alone. They certainly do this, but their actions serve to highlight the imbalance that lies at the centre of all of the films discussed in this chapter.

Clearly Keloid is meant from the outset to represent the arbitrary nature of society's disciplinary mechanisms: he is, after all, a plastic surgeon responsible both to and for notions of body image and image-culture. Certainly *Rabid* does make some attempt to grant Keloid a measure of morality by having him resist, during a board meeting, attempts to turn the clinic into 'the Colonel Sanders of plastic surgery' (Cronenberg, 1977).[7] Nevertheless, plastic surgery is both arbitrary (reliant on the fads and vagaries of fashion and image-culture) and disciplinary (involved in offering models of the body to be conformed to, and which are confirmed with each procedure). Keloid therefore functions as an example of society at both its most arbitrary and its most disciplinary, and these factors are involved in his decision not just to operate on Rose, but to experiment upon her. Here the hubris of the mad scientist is veiled by a veneer of pubic service and expedient necessity, yet Keloid is no different from Hobbes. Rose's passivity mirrors Annabelle's in *Shivers*: of course, the fact that Rose is in a coma when Keloid encounters her neatly sidesteps (but does not resolve) the issue of consent and thus, with the premise of needing to save her life, the narrative of *Rabid* conspires to enforce Rose's participation.

Still, Keloid's (and Hobbes') role as a disciplinary exemplar is problematic, to say the least. Certainly as a doctor he is well placed to impose disciplinary measures surrounding the health and maintenance of the bodies he encounters that would be both socially and morally 'correct'. Hobbes, too, could presumably function in this harmless – which is to say, disciplinarily invisible – fashion and yet neither of them do. Hobbes' desire to force one side of the Cartesian divide to prominence seems to be a rather elaborate, and ham-fisted, attempt to either resolve or rationalize his predilection for his underage students. If anything, Keloid's unthinking rationalism is more horrifying because of the way it reveals so fully the entrenched discourses of power that justify and validate his position and his actions. Both of these men, by violating the tenets of their authority, work to render visible the articulation of power inherent in their positions.

These two examples, Keloid and Hobbes, demonstrate the degree of criticism inherent in Cronenberg's narratives: in both films, there are discourses of scientific imposition and its relationship to both sexual and social relations (as well as general sexual impropriety). In both films,

women are utterly passive before the powerful men who intrude into
their lives and bodies, and in both the women suffer at the hands of
these men and the scientific community they represent. Yet the manner
with which these films play out seems to undercut this relatively straightforward critique by offering the possibility for further interpretation. In
both of these films it is the woman's body that is (at least at first) rendered monstrous and overproductive. Despite Rose's plaintive appeals
that 'it's not my fault . . . it's not my fault' (Cronenberg, 1977), the film
leaves open the question of how we are to assess Rose: is she, as the television reporters in *Rabid* suggest, a kind of active and knowing Typhoid
Mary who should be held solely responsible for the outbreak of rabies, or
does the responsibility lie elsewhere for her transformation and its concomitant effects upon the society that is demonstrably ill-prepared for it?
Given that Keloid functions as the representative of society in *Rabid*, the
issue of assigning blame or responsibility turns in on itself. This is not to
suggest, however, that it is irresolvable, at least in the film's own terms.

The fact that Rose's particular infection is generative (i.e. her feeding
activities produce the rabies which she herself does not suffer from)
means that her body, rendered 'over-full' with the development of a
spiked neo-phallus that nestles in her armpit within a puckered neo-anus
of its own, is both a site of horror and is also capable of producing and
transmitting horror. She is, in effect, both the mother of the 'crazies',
insofar as she incubates the rabies they catch, and the father who impreg-
nates them with the virus. The problem that Rose becomes is resolved
with the film's conclusion as she is, quite unceremoniously, collected
and deposited in a trash compactor. Here Cronenberg's ambiguity is at
its most difficult: both sides of the disciplinarian structure seem equally
viable as sites of criticism, for even as Rose is consigned to the trash, the
surgeon who has interceded is also punished (he is fed upon by Rose,
develops rabies and, presumably, dies).

Rose's Ambiguity and the Porn Aesthetic

Rose's presence as a site of ambiguity in the film's narrative (and the various interpretations we might come to make of it) is nowhere as visible as
in the various attacks she performs during the course of her transformation. The first of these, which occurs as she awakens from her post-
operative coma, is confusing for both us and her, and this confusion is
reflected in the ways in which the film does not, at first, seek to explain

what is happening. Rose, awakened from a coma in a state of comely undress, is comforted by Lloyd Walsh (Roger Periard), a fellow patient in the clinic. Despite his insistence that he get further medical help, she holds onto him and, without fully realizing her actions, punctures his neck and begins to feed upon him. This sequence is itself punctuated by an extreme close-up shot of her hypodermic phallic spike emerging from its neo-anal sheath. This image, while horrifying, occurs without any kind of framing or context and so hangs unresolved amidst Rose's actions, which are more conventionally framed. What we instead might choose to focus our interpretive energies upon is the sight of Rose, top-less, pulling an older man towards her while imploring him to comfort her. It is here that Ivan Reitman's decision to cast Marilyn Chambers as Rose generates interest, with the famous porn-actor playing Rose against type as a gentle and innocent victim who, in this scene, seems to coincide with Chambers' other, more notorious roles. Regardless of this collapse of inter- and intra-diegetic information, Rose's actions are not malicious despite their disturbing nature: she is clearly unaware of the import of her actions, and her innocence (aided by the slightly naïve mannerisms of Chambers' performance) seems to leave her untainted by the fleeting shot of her new viscera.

Her next attacks, however, render this condition as a mistakenly maligned innocent more problematic. Her second attack, coming after an unsuccessful attempt to feed on a stabled cow leaves her retching, sees Rose use her spike to blind a drunken farmer who tries to rape her. This action further develops our sympathy for her: we see her vomiting the cow's blood and understand the nature of her condition even if she herself is slower to comprehend its import. Further, the use of this new organ in self-defence is acceptable, only because we do not yet know that her attacks inevitably lead to fatal cases of rabies. Here, her actions are simply in self-defence, if bizarre in execution. However, while Rose's assault on Lloyd could potentially be explained away due to her post-operative condition and her lack of understanding about her condition and transformation, there can be no such excuses for her subsequent attack on a clinic patient. Immediately after her abortive attempt to feed on the cow and the attack on the farmer, Rose returns to the clinic and finds fellow patient Judy Glasberg (Terry Schonblum) luxuriating in the clinic's hot tub. Despite Judy's increasingly insistent protests, Rose joins her and then pulls her close, impaling her on her vampiric spike. As the two thrash about in the hot tub, Judy in her bikini and Rose in a translu-cent hospital gown, the sequence cuts to a close-up filmed in slow motion.

This is clearly not so that we can see the event in any greater detail; throughout the images are grainy and indistinct, given the mood lighting of the clinic's hot tub room.

This sequence contains clear formal echoes of the parasite-passing kiss that moves the child in *Shivers* from victim to eroticized antagonist. Similarly, the embrace between Rose and Judy suggests a scene in *Shivers* between Janine Tudor and Betts, her sexually active friend and neighbour, during which Betts passes the parasite on to Janine. There, as here, the moment is detailed in close-up and in slow motion, utilizing lighting designed to soften and render intimate sequences which are, at a superficial level, straightforward erotic exchanges. However, what these sequences have in common is more than their utilization of certain formal techniques mobilized by a male director in the delivery of erotic material. Both of these sequences reveal a variety of disciplinary structures to be in operation. The utilization of a porn-aesthetic at these moments draws on our recognition and understanding of these techniques; as the elements of this aesthetic begin to coalesce, they direct us towards a particular interpretation and, therefore, a certain kind of spectatorial pleasure. Thus the diegetic components of all of these sequences – intimate or private location, revealing costumes, isolation, softened lighting in warm tones, slow motion and close-up at certain crucial moments and, importantly, two attractive women – all function invisibly by drawing upon our prior knowledge of these same factors and steer us towards a desired interpretation that this is an erotic encounter, not a vicious assault. However, what both of these sequences do is undercut the possibility for spectatorial enjoyment by providing an added element of narrative information that is much harder for us to reconcile.

With Janine and Betts in *Shivers*, the pleasure which we might otherwise draw from their performance of socially illicit yet not troublingly transgressive contact is prevented with the close-up of the parasite moving from Betts' throat and into Janine's. The phallic nature of the parasite (this particular one had invaded Betts' vagina while she bathed) makes this a complex sexual encounter indeed. Rose's attack on the patient in the hot tub, which superficially is another lesbian encounter, brings forth not only the same kinds of spectatorial pleasures, but also issues of rape and violence when we finally, and fully, comprehend her actions. It is on the issue of Rose's actions that this sequence hinges, since it, like its predecessor in *Shivers*, makes clear the correlation between agency and its manifestation as sexual performance. What the parasites in *Shivers* and Rose's affliction in *Rabid* have in common is the way they focus attention on issues of agency and its relation to the body. As noted, while Hobbes may operate along strictly Cartesian lines, *Shivers* does not, utilizing the body as a central term that mediates between the disciplinary forces of society and culture and the identity that emerges as a result of these. Altering one of these terms will have profound effects on the other two and on the nature of their interrelationship.

In *Rabid* the same critical structure is in place, meaning that one cannot trust a reduction of the film to a simple Cartesian binary. Rose's attack on Judy is significant as it should mark Rose's growing awareness of her condition and its implications; it is the first attack in which her desire to feed is clearly evident and cannot be hidden behind some other explanation. Yet throughout *Rabid*, Rose is continuously constructed as a victim, and her protestations (and eventual suicide) support this sense of her as unwilling subject to the demands of a different kind of bodily agency. Thus Rose's agency is called into question by the very actions that would appear to demonstrate that she is an agent, just as Janine and Betts are rendered problematic by their actions which seem, on the one hand, to emerge 'naturally' out of the plot (frustrated wife falls prey to experienced older woman) and yet, on the other hand, are motivated by the presence of the venereal parasites. Rose's attack on Judy, the first to be visibly and concretely marked by Rose's own awareness of her body's new requirements, throws our previous interpretations of her into disarray. If she is a victim, subject to the demands of an alien condition, she cannot be held responsible for her actions. Yet the attack on Judy reveals a degree of complicity that cannot be explained within a Cartesian schema. As with *Shivers* we are encouraged by Cronenberg to consider the possibility of alternate forms of agency with demonstrably different desires and bodily demands, the understanding of which eludes us because of their very difference to us.

Rose occupies a liminal position, neither simply a monstrous woman nor a powerless victim.[8] The manifestation of Rose's transformation – the phallic spike she uses to penetrate her victims – places her in a powerful position to negotiate between strictly phallic (i.e., masculine) violence and a feminine response to the violence performed upon her by Keloid. Thus the violence in *Rabid* is gendered in a way that it is not in *Shivers*, though this gendering remains unstable (with a single exception, Rose's victims are men and she penetrates them with her own phallus, itself the result of masculine medical intervention). The film's final moments, which see Rose literally reduced to trash, stand as a complex sequence that, again, cannot be so easily consigned to a single interpretation.

Rose's generative vampirism marks her as abject, certainly, but her actions in trying to comprehend her condition do not permit us to reach a stable understanding of her own self-awareness and, hence, agency within that condition. Similarly, the anarchy that emerges as a result of the second-stage rabies is met with swift and deadly force by a group of authorities that seems only too prepared to mete out violence with little consideration of alternative avenues of response.[9] Therefore, *Rabid* both satisfies the demands of the Body Horror genre and exceeds them, rendering impossible the possibility of arriving at a stable interpretation of the film. Throughout all of this, it is the notion of Rose's agency (and hence complicity) that remains the most troubling; in identifying (with) her as a victim, our own desire to reach a stable interpretation of the film emerges as much from a desire to resolve the conditions of our own agency as the wish to find a point of narrative interpretive stability.

The Fly

It is in *The Fly* that the elements at play within *Shivers* and *Rabid* come to fruition. Here we see a central protagonist who fulfils both the role of the scientist figure whose hubristic actions give rise to the crisis at the film's centre, and the role of sole victim of that crisis. Further, the body of the victim continues to serve as the site upon which disruptions of the usually invisible assumptions of the Cartesian dialectic occur, with the added implication that here, finally, it is the flesh itself that seems to have its own wants and needs, its own agency that takes the brilliant mind inhabiting it merely along for the ride. While in *Videodrome*, Cronenberg's discussion of the body, and particularly of the transformative possibilities of the flesh, reaches a discursive maturity, it is *The Fly* that contains the most articulate and sustained discussion[10] of the body and the disciplinary structures that surround the body. The entire film is focused on the development, transformation and fate of its central protagonist, Seth Brundle (Jeff Goldblum), as he negotiates and, importantly, fails to fully control the fact that his body is subject to 'a disease with a purpose' (Cronenberg, 1986). This shift, represented by the notion that the flesh itself has a purpose that renders it at odds with the subjectivity that inhabits it, is something we have seen as central to Cronenberg's films from *Shivers* forward. In all three of the films discussed in this section, it is the flesh that rebels, striking at the bonds of the mind to which it is subject and which holds it in thrall. Indeed, as has been noted elsewhere,

Cronenberg's 'practise of cinema seems, then, to be driven by a desire to annihilate the "bar of repression" which separates the signifier from the signified' (Roche, 2004). This means that his desire to 'make the word be flesh' is tantamount to overcoming, as he sees it, the entirely artificial Cartesian distinction so as to release the fear that the Cartesian dialectic elides. As Roche so forcefully explains,

> . . . the fear of the body is ultimately the fear of the other within me (the fly), whether it be my unconscious flesh (Seth's disease) or my unconscious desires (his newfound superhuman strength and sexual stamina) which often expresses itself through my flesh. (Roche, 2004)

In this manner, *The Fly* is the clearest articulation of Cronenberg's notion of the 'creative cancer'[11] that seeks to articulate its own fate, regardless of the consequences.

The Fly is, more than Cronenberg's other films, sui generis, partaking in nearly equal amounts of aspects of the love story, the science-fiction narrative, the monster movie and the horror film. Each of these genres necessarily brings its own generic requirements and Cronenberg is able to negotiate them much more readily in this film than in the two earlier examples previous discussed. Further to this, Cronenberg's particular technical innovations – in this film concentrated most obviously in the arena of special and creature effects – are much more comprehensively integrated into the film. Another significant development lies in the manner with which Cronenberg's camera (here manned by Mark Irwin, who had worked with Cronenberg since *Fast Company*) is much more empathetic to Brundle and his relationship with Roni Quaife (Geena Davis). Where both *Shivers* and *Rabid* utilized a mode of cinematography that maintained a clinical distance from the subject, and particularly from whatever protagonist the films could muster, here the camera is much more attuned to the requirements of sympathetic character construction, moving closer and providing us with the intimacies that are essential for a central love story. These formal elements will be discussed more completely below.

The Fly stands apart from *Shivers* and *Rabid* in that it is not a Cronenberg story but is an adaptation of a now-classic B-movie of the same name (1958) and, prior to that, a short story. However, Cronenberg notes that the draft of the adaptation he was offered by Mel Brooks (whose company produced *The Fly*) contained material 'detailing the transformation of this character that felt like I could have written myself' (Cronenberg, 1986; DVD special features). This material, when supplemented by Cronenberg's own input,[12] means that *The Fly* does not appear dissimilar from the kind of nascent text being developed in *Shivers* and *Rabid*. What is unique about *The Fly* is that it marks a transition point, after which Cronenberg's discussion of transformation and transgression becomes internalized and subject to other psychic forces. Certainly his later films all continue this discussion of the role of the flesh; after all, the body, for Cronenberg, is the first fact of existence. But in all of the later films the flesh plays a different role. The possibility for a bodily agency becomes less central and the body, if it is altered at all, is either transformed as a result of fantasy (*Naked Lunch*, for example) or other transgressive practices that have their origin in the mind first (*Crash* is a prime example of this).

The Fly is more complex than the other two films discussed in this section, both in terms of its narrative and the underlying concepts it seeks to demonstrate. Brilliant scientific researcher Seth Brundle is involved in ongoing research into teleportation and, at a function, meets science reporter Roni Quiafe (Geena Davis). Despite his ham-fisted attempts at seduction, Roni accompanies Brundle back to his warehouse-cum-laboratory and witnesses the teleportation of an object (one of her stockings) between two of Brundle's telepods. Convinced by Brundle's claims that his invention 'will change the world as we know it' (Cronenberg, 1986), Roni takes Brundle's story to her editor and former lover, Stathis Borans (John Getz). While Borans claims that Brundle is a fake, Roni agrees to document 'the Brundle Project' and, shortly after, the two become lovers. After a failed teleportation experiment, which sees Brundle's test baboon literally turned inside out, Brundle has an epiphany sparked by Roni's post-coital comments about the body, flesh and its influence. Brundle, having decided that his computer needs to be taught how to be 'made crazy by the flesh' (Cronenberg, 1986), successfully teleports another baboon and then, in a fit of jealous pique at Roni's past relationship with Borans, teleports himself. It is at this point that a housefly is trapped in the telepod and, when transported, is entirely assimilated by Brundle's body.

At first Brundle only notices that he has somehow been improved by the experiment, commenting that his presumably purified body has left him feeling 'a king amongst men' (Cronenberg, 1986). However the genetic material of the fly soon begins to assert itself and Brundle's irrational behaviour and increasingly aberrant body alert Roni to the changes he is undergoing. It takes some time for Brundle himself to recognize the change for what it actually is and much of the film's third quarter is taken up with his attempts to fathom his body, which is increasingly beyond both his control and his ability to understand it. Finally, after a climactic fight with Borans, Brundle's attempt to further purify his body by assimilating it with Roni's leaves him fused with his telepod. No longer able to speak and barely able to move, the horribly disfigured Brundlefly-pod is killed by Roni in a final act of mercy and love.

Among the most important moments in *The Fly* for this discussion are those in which Brundle attempts to make sense of the changes he is undergoing. Beard sees Brundle's growing awareness of his condition as moving through three broad stages:

> The first is a transitional period where Brundle misreads the earliest 'fly' symptoms as heightenings of his human powers; the second coincides with the recognition of his state and to continual growth of 'fly' characteristics; the third arrives when Seth's self has finally been obliterated by 'flyness'. (Beard, 2001, 207)

This account is useful as it alerts us to the divergent narratives at work in *The Fly*. Aside from the film's own narrative, Beard's structure demonstrates that the narrative Brundle assumes he is following (talented researcher cracks monumental puzzle to general accolades and global fame) is entirely at odds with what becomes the film's central concern, the narrative of his increasingly independent body. Further, it demonstrates the retrospective rationalizing Brundle is forced to enact with each change as he seeks to explain the transformation that is increasingly removing him from the realm of human discourse. Thus Brundle's 'politics of insects' stands as a way of drawing the alien and unknowable (i.e., the insect) into a realm of discursive representation and, therefore, of containing (however partially) the threat that the unknowable 'politics of insects' offers. However, each rationalization, coming as it does after the specific change it seeks to explain has already occurred, must necessarily fail because Brundle does not know his own body. By implication, the body – a metaphoric representation of the spectator's own – is itself unknowable and thus belongs from the start to another order that necessarily and inevitably eludes representational attempts to force a stability of meaning upon it.

Self-Knowledge and Knowledge of the Self

The film clearly indicates that Brundle is, if not a virgin, then sexually inexperienced prior to his relationship with Roni. Many diegetic indicators of his life of solitude are given, from the fact of his wardrobe containing identical sets of the same conservative outfit to prevent time wasting to the conflation of his living and work space. Indeed, as Brundle notes when offering Roni the chance to document 'the Brundle Project', 'I don't have a life so there's nothing for you to interfere with' (Cronenberg, 1986). The implication is that Brundle does not have a life aside from his work or, rather, that his life *is* his work. All of these facts of Brundle's character and backstory combine to provide us with a picture of a man who, like Hobbes and Keloid before him, has made a specifically Cartesian choice. However, where Hobbes' and Keloid's choices are acted out arrogantly on the bodies of others, Brundle's decision to deny his body (insofar as such intellectual practice, when combined with mise-en-scène detail, suggests an ascetic lifestyle) in order to further his mind and his career affects, at least initially, him alone. This innocence about his own body is, of course, an innocence about his own sexuality.

Thus *The Fly* replays and explores the relationship between sexuality (and sexual practice) and agency that has been a feature of both *Shivers* and *Rabid*, with the understanding both of these factors are central to the kinds of transformations that occur. If *Shivers* demonstrates, at its conclusion, the kind of agency that emerges as a result of a solely body-oriented knowledge (i.e., entirely libidinal), Brundle's life prior to his transformation is at the other extreme but represents an equivalent imbalance. After all, when it is well, when its multitude of biological processes function as they should, the body as an object is invisible. It is not noticed because there is nothing *to* notice, nothing out of the ordinary. Therefore, it is only when the body's processes, and the body itself, display something *extra*ordinary that attention is drawn to the ways in which the body is conceived and utilized. Thus, as Sontag notes,

> Illness reveals desires of which the patient was probably unaware. Diseases – and patients – become subjects for decipherment. And these hidden passions are now considered a source of illness. (Sontag, 2002, 46)

Given the conditions within which Brundle exists, it should come as no surprise that a specific 'knowledge of the flesh' is central to *The Fly* and

Brundle's transformation. The reason, he discovers, that the telepods cannot initially transport organic material is because they do not 'know flesh'; the computer program that controls the entire enterprise only knows what it has been taught and the implication is that Brundle's lack of bodily knowledge is the missing piece of the puzzle. As soon as he and Roni become lovers, Brundle begins to learn about flesh, about bodies, and is then able to transfer this knowledge to the machine to aid its own development. One cannot help but posit the suggestion that what the machine lacks – which is another way of articulating what Brundle lacks – is not knowledge of the flesh, but knowledge of desire and satisfaction. Leaving aside questions about machine intelligence, the sequence in which Brundle intuits the problem at the centre of his experiment is a fascinating one. After he and Roni have consummated their relationship, she playfully bites him in bed and comments 'I just want to eat you up. That's why old ladies pinch babies' cheeks. It's the flesh . . . it just drives you crazy' (Cronenberg, 1986). Brundle seizes on this notion and, dividing a steak in half, teleports one portion and then cooks both to demonstrate to Roni that the machine does not understand the intricacies of organic material. As she complains about the synthetic taste of the teleported half, Brundle explains that:

> [t]he computer is giving us its interpretation of a steak. It's translating it for us, it's rethinking it, rather than reproducing it. And . . . something's getting lost in the translation. (Cronenberg, 1986)

What is getting lost in the teleportation process is

> the flesh. It should make the computer crazy. Like those old ladies pinching babies. But it doesn't – not yet. I haven't taught the computer to be made crazy by the flesh. . . . So I'm going to start teaching it now. (Cronenberg, 1986)

Of course, the exact method by which one encourages a computer to be 'made crazy by the flesh' is not explained by the film. What is important is that it is Brundle's own growing knowledge of the body – his body and Roni's – that provides him with the information to translate Roni's idea into a form that the computer can recognize. This structure is, in effect, a chain of translation that works from Roni's intuitive understanding to Brundle's scientific comprehension and then through the computer as an objective 'flesh-effect'. In this fashion Brundle becomes the one who, even if only momentarily, occupies the interstitial position between the two poles of body (as represented by Roni and the physical intimacy she provides) and the computer (with its connotations of intellectualism devoid of bodily and interpersonal contact).

Brundle's oversight that permits the fly into the telepod chamber is just that, an accident. But its value, aside from its obvious centrality to the narrative, lies in the way it permits us to witness Brundle's attempts to rationalize his transformation in Roni's terms – a continued discussion of the flesh and its own wants, needs and desires. The imposition of a bodily subjectivity is something Cronenberg has been exploring throughout his films and Brundle's articulations of his own flesh and its development is, as noted, the most comprehensive thus far. What becomes clear, however, is that it is Brundle's unfamiliarity with his flesh that leads him to misrecognize his transformation until much later in the film. His messianic discourse regarding the power of his 'new flesh', which occurs in a café as Roni watches him spoon enormous amounts of sugar into his coffee, seems, for Brundle, to emerge from his new-found boundless energy. We, however, encounter this enthusiasm with Roni as our filter and, when compared to her 'naturalism' (both of performance and appearance), Brundle's 'crazy flesh' is obvious. During his café speech (which, despite Roni's presence, plays out as a soliloquy) Brundle asserts that

> I'm beginning to think that the sheer process of being taken apart atom by atom and being put back together again . . . why, it's like coffee being put through a filter . . . it's somehow a purifying process, it's purified me, it's cleansed me. And I'll tell you, I think it's going to allow me to realise the personal potential I've been neglecting all these years. . . . (Cronenberg, 1986)

Of course, Brundle's flesh is anything but pure, but it is interesting that this discourse occurs, that Brundle associates what are initially the positive effects of his transformation (and which, one presumes, are a result of the fly's abilities being scaled up to Brundle's size) with a becoming-pure, a state of being better than he was. This misrecognition of his own condition, and the act of casting his renewed vitality and libidinal excess as a teleological triumph, is viewed by Brundle as the successful removal of 'impurities' generated by a life lived without attention to the body. In this fashion, *The Fly* demonstrates that Brundle's 'project' (though derailed by the accident) is not that far from Hobbes' and Keloid's own attempts to promote a form of 'better living through science'. At the same time, *The Fly* completes the trajectory of *Shivers* and *Rabid*. Both of those films made use of environments and, hence, social and cultural situations that presumed

> . . . order and control, yet nothing could be further from the truth. Beneath the appearance of order, repressed forces of sexuality, passion and desire are lurking, waiting to be released on an unsuspecting society. (Handling, 1983, 101)

It is with *The Fly* we see recognition of the fact that it is exactly these disruptive forces of sexuality, passion and desire, which are required in order to break through the stasis of Brundle's pre-teleportation life.

The Agency of the Flesh

The coffee shop incident described above is pivotal: here is Brundle's first attempt to comprehend the changes undertaken by a body he has previously ignored and which he hardly knows. The terms of his attempted explanation may be Roni's, within a discourse of common-sense understandings of pure and impure bodies, but the explanation is Brundle's and remains coded with his bodily naïveté. Here we see the retrospective explanation – if he feels good now then he must have previously felt bad (when we are given to believe that he, in fact, felt very little at all) – while the notion that a life of the body is somehow more pure or natural than one focused on intellectualism could have come straight from Hobbes' actions in *Shivers*.

Soon after, Brundle associates the teleportation device with his new-found strength and well-being. Visually, by this stage the transformation is already beginning to manifest itself, with his skin demonstrating signs of his internal condition. Clearly Brundle's attention to the flesh remains abstracted as he does not notice these things in his fervour. Instead, his evangelical dedication to the notion of a new flesh leads him to attempt to pressure Roni into teleporting so that she too can 'feel the power surging inside . . .' (Cronenberg, 1986). She resists his 'born-again teleportation crap' (Cronenberg, 1986) which prompts the first of his post-teleportation irrational outbursts:

> You're afraid to dive into the plasma pool, aren't you. You're afraid to be destroyed and re-created, aren't you. I bet you think you woke me up about the flesh, don't you? But you only know society's straight line

about the flesh. You can't penetrate beyond society's sick grey fear of
the flesh. Drink deep, or taste not the plasma spring. See what I'm saying? I'm not just talking about sex and penetration. I'm talking about
penetration beyond the veil of the flesh. A deep penetrating dive into
the plasma pool. (Cronenberg, 1986)

One should note the elision that occurs in Brundle's speech here – the
move from a discussion of the flesh to suggestions about the means to
transcend it, to move 'beyond the veil of the flesh'. In this fashion, the
discourse of the flesh that occurs in *The Fly* becomes increasingly complex as we are asked to consider the discursive positions represented by
the two protagonists. Roni, who previously represented a knowledge of
the flesh has come to stand for a bodily conservatism that is clearly the
more rational position, when compared with Brundle's desire to transcend 'society's sick grey fear of the flesh'. Brundle's outburst occurs
before he discovers the manner with which his body has fused with the
fly's and it is interesting that, after this discovery, Brundle's notion of his
body shifts from transformation (which, as he considers it, is inherently
positive) to disease (which is wholly negative). Of course, as should be
clear, Cronenberg's own considerations of disease are that it is transformation pure and simple, without any kind of moral compunction. Whatever moralizing occurs around transformation, Cronenberg suggests,
happens at the social level and functions as a way of containing, isolating
and hence disciplining the body undergoing change.

Of course, Brundle's retrospective rationalizing occurs until, as Beard
notes, the identity that was Brundle, and which had survived the transformation into Brundlefly, is entirely overcome by the fly. Nevertheless, with
each adaptation, Brundle's discourse reflects an identity desperately trying to posit not just an agency in the body it can no longer control, but
an agency that is rational, logical and human. With this in mind, his
claims about a politics of insects mark his attempt to find a place for his
identity within the actions of a body that is becoming increasingly
unfamiliar, and which is increasingly moving beyond his ability to contain
(both literally and discursively). Having initially tried to explain away his
fusion with the fly in terms of purity and impurity, he finally grants the
transformative agent – now refigured as a disease – a specific agency of its
own. After asserting that 'it's showing itself as a bizarre form of cancer
[involving] [g]eneral cellular chaos and revolution' (Cronenberg, 1986),
pitting the agency against his own (and thus against his body as well),
Brundle eventually comes to believe that

[t]he disease has just revealed its purpose. . . . I know what the disease
wants. It wants to turn me into something else. That's not too terrible,
is it? Most people would give anything to be turned into something
else. (Cronenberg, 1986)

When Roni queries this position, Brundle concludes that he is becoming
'something that never existed before. I'm becoming "Brundlefly". Don't
you think that's worth a Nobel Prize or two?' (Cronenberg, 1986). As
before, each of these explanations is an attempt by Brundle to locate
himself alongside the agency of his flesh. But they also mark how difficult it is to continue to assert one's identity in Cartesian terms in the face
of what Cronenberg offers as a model that appears to recognize the
insect as representing an as-yet-unrealized transformative possibility.

As discussed in some detail above, each of the terms in Cronenberg's
continued revision of the Cartesian dialectic leads to a revised set of
terms – identity/body/society – that are more closely related than the
invisibly functioning Cartesian model would have us believe. Cronenberg's structure both demonstrates the possibility for transformative
action that occurs with the identity/body dyad, and the disciplinary
actions taken by the social axis to limit or govern such transformation.[13]
Thus Brundle's ignorance of his body is not necessarily the sin of impurity or wasted life that he makes it out to be once he gains knowledge
(however partial) of the flesh. Brundle is merely living as we all do, with
scant regard paid to the body qua object until some event occurs to upset
the balance (itself figured on the very invisibility of the correctly functioning body).

To return to an earlier point, Brundle believes it is possible to comprehend, first, his body and flesh and then, second, the forces of transformation to which he is subject and which he has cast as his 'creative cancer'.
The point he misses is that he is, in effect, attempting to put words in the
place of this foreign agent's actions. To be suffering from a disease with
a purpose, while desperately sad, does make a recognizable kind of sense
and can provide some small comfort (the comfort of the afflicted). The
politics of insects is achieved in this film, but only at the moment when,
as Fly, Brundle can no longer speak and is, in effect, no longer human.
The disciplinary structures that surround Brundle provide him with the
means to understand his body. This is evidenced with the various attempts
at rationalizing that occur as he moves towards utter unknowability. As he
moves to integrate the two parts of the Cartesian binary into a comprehensive whole, gaining knowledge of his flesh such that he can transfer

that information into a site of pure intellect (the computer), he violates a series of discourses that work to maintain the body in its functioning invisibility. As with all Cronenberg films, violation of a disciplinary structure – the act that renders such structures visible – brings with it the harshest of all punishments which, for Brundle's growing self-knowledge, is to be moved towards a horror of the body in its very unknowability.

Chapter 3

The Mind Erupts

Frames and Framing

In the introduction to *The Fright of Real Tears* (2001), Žižek recounts an occasion when, as part of a conference, he was caught out by an unexpected question regarding a painting he had only seen once before. In response to this, he notes that he

> . . . engaged in a total bluff, which went something like this: the frame of the painting in front of us is not its true frame; there is another, invisible, frame, implied by the structure of the painting, and these two frames do not overlap – there is an invisible gap separating the two. The pivotal content of the painting is not rendered in its visible part, but is located in this dislocation of the two frames, in the gap that separates them. (Žižek, 2001b, 5)

As he goes on to explain, this notion of 'the dimension in-between-the-two-frames' became a huge success, a fact that

> . . . made me sad, really sad. What I encountered here was not only the efficiency of a bluff, but a much more radical apathy at the heart of today's cultural studies. (Žižek, 2001b, 6)

Of course, Žižek's anecdote demonstrates his point; the 'pivotal content' of his comments, at the conference, relates to the fundamental role context plays in the manner with which an audience interprets the object before them. Thus the anecdote reveals a variety of layers in its application: leaving aside the possibility of a 'radical apathy at the heart of today's cultural studies', what makes the bluff possible (and, hence, useful), along with its context, is the fact that it is uttered by, and framed by, the person who utters it. Thus the content of the bluff is authorized as legitimate by Žižek's presence, and the fact that the bluff *is* a bluff (for Žižek) in no way diminishes the efficacy of the comments for the audience, which seizes upon them readily, interpreting them not as bluff, but as a legitimate response from so authoritative a figure.

The notion of framing and the relationship of the frame to the context (and, thus, to content) is made clear when, later in the same book, Žižek is discussing Kieslowski's *Decalogue* (1988) and its relationship to the Ten Commandments. At a pivotal point in his argument, Žižek has cause to return to the notion of frames and framing, to the context of interpretation and the manner with which the text's content is encountered and interpreted. At this moment, he comments that

> [o]ne of the minimal definitions of a modernist painting concerns the function of its frame. The frame of the painting in front of us is not its true frame; there is another, invisible, frame, implied by the structure of the painting, which frames our perception of the painting, and these two frames by definition do not overlap – there is an invisible gap separating them. The pivotal content of the painting is not rendered in its visible part, but is located in this dislocation of the two frames, in the gap that separates them. (Žižek, 2001b, 130)

Certainly there are some minor differences between the two passages, but they are essentially identical; the irony (and purpose) is that while the first use of this notion was a bluff, a joke, here he means it – here it is 'for real'. The point is thus clear because, as Žižek demonstrates, the frame within which interpretation occurs fundamentally alters the content as it is encountered. The only actual difference between the two uses of this paragraph is context, not content; the context within which he utters the same comments has altered (from bluff to analysis), and as a result of this shift of interpretive frame, the content is radically altered. In this manner, an understanding of the conditions of framing and the manner with which content is framed is vital to the process of interpretation that occurs as a result of one's encounter with a text's content. This is the point which Žižek so forcefully makes and which is rendered visible through the very process of enacting it.

In the interplay of the same phrases and thoughts in these two instances, we are able to discern a number of key insights that carry forward to an exploration of cinema in general and Cronenberg's cinema in particular. First among these is the fact that an audience's reading (and, indeed, expectations) of the text in question (be it Žižek's impromptu statement or images upon a screen) is framed by the context within which the text is delivered. Thus the fact that it is Žižek delivering this address adds a particular valence to the comments he makes, just as Cronenberg's name as an authorial presence leads an audience to expect a particular kind of text prior to its screening.[1] The second insight Žižek provides is that the context within which the text is encountered is part of a larger interpretive structure, a larger interpretive frame: it is this that allows us to discern when Žižek is using his paragraph to make a point about theoretical apathy and when, later, he actually means (so we assume) what he writes. Third is the fact that these previous two insights rely on the presence of rules through which the performance can be encoded and, later, decoded, and that crucially these rules must be held in agreement between both parties. Žižek's specific example demonstrates the complex relationship that exists between an audience and the ways in which its members can be led to interpret a text depending on the manner with which that text is framed and, crucially for this study, the manner with which the text itself makes use of frames in order to guide interpretation. This interpretation is therefore directed towards a narrative and diegetic field both located by, and locked into position with, a series of frames.

The three films of this chapter, *The Dead Zone* (1983), *Spider* (2002) and *eXistenZ* (1999), are all concerned with altering the frames to which they are subject by shifting – or sometimes doing away with – the parameters of context. This is visible in two ways. First is the manner with which an audience encounters and interprets the character of the protagonist(s). Altering those formal devices utilized in the delivery of character-specific information will impact on the construction and interpretation of the protagonist as they act within the narrative. Second is the way that manipulation of the frames of interpretation will impact on an audience's understanding any formal shift from a 'standard' objective narrative position towards something approaching a subjective experience of the narrative and diegesis. It is important to note, then, that the movement between an objective diegetic position and a subjective experience of the diegesis is central to the narrative of all three films. Key to this discussion is some consideration of the means by which an audience comes to utilize the frames that guide their interpretation of the texts they encounter. One method for understanding this process is offered by Joseph Anderson, who utilizes the concept of 'play' as a model through which we can come to fathom this deceptively simple (and ideologically invisible) process. For Anderson, this analogy works because our '. . . capacity to pretend, to set apart certain of our activities as having special status . . . is a part of *play* . . .' (Anderson, 1996; 113; emphasis in original). As he goes on to note, the kind of play that is enacted in cinemagoing allows an audience to

> . . . enter into the make believe play of a motion picture, observe the consequences of certain actions and share the emotions of certain characters in the film, without being exposed to the same extent or in the same way to the physical and/or psychological dangers to which the film's characters are exposed. (Anderson, 1996, 114)

All of this, for Anderson, is predicated on the fact that, just as

> . . . the 'rules' of visual and auditory processing allow for the illusion that we are surrounded by the diegetic space [of the film being screened], there is yet another set of 'rules' that allows us to sustain the illusion of the reality of the motion picture's fictional world. (Anderson, 1996, 113)

Thus our encounter with film is framed by a shared understanding of the various devices that work to constitute the diegesis, up to and including the fact that

> the usual moviegoing experience is overtly, even verbally framed. We have a word for the object of our attention that separates it categorically: movie. And we go to a place specifically designed for that activity. . . . (Anderson, 1996, 122)

All this is a way of demonstrating both the entirely consensual nature of the moviegoing practice and the fact that this practice, and the 'play' that occurs as part of that practice, both happen within a very tightly regulated set of circumstances. For example, the invitation to 'pretend' or 'play' is '. . . issued in the traditional narrative by that opening sequence of shots that all of us recognise . . .' (Anderson, 1996, 122). This point demonstrates that the formal devices at work *within* the diegesis are as important to the manner with which we interpret it as are the various framing devices that signal this event to be a type of activity distinct from any other.

Again, utilizing Žižek's points, we can see that the content of the text, which contains a series of rules that guide any interpretation of it, is further framed by and against related interpretive guidelines that govern the context of the moviegoing event. Thus the rules that govern 'play' serve both to control and guide the interpretation of the text that occurs as a result. Certainly, the reason these rules (which are, in effect, disciplinary structures) surrounding the creative activity of play exist at all is to ensure that all participants are guided towards an equitable and equivalent viewing experience. Furthermore, as noted, these rules extend from the viewing context (itself an interpretive frame) into the construction of the diegesis. Anderson provides a clear (and, for this study, entirely pertinent) example:

> Similar signals or frames [to those that indicate the beginning of a narrative] are necessary within a film/video narrative to introduce any shift from one realm to another: into (or out of) flashbacks or flash forwards, imaginary or fantasy sequences, dreams or hallucinations. Many such devices have been used precisely for the purpose of marking the change in level: blurred focus, gauze or filters over the camera lens, shifts from black-and-white to colour or vice versa, iris shots, and a variety of mattes. (Anderson, 1996, 122–3)

Thus the process of indicating movement within the diegesis from objective to subjective states has seen the development of a highly codified set of formal devices whose utilization clearly indicates that such a diegetic shift is occurring. These techniques are both normative and normalizing, for

> [f]ailure to supply adequate signals for a change in the image's status (for example, into or out of flashback, dream or fantasy) results in viewer confusion. Even when part of the filmic style, . . . if the viewer is either unable or unwilling to supply the transitional signals himself [sic], the result is at least temporary bewilderment if not aversive incomprehension. (Anderson, 1996, 123)

Therefore Anderson's point regarding the purpose of play, insofar as it allows those playing to explore within boundaries, demonstrates the disciplinary nature of the exercise: within cinema an audience may 'observe the consequences of certain actions and share the emotions of certain characters in the film' (Anderson, 1996. 114) without having to undergo the same travails in their own lives. But, more than this model of instructive passivity, Žižek demonstrates the role of the spectator in the creation of this experience, in the active utilization of the 'rules' governing this 'play' in order to provide an experience that is intelligible within its context. As Anderson notes above, failure to follow the rules surrounding the delivery of material (for example, in indicating diegetic shifts) risks textual intelligibility. Thus the spectator's potential for interpretation is framed by the experience of watching the film (i.e., the context), and the film's content is further framed by the formal devices utilized to deliver it. The use of these devices is predicated on their familiarity, a familiarity bred on the repetition and, hence, on the naturalization of their use, which in turn renders them – as ideological and disciplinary devices – invisible and therefore effective. In this manner both the viewing experience and the way in which the audience is guided towards a shared experience of the narrative and plot serve a disciplinary outcome insofar as these framing devices work together to render the text, its context(s) – of reception and interpretation[2] – and its content natural and invisible.

What Žižek reveals is both the presence of a gap between the frames and the fact that this gap is invisible because the processes that occur within, between and around the frames are naturalized by repetition and familiarity. This effaces the active role the audience plays in constructing that meaning (regardless of the ways in which they are guided towards that meaning). What is important to carry forward is the idea that film, generally, works to direct its audience towards a particular interpretation of its narrative and therefore utilizes its formal repertoire as the means to accomplish this. Anderson notes that

> . . . a seamless fictional world is a source of tremendous power in the cinema – it provides a stable and continuous basis for the involvement of the viewer in the experience of the film. (Anderson, 1996, 124)

Anderson's comment therefore alerts us to the potential for conflict between an audience trained to recognize the use of certain formal codes as indicative of particular interpretive techniques, on the one hand, and a film whose diegesis works to disrupt, for whatever end, those interpretive techniques or strategies.

In each of the films in this chapter, a similar troubling of the frame occurs. Given that I claim Cronenberg's overriding interest – the content of the 'Cronenberg project' – is a desire to critique disciplinary structures by revealing them in operation (most often through the heretical action of taking them too far or too seriously), the three films of this chapter all, in their ways, utilize framing devices as a way of achieving this. Necessarily each film attends to its own issues of framing and interpretation in a different way and to different ends, but overall the purpose of these disruptive actions is the same: to force heretical attention on the disciplinary structures that work, first, to consolidate meaning and, second, to guide an audience to this consolidated meaning in a consistent fashion. *The Dead Zone* works to interrupt the movement from objective to subjective states in such a way as to render unreliable the actions of the film's protagonist. This interruption occurs even as the narrative and the various devices through which character is constructed and transmitted move to demonstrate Smith's honesty and belief in his own course of action. Thus a conflict emerges between two representational systems: the construction of the protagonist within a generic and broadly industrial context (i.e., mainstream narrative film), and the reliability of the subjective experience delivered as objective representation. *Spider* continues this exploration of the relationship between subjective and objective states by removing entirely those transitional devices that usually work to indicate such shifts in interpretive position. With these devices missing, the audience is deliberately forced to experience the narrative and diegesis of *Spider* as the protagonist does. Finally *eXistenZ* undermines the stability of the diegesis itself, utilizing what are effectively frames-within-frames to dislocate interpretation and prevent any kind of objective spectatorial positioning. As well as this, both *Spider* and *eXistenZ* add the possibility of endlessly multiplying narrative and spectatorial positions, developing on the disruptive ground opened up in *The Dead Zone*. Therefore, because the frame must be accounted for by the audience in order to achieve a satisfactory interpretation of the text's content, it becomes obvious that in this accounting (even if, and especially if, this involves an audience ignoring it) the frame functions as a disciplinary device that guides its audience towards interpretation. Thus Cronenberg's heretical texts will utilize frames and framing – and, especially, the act of revealing the frame in action – either as a way of situating the audience differently in relation to the material, or in order to upset or estrange the viewing experience.

The Dead Zone

The Dead Zone (1983) is the story of John (Johnny) Smith (Christopher Walken), a New England schoolteacher who awakens after a five-year coma, brought on by an automobile accident, to discover that he has psychic and, vitally, precognitive abilities. At first his visions are concerned either with events occurring at that moment (his first vision enables his nurse to rescue her daughter from a house fire) or in the past (he is able to tell his doctor, a Polish émigré, that his mother survived the war). However, events conspire to force John increasingly into the public eye: he assists the town sheriff in stopping a serial killer and, later, successfully prevents the death of a pupil in a lethal ice-hockey game. These events, worrisome though they may be, are offset by two further developments. The first of these is the discovery that each vision appears to be draining Johnny of his 'life force', sapping his strength and shortening his life. The second concerns Johnny's most comprehensive vision: while shaking the hand of presidential candidate Greg Stillson (Martin Sheen), John sees him as an unhinged leader launching an unprovoked nuclear first strike. Deciding that this potential Hitler (a comparison made directly in the film) cannot be allowed to come to power and bring about Armageddon, John resolves to assassinate Stillson at a public rally. However his first shot misses Stillson, who seeks cover by holding a baby in front of him as a shield, and John is mortally wounded by Stillson's bodyguard. John's final vision reveals Stillson's suicide, his career ruined by photographs of him using the baby as a shield. At this point, and with his task accomplished, Johnny dies in the arms of his unrequited love.

Johnny's visions are of central importance to this film as they provide us with the means to comprehend his interior psychic condition and, therefore, colour our understanding of his character as developed by the film from its outset. Johnny, it must be said, is the most ordinary of Cronenberg's protagonists and *The Dead Zone*, without a doubt, the most mainstream and conventional of his films – in its use of stars, its reasonably conventional plot and the clearly articulated character arc that forms the heart of the narrative.[3] At this most superficial of levels, *The Dead Zone* is, like *The Fly* which followed it, a tragic love story and Johnny Smith is perfectly placed to function as an 'everyman' protagonist whose selfless and simply 'good' life seems only to reward him with injury, disappointment and death. Without the psychic phenomena, this would be a very ordinary film indeed. Rather it is the interruption of Smith's dream-like pre-accident life by these uncalled-for and uncontrollable visions that places the film at the end of a generic spectrum more familiar to Cronenberg. It is interesting to note, therefore, that original drafts of the screenplay, including Stephen King's own reworking of his short story that is the basis for this film, tended to ignore Smith's visions altogether. *The Dead Zone*'s final screenwriter, Jeffrey Boam, has commented that the basic difference between earlier versions of the screenplay and the final version he and Cronenberg developed was that Cronenberg

... ultimately wanted to see the story through Johnny's eyes. . . . This is when David first introduced the notion of visual representation of Johnny's visions. [Previous screenwriter] Stanley [Donen] perceived it as a drama in which nothing weird was shown happening on the screen. We would see Johnny experiencing the vision, but never the vision itself. Once we began the revision of my script, David never once looked back at the novel. (Boam, quoted in Rodley, 1997)

The visions themselves fall into three categories, corresponding roughly (although not exactly) to the past, present and future, and clearly an audience needs to comprehend these visions in order to understand, and thereby empathize with, Smith. It is vital, then, to explore in some detail the first of these visions in order to understand the manner with which *The Dead Zone* works to provide its audience with the means to interpret the protagonist's subjective experiences, as well as the movement from an objective diegesis to a subjective state. As Smith is the film's protagonist, this movement is vital as it will affect the manner with which an audience develops an empathy for, and an understanding of, his condition (and, hence, of his character arc). Thus this first vision, of Smith 'seeing' his nurse's daughter trapped by a house fire, demonstrates the manner with which Cronenberg is using this subjective moment as a way of implying supplementary character information, as well as ensuring that the audience will become necessarily involved in Johnny's experience. The form of this sequence, in particular the architecture of the editing, works to align the audience with the protagonist even as he becomes socially (and hegemonically) problematic.

Saving Amy

The construction of Smith's first vision is important as it is required to give the audience an enormous amount of information, both regarding Smith (and character detail as we assess him in response to his own responses) and, importantly, about the film itself. This vision announces that visions, per se, will play a part in the plot and must therefore be distinguished from the rest of the film's diegesis, lest we become confused about the relationship of the visions to the rest of the film's inhabitants. After all, these visions are Smith's alone – and while they can be represented to the film's audience, they cannot be communicated to any other diegetic inhabitant without Smith present to do the telling.

The sequence that contains Smith's first vision begins conventionally enough. The first indication we have of anything untoward comes as the score, which had previously been kept innocuously in the background, ceases entirely at the moment when Smith's nurse leans over him to wipe his fevered brow. Entirely in keeping with generic requirements,[4] this is a sure sign to an audience that some kind of on-screen event is about to occur. Sure enough, as we cut to an over-the-shoulder shot looking past the nurse to Johnny, he lurches forward (i.e., at us) to grasp her forcefully by the arm. Undercutting this moment is the score itself: at the point where Johnny clasps the nurse's arm, we hear sustained bass notes, cellos and violins that are clearly designed to encourage our fear *for* Smith, not *of* him. This moment, and the manner with which the score of *The Dead Zone* is working to direct our interpretive practice may be usefully compared to Bernard Herrmann's score for the shower sequence of *Psycho*: there, at the moment of shock as the shower curtain is pulled back, we hear high-pitched glissando violin notes instead of this sequence's sustained bass notes. There we are meant to fear the anonymous figure that pulls the curtain back, while here we are asked, if not to identify with, then at least to remain open and sympathetic to the person who causes the shock.

However, the way the score is utilized to align our sympathies with Smith is just one of the film's mechanisms at work here: supplementing the orchestration is the fact that we see Smith undergoing an experience he clearly has no control over. In fact, we are given a shot of Smith lurching forward into mid-shot, looking past the camera and into the middle distance. Because of this, we can reasonably expect the next shot to give us some insight into what it is Smith sees. Sure enough, we cut from this shot to a shot of a very brightly lit doll's house in flames and it is clear that the mise-en-scène in this shot, including the way it is lit, differs from the mise-en-scène of Smith's room as established by the scene's introductory sequence. In this fashion a distinction is drawn between the objective mise-en-scène of the film's narrative (which is typified by a dour, grainy light) and this second phantasmatic space which Smith alone (apparently – at this stage) can see and which, by contrast, is very brightly lit.

At this stage a conventional rhythm is established, cutting from shots of Johnny in his hospital room, looking past the camera and twitching at what he sees, to shots of the events of his vision (each shot providing us with incrementally more detail of the child's room on fire). This rhythm allows us to establish the two diegetic spaces, to distinguish between them and to understand the rationale (we are seeing what he sees) that dictates our movement between them. The real surprise comes when we cut from a shot of Smith, in hospital room, looking and flinching, to a shot of Amy cowering in the corner of her bedroom, and then back to a shot of Smith, still in his hospital bed but now occupying a similar space within Amy's room. This is the key to this sequence and also the start of our own interpretive difficulties as, at the moment he utters the child's name, Smith emerges as both a witness and a participant (although not an agent) within the vision we have already seen established by the film's form as phantasmatic.

This sequence, which shocks us because it places Smith within his own vision, necessarily impacts on the manner with which we interpret his character and understand the narrative. The insidiousness of the visions, which occur seemingly without warning, rests on the fact that Smith is powerless to do anything but report on what he sees; this power which he has been granted, presumably as a result of the accident, actually renders him powerless. In this manner, one of the reasons for placing Smith within his own vision is made clear. Cronenberg could certainly have continued the shot–reverse-shot sequence that began the vision, cutting from what Smith sees in his vision (distinguished by being overlit and with a slight reverb on the diegetic sound, thereby indicating its status as vision) to shots of Smith in his hospital bed, actually engaged in 'seeing'. Yet none of this would transmit both the power (as in effect) of the vision and the resulting sense of Johnny's powerlessness. Crucially, this sequence is important as it marks our first experience, as an audience, of Smith's visions and, as such, it functions also as the means to train us in the interpretation of these events, in this context and within this film. A great deal of weight therefore rests on this first visionary sequence: it must make clear to us that we are moving between a 'real' (i.e., diegetic) space and a phantasmatic one; it must provide us with the means to understand who is experiencing this vision, how they are seeing it and, to some extent, why; and it must ensure we understand the way in which this event impacts upon Smith as he experiences it.

Smith's Dream

Smith's fear of his visions is best expressed by Cronenberg, who explains,

You have someone who thinks he is a normal, well-entrenched member of society – low profile, nothing special, an okay guy who teaches at school. [These visions destroy] . . . his life as he has known it. . . .

> He's an outsider even though he looks like a normal guy, but he knows
> he's not. He's cut off from the life he thought he had as his birthright
> as a normal human being. His girlfriend, his mother, his father, the
> town he was living in, the school that he taught at, are all gone sud-
> denly. (Cronenberg, Beard, & Handling, 1983, 196)

Contained in Cronenberg's comment are a number of important points,
not least of which is the relationship between the individual citizen's
expectation of a 'normal' life as a birthright, and the pressure that one
be 'normal' in order to either obtain or qualify for that birthright. *The
Dead Zone* takes great care to establish exactly how normal Smith is and,
indeed, his normality comes to resemble a type of repression that reflects
the self-denial practiced by Brundle before his own (in this instance,
bodily) transformation. Perhaps the best example of this, by which we
can (and, in watching the film, do) assess Smith's character, comes as he
escorts his girlfriend home after an after-school date at an amusement
park.[5] As the couple stand awkwardly on her front porch, sheltering from
the rain, she invites him in to spend the night. His response, 'No, better
not . . . some things are worth waiting for' (Cronenberg, 1983), demonstrates clearly the nature and history of their relationship and Smith's
role within it. Moments later, in case we missed the full import of his
statement, he adds, 'I'm going to marry you, you know' (Cronenberg,
1983). As Beard correctly notes, '[h]e wants Sarah, but in the context of
a safe, permanent, institutionalized relationship, not on the basis of an
impetuous instinct or indeed any kind of *act*' (Beard, 2001, 169; emphasis
in original).

Beard's note regarding Smith's desire for an 'institutionalized relationship' is undercut by Smith's own ambivalence: clearly he does desire
the markers of a 'normal' existence (in the order deemed most socially
acceptable, hence no sex before marriage) and yet, because of his power
(or rather, powerlessness),[6] actively seeks isolation in order to avoid
being subject to the whims of others. Smith is, we begin to understand,
subject to conflicting social (hence hegemonic) demands: because he is
abnormal he believes he must either remove himself from the broader
social fabric, or be removed. Yet, for all his abnormality, his powers do
offer benefits to the society he seeks to remove himself from. And, to be
entirely fair, aside from one slightly haphazard press conference, there is
no indication that Smith is treated unfairly by those citizens around him.
We can only conclude, then, that the ambivalence of Smith's actions
regarding his social position and membership occur as a result of his

own interpretation of his position, his own reading of the various social demands he is subject to (including the requirements of a 'good' citizen, a 'good' partner and husband, a 'good' son). Perhaps it is fairer, then, to note that Smith's deliberate course of inactivity is marked by a single action, his own self-exile.

Smith's ambivalence leads him to first refuse and then (after a day spent in the arms[7] of his now-married ex-fiancée) accept the appeal of Sheriff Bannerman (Tom Skerritt) for help with an ongoing serial-killer investigation. The vision that occurs as a result of this is more complex in its structure than the 'Saving Amy' episode because it has a dual purpose to serve. First, it allows us to deepen our understanding of Smith's ambivalence at being asked (and being able) to help the side of normalizing law and order with the use of an abnormal power that will forever mark him as an outsider to that hegemonic position. Further, this vision (which can be structurally more complex because we have already experienced the 'Saving Amy' vision) provides us with the means to remain aligned with (and empathetic to) Smith's character despite his reticence. As we see Smith negotiate his position, it becomes clear that Cronenberg wants us to empathize with Smith's social position without necessarily identifying directly with him. It is for this reason that Smith's visions do not include point-of-view shots (indeed, *The Dead Zone* does not have a single point-of-view shot) but do include shots that approximate Smith's position without replicating it. For all of this overt structuring, however, the revealing of Smith as a visible presence in his own vision occurs, as with 'Saving Amy', entirely naturalistically.

As this sequence begins, we shift from shots of Smith beginning to experience his vision, with requisite flinching and grimacing, to a shot of the same setting – an outdoor gazebo in the middle of a snow-covered park beside a frozen lake – but earlier that day.[8] Beginning with a high-angle shot of the murder victim approaching the gazebo, the camera cranes down to reveal, first, the figure of the murderer (with his back to us) calling the victim to him and then, as she walks up the stairs of the gazebo, Johnny himself. All of this occurs while intercutting from this sequence of events to shots of Johnny, in the diegetic present, clasping the hand of the murder victim and then falling backwards muttering, 'She knows him. . . . She knows him' (Cronenberg, 1983).

The revelation of the murderer's identity, when it comes, certainly fulfils all of the formal generic requirements of a suspense/horror film. However, while the 'Saving Amy' vision was careful never to stray too far from what we could assume was Smith's point of view from his position on the bed, here the camera assumes a degree of omniscience that is more familiar insofar as it is more conventional. Thus shots of the killer opening his 'murder-coat' (Beard, 2001, 196) to reveal his weapon of choice, and of him looming over the victim are clearly from the victim's point of view. Other shots, of him stripping her prior to stabbing her, are neither Smith's nor the victim's but pass by so quickly that their authorship or spectatorial location is never questioned. These shots register not as positioning mechanisms as such, but simply as part of mainstream cinematic form. Finally, the shot of the killer raising his arm to deliver the fatal blow (which we never actually see) is cut short to show us Johnny shouting impotently 'No . . . Wait' (Cronenberg, 1983) before falling forward beside the body, his movement serving as the means to mask the cut from his vision to the diegetic present.

The simplicity of this sequence belies its complex purpose. As noted, Smith is undergoing a shift in characterization from passive victim to noble self-sacrificing hero, and this vision – the film's centrepiece – is the diegetic marker of that character arc. This shift in characterization works also to recuperate Johnny, meaning that as well as remaining a figure of spectatorial empathy, he becomes more closely aligned to a standard character 'type'. Therefore just as the formal devices that framed and delivered the first vision worked to unsettle the spectator with the inclusion of Smith inside his own vision, this vision and the movement towards an omniscient third-person camera move the frame back towards a hegemonic invisibility, just as Smith's characterization is itself becoming more 'normal'. Given this, what stands out (and what is meant to stand out) is Smith's reaction. Coming to his senses in the darkened gazebo, he is grilled by an anxious Bannerman, and yet revealing the killer's name comes almost as an afterthought:

> **Smith:** I saw him . . . I was there . . . I saw him. I stood there . . . I saw his face.
> **Sheriff Bannerman:** Who?
> **Smith:** I stood there and watched him kill that girl. Dodd!
> **Sheriff Bannerman:** Wait a minute . . . wait a minute. What are you saying?
> **Smith:** I did nothing. I stood there and watched him kill that girl. Dodd! I stood there . . . I did nothing.

This moment stands out because Smith's defining character trait has, until this point, been one of near-total inaction. He refuses, however gently, his fiancée's offer and spends much of the film prior to this point ignoring requests to utilize his power, viewing it as a curse rather than a gift. Each of these refusals is cast so as to place the onus of refusal in another's hands, this 'Other' coinciding with a social structure too authoritative to deny. This refusal to act works to bring him to the continued attention of the very authoritative structures he has previously acquiesced to and, in so doing, demonstrates the conflicting hegemonic requirements Smith must negotiate. Thus while refusing Susan is cast as 'the right thing to do' ('Some things are worth waiting for'), his condition forces him into a situation where both action and inaction are 'wrong' insofar as acting to help Bannerman would also 'be the right thing to do', but would further draw attention to the condition that alienates him. Smith's only recourse is to make clear to Bannerman that the fault lies with God, who is ultimately responsible for the automobile accident in the first place. It is worth noting that, in each instance, the structure Smith acquiesces to is 'larger' (ideologically and hegemonically) than the one that makes the demands upon him, so he can, in all good conscience, refuse those demands and still feel as though he is fulfilling some kind of broader social duty. Further to this, we can see how Smith's actions, which are designed to resist fulfilling the desires of the Other (which would render him perverse-by-default), work to further draw the Other's attentions to him.

At its centre, therefore, *The Dead Zone* contains a discussion of social responsibility and the role of the individual within a system that is, at best, ambivalent towards its participants. Smith's actions reveal the difficulty he has in resolving his position (white, educated, heterosexual) within the broader social framework, particularly with regards to the fact that his position carries with it a series of concomitant responsibilities. His ambivalence (which, in itself, can be viewed as emerging in response to the broader conditions of social ambivalence his abnormality reveals) comes from his inability to derive meaning from his accident and power and, particularly, the inability of the larger social framework to provide those events with meaning. Smith views the system as having failed him; moreover, because his maltreatment does not issue from an identifiable source, blame must be located in some other authority. Hence, Smith is claiming for himself a form of social powerlessness, and in this claim is making clear the terms of his self-conceived social contract: one gives up the right to act for one's self in exchange for the stability and normality that functions as one's birthright and reward for this sacrifice. The price of belonging, at least insofar as Smith demonstrates this, is a social and personal meekness and obedience. Therefore, within the binary of action/inaction established by *The Dead Zone*, acting in the service of a hegemonic structure becomes perverse insofar as Smith's ability works to satisfy the demands and desire of the Other. While *The Dead Zone* does not develop this point further, it seems clear that Cronenberg is working to explore the relationship between the demands that one fulfil one's social obligations and the manner with which such obligations will affect the subject who performs them.

It is for this reason that Smith, initially at least, refuses what he later comes to view as his responsibility, and it is only after he spends a day basking in the love of his ex-fiancée, spending time with her and her child in his family home (and thereby partaking in the normality previously denied him), that he is able to reassess his position and come to some understanding of his fate. His self-imposed exile, it would appear, does not absolve him of the responsibility to act, and his acceptance of Bannerman's request, coupled with his horror at his inability to prevent the girl's death, demonstrates this. Smith's shift in position from self-imposed exile (thereby allowing him to luxuriate in an 'outsider' status) to socially responsible agent becomes the focus of the film's second half. Thus it seems as though the day spent in the arms of his lover functions to remind him of the society that requires his assistance in preserving itself from threat, meaning that the lesson Smith learns from his day of suburban bliss is that, to paraphrase another great hegemonic moment, with great power comes great responsibility.

Of course, the ambivalence that is revealed through the movement of this narrative is not Smith's but is that of the film itself, at least insofar as it is required to resolve itself satisfactorily, which is to say, within the acceptable bounds of a hegemonic system. At one level, Smith's responses to the social structures that brand him an outsider are perfectly understandable. Yet such a realistic figure does not necessarily make a good cinematic protagonist; hence Smith's recuperative character arc. The day Smith spends with his ex-lover is actually a demonstration of interpellation-in-action – both of him and, hence, of the audience, which, as a result of this moment, remains empathetic with his continuously noble gestures and his act of self-sacrifice. Indeed, it is perfectly possible to imagine a similar scenario in which Smith does not go willingly to his death as 'the right thing to do' but, instead, surrenders to it recognizing that there is no place he can go that is far enough away from his social responsibility. The difference between these two scenarios lies not in their diegetic result, which would be the same in both cases. Instead, the difference lies in our assessment of Smith's character; to alter Smith's motivation (willingness to achieve a 'good' death versus the broken victim resigned to his inescapable fate) would fundamentally affect our experience of the film.

It is no accident then, that the structure of the visions Smith endures after catching the killer alters. There are two of these visions – the vision of Roger's son falling through the ice while playing ice hockey and the vision of Stillson's nuclear war – and what distinguishes them from the visions described above is the fact that Smith does not appear in them. In conversation with his doctor, Smith posits his absence from his own visions as indicating a point of indeterminacy, a 'dead zone' that demonstrates that the future is malleable and can be affected by actions in the present. This fact, Smith's absence as a site of potential where, in previous visions his presence is a marker of impotence, further illustrates the kind of social discourse Smith (and hence the audience) is subject to: visibility is equivalent to helplessness while invisibility is an indicator of one's potential for service to a 'greater good'. This invisibility is crucial and should be understood both literally and metaphorically. Smith's visibility in his own initial visions works to mark him as different, and it is only after he accepts his social burden that he becomes, in effect, invisible to himself. This invisibility is the marker of the correctly interpellated subject, or, as Foucault would have it, the distinguishing marker between the subject (who, in behaving correctly, is invisible to the disciplinary functioning of the hegemony) and the individual who, through whatever deviance, becomes visible and is, therefore, individualized (Foucault, 1995, 193).

Thus the film's broader disciplinary message is made clear, a fact that goes to explain the absence of point-of-view shots (which would work to affect an identification with Smith as an individual) as opposed to the plethora of shots that position an audience alongside Smith's putative gaze. The effectiveness of this formal construction, when coupled with this narrative, lies in the fact that we are asked to identify with Smith's social-structural position and not with him specifically, and in this manner what we find emerging in *The Dead Zone* is a discussion of the relationship of individuals to the social or cultural network that surrounds them. The discrepancies we find in any assessment of Smith's actions over the course of the film are, in actuality, discrepancies inherent in the broader disciplinary structures that are implied but invisible in the actions of each individual. In essence, then, Smith is required to both not act in certain circumstances (i.e., in refusing his fiancée) and then act forcefully in others (to assist the forces of law and order) with the inherent understanding that all actions and inactions occur within a social structure that is ultimately inescapable.

Character, Narrative and Interpretation

It is worth noting that there is more occurring in *The Dead Zone* than just a straightforward exploration of civic responsibility. What becomes clear while watching the film is the degree to which Cronenberg plays on the ambiguity of both the social responsibility Smith is subject to and the manner with which an audience interprets Smith's actions, particularly as the film moves toward Smith's self-sacrifice in the attempted assassination of Stillson. As Cronenberg, in conversation with Beard and Handling comments:

> I think on a very straightforward dramatic level, people will believe his visions are real, and therefore will believe he is justified in going to kill this potential presidential candidate. . . . Emotionally you will go along with it – there is some proof of other visions that Johnny has had that have turned out to be true, so you'll totally believe, I think. But the demon in *The Dead Zone* is . . . that in fact nothing Stillson does in the movie would be enough to condemn him to death. . . . That's not enough to have him killed, and finally you begin to realize that all you're left with is Johnny's belief in his vision. (Cronenberg et al., 1983, 197)

Cronenberg is making clear the ways in which *The Dead Zone* has constructed Smith in order for the audience to identify with his position and empathize with his character, only to make it clear that Smith's own belief in the veracity of his visions need not absolutely justify his actions. Smith is constructed so that the film's dwelling on his particular motivations, especially including his decision to 'come in from the cold' of his self-imposed exile, overwhelms any hesitation we might have as to his actions. In this fashion Cronenberg is undercutting King's original story in order to draw attention to the manner with which systems of identification and empathy can be so powerful as to result in the wilful overlooking of this very important point: despite the film's formal construction of Smith's visions, they remain both subjective and phantasmatic.

The Dead Zone, then, utilizes a variety of framing devices to upset any kind of standard interpretive practice. It is, admittedly, not entirely successful either in its heretical intentions (as revealed by the number of entirely conventional readings that, as Cronenberg predicts, miss the ambiguity inherent in Smith's visions)[9] or as a mainstream piece of filmmaking,[10] but these responses reveal the manner with which the film does work to unsettle its audience and critics. This unsettling comes, I believe, through its constant reformulating of its various frames – both diegetic and, in line with Anderson's discussion, extra-diegetic. At every point where its frames are in motion, and despite the fact that it is not entirely consistent in this motion, what is upset is the single stable frame imposed by a dominant hegemonic position. This is the frame that Žižek works to critique, the frame that, through its actions, is functionally invisible despite its very active presence in framing and, hence, directing interpretation. Thus Smith's presence in, and then absence from, his own visions unsettles us; first, because we are unused to encountering the source of the vision in his own phantasmatic space and, second, because by the time we get used to this framing device, Cronenberg removes it. In a similarly heretical action, Smith's decision to remove himself from and then re-enter civil society (with his abnormality as the reason in both cases) functions to reveal the contradictory requirements made upon the citizen and subject.

Spider

Spider (2002), like *The Dead Zone*, offers two directions for analytical inquiry. The first of these concerns the ways in which subjective interior processes are represented, providing the possibility for an exploration of the relationship between those processes and the visible actions of agency. This necessarily works to draw attention to the film's framing devices, which in turn work to deliver these subjective processes to the screen. The second concern is with the ways in which these framing devices both position and undercut an audience engaged in interpreting them, leading to narrative instability. As with *The Dead Zone*, the first of these analytical directions marks the way in which the film both corresponds to and deviates from the various normalizing conventions surrounding characterization-on-screen, while the second is the area in which Cronenberg's own directorial decisions mark this film as heretical.

FIGURE 3.1   Spider imagines an empty London.

Spider tells the story of Dennis (Spider) Cleg (Ralph Fiennes), a mentally disturbed man who, when released from the asylum where he has
spent the better part of his life, finds himself revisiting the locations and
memories of the events that generated his illness in the first place. *Spider's*
first shots reveal Spider as an adult, arriving in London and making his
way to the halfway house that is to be his new home (see Figure 3.1).
Thereafter, the film plays out as a series of confused flashbacks, memories and fantasies that witness the spilling over of events from Spider's
past into his contemporary existence. It is through these flashbacks that
we see the Boy Spider (Bradley Hall) attempting to come to terms with
his parents' marital difficulties, and it is in these memories, within which
the adult Spider often features as an onlooker, that we see Boy Spider's
confusing of actual events with his own fantasized interpretation. What
results is a situation where the audience is required to sift through the
growing narrative much as Spider himself is attempting to. As we initially
encounter it, the marriage between Bill (Gabriel Byrne) and Mrs Cleg
(Miranda Richardson) is one marked by general long-suffering antag-
onism and difficulty. Mrs Cleg's[11] favourite story to Boy Spider is of her
own memories of encountering spider webs, like 'sheets of muslin', that
were the product of mother spiders who had exhausted themselves in
the process, giving up their own lives so as to foster the health of their
youngsters. Bill, for his part, is a picture of quietly simmering hostility,
given to explosions of anger if roused. With Spider as our guide to his
own memories, we see Boy Spider exposed to the aggressively sexual

women who frequent the Dog and Beggar, the same pub Bill drinks in. One of these women, Yvonne (Miranda Richardson), becomes Bill's lover and, when the two are discovered by Mrs Cleg in Bill's allotment shed, assists in the murder and disposal of Mrs Cleg's body. The fact that Yvonne and Mrs Cleg are played by the same actor illustrates the manner with which Spider is conflating both events and people in his memory, and this is further compounded when, after remembering the death of his mother, Spider discovers that Mrs Wilkinson (Lynn Redgrave), the manager of the halfway house, has transformed into an Yvonne-esque character as well.[12] After confronting his father and his new lover about the death of his mother, Boy Spider decides to take action, lest he be their next victim. As Bill and Yvonne go out for an evening at the pub, he runs a length of twine from his upstairs room to the gas cooker, meaning that when Bill and Yvonne return home drunk, he can open the gas remotely. After doing so and being rescued by his father, Boy Spider waits outside for his father, only to discover that the body his father retrieves is not Yvonne but his own mother. Spider, finding that Yvonne has somehow inserted herself into his adult life, decides to repeat the action that removed her in the first place, only to discover, again, that the woman he is about to kill is not Yvonne at all but the original Mrs Wilkinson. *Spider* ends with Spider being driven back to the asylum, a shot that dissolves into an image of the Boy Spider undertaking the same journey.

Shifts in Time and (Subjective) Space

As is clear from the above synopsis, *Spider* is a deliberately convoluted film that does not make for easy retelling and requires multiple viewings in order to understand its multiple narrative pathways and possibilities. Here, though, the obstacles to an easy interpretation are designed to foster an audience identification with Spider, which Cronenberg makes explicit in the DVD's commentary:

> I really didn't want there to be any distance between the audience and Spider. I really wanted the audience to become Spider by the end of the movie and to live not just in his world, but in his mind. (Cronenberg, 2002b, director's commentary)

This intention has clear implications for both the film's formal strategies and for its narrative. There are many moments in *Spider* when the narrative becomes unclear; as Spider attempts to both collect and interpret his memories, he faces the inevitable resistances of repression, meaning that '. . . if the audience is really going to be Spider then, when he's confused, they will also be confused' (Cronenberg, 2002b, director's commentary). *Spider*, therefore deals with time and memory and utilizes the shifts in diegetic space as a way of understanding Spider's trauma. Thus it is important to examine how the film signals these shifts, and how it signals its movements from what might be an objective diegetic reality to an entirely subjective memory or fantasy. This, however, places a strain on an audience's relationship with the narrative that attempts to deliver these shifting positions because, as with this film in particular, there is no interpretive centre from which a 'safe' (i.e., stable) interpretation can proceed. This, indeed, is the purpose to *Spider*'s narrative structure and, at the film's conclusion, whatever sense we have of Spider's own self-discovery is as tenuous as our understanding of Smith's actions in *The Dead Zone*. However there is nothing in *Spider*'s form to immediately suggest that Spider is an unreliable guide to the events that unfold or even that Spider will in any way affect the manner with which we encounter these events. It is here that *Spider* deviates from the course set by *The Dead Zone*. Smith's experiences occur in the objective diegetic space of the film, and while his visions are his alone, Cronenberg works to undermine our allegiance to a specific character type. This occurs as a result of our being led to mistake Smith's (subjective) visions as an acceptable (objective) basis for his actions. It takes us some time to discover that not only are the events we are witnessing in *Spider* the memories of Spider himself, but that they are actually filtered through his experience of the diegesis and, as such, never have the same (however tenuous) claim to objectivity as the events in *The Dead Zone*.

As Cronenberg comments, all of the film's formal considerations were dictated by the central character and the pivotal role audience identification would play in interpreting him. This means that the film, as shot and edited,

> . . . would accept the pace of Spider. If we were going to live in Spider's mind and space, which is really what I wanted the audience to do, the movie would have to accept his rhythms, which are slow and deliberate and confused. (Cronenberg, 2002b, director's commentary)

Thus all camera movements match Spider's hesitant movements through the landscape, pausing as he does and maintaining, through framing, a clear distance from this obviously damaged man. This distance, however, is not so designed as to keep us from Spider. Instead, the very emptiness of the frame, often with Spider shuffling alone in its centre, works to draw us to him by demonstrating his isolation. Similarly, the film's editing style is equally slow and hesitant, often leaving the various shots and takes to run on for a second or two before cutting. Because there is little actual action or, indeed, dialogue in these introductory moments in the film to cut between, the pace of the film is entirely in keeping with the establishment of Spider's world, crucially, as he experiences it. It is in this manner that Cronenberg works to enable audience identification with Spider; not by providing us with his point of view[13] but by demonstrating to us how Spider experiences the world by making his diegetic experience ours.

It is with the film's first movement from an objective diegesis into Spider's memory that the specific techniques this film utilizes become clear. As with Smith's first vision in *The Dead Zone*, this moment is our first experience of the way in which shifts in diegesis (both for the protagonist and for us) will be demonstrated. Our first experience of Spider's memory occurs as he is sitting in a café, shortly after establishing himself at Mrs Wilkinson's. This is a location that will accrue significance as the film continues, but for now its general shabbiness works to further demonstrate Spider's isolation. As he sits drinking a mug of tea, the shot is framed so as to position two poorly laminated images of the English countryside above his head. These generic images are rendered important by a close-up of Spider glancing up at them. Immediately this connection is made, we cut abruptly from the café to another location, with Spider and two unidentified men, dressed identically in corduroy trousers, green woollen jumpers and work boots, standing in a field and clearly taking a break from their labours.

We are clearly given to understand this pastoral sequence as a flashback, and Spider's presence in what is clearly his own memory of the event is unproblematic as, thus far, everything we have encountered conforms to standard narrative and formal practice. Yet consideration of this sequence raises a series of important issues, important because of the way they inflect our narrative experiences yet-to-come. This flashback is our first movement away from the film's seemingly unproblematic continuous-present. Prior to this event, the film has unfolded seamlessly, and what questions seem to arise from Spider's unknowability exist as questions waiting to be answered by the unfolding narrative. For much of its length, and certainly until this abrupt cut, *Spider* is a film marked by its stillness: camera movements, editing styles, indeed, even Spider's own meanderings through the mise-en-scène are all marked by this hesitancy. However, the flashback that begins with Spider in the café, is signalled, if anything, by a sudden cut that, because of its swiftness, stands out from the deliberately slow editing up till this point. Thus this cut moves us from a presumably objective diegetic reality to Spider's memory itself. There is no other cinematic device enabled, and because the device here is simply a ubiquitous cut, this suggests that the relationship between Spider and his memories is much more immediate than his relationship with objective reality. With this in mind, this sudden cut demonstrates that as we experience Spider's own experience of his world, the movement from any kind of objective spectatorial position to one subjectively impacted by the influence of memory will be equally sudden. Similarly the cut back from the memory to what is the film's continuous present occurs without warning.

Our next chance to compare the film's strategic temporal shifts comes with the second flashback sequence. Of course, because we understand that we have already experienced a flashback, or memory, that is not formally announced so much as suggested by the character's actions in the mise-en-scène (Spider nodding and muttering), we face a difficult task with this sequence. We see Spider in his bedroom at the halfway house as he walks to the edge of the rug that lies over the hardwood floor. The camera is at ground level and so we see his worn shoes approach us, and then Spider bends into frame as he pulls the rug back to retrieve his notebook. The next few shots show us Spider writing carefully with the worn stub of a pencil and then, finally, the contents of the pages themselves. It is at this point we see that what Spider is writing is a kind of cuneiform,[14] and this fact, coupled with the constant muttering that is a clear self-narration, demonstrates that the events we see unfolding are as much a mystery to him as to us or, at the very least, form an enigma that requires ongoing narrativizing.

This sequence ends with an abrupt cut to a shot of Spider creeping through a back alley, moving through an open gate and into the back garden of a terrace house. With no establishing shot to announce the rationale for this cut, we have no way of knowing our temporal diegetic location or its relationship to the previous location, Spider's room. Unlike the flashback sequence, which was distinguishable because of both a shift in formal consideration (the sudden use of a sharp cut where none had previously occurred) and a change in mise-en-scène detail (cutting from the café to the field, alterations in wardrobe, the addition of two extra characters), here we have only the cut from Spider working at his desk to guide us. It is not until we see Spider, still outside the ter-race house, draw back the netting curtain to peer inside, an action which is our motivation to cut to the interior, that we begin to notice period details that allow us to locate this action in time (the past) and then, as a result, in space (interior [mentally] and subjective).

Once provided with the motivation to enter the house, we cut between close-ups of the mother, the boy and Spider outside the house. The cam-era is now inside the kitchen, and after two circuits of the room, we cut away to a medium long-shot to give us a sense of the room itself, with the mother centre-left, the young boy centre-right, and at the extreme right-hand side of the frame, Spider is just visible peering through the kitchen window; in effect he has delivered us into this space that he cannot enter (or not yet, at least). It is not until we see Spider's engagement with the dialogue being spoken that we are finally given enough information to make sense (in a broader narrative sense) of this sequence and place the participants in some kind of spatial and temporal relationship with each other. As the as-yet-unnamed boy chats with his mother, we see Spider moving from repeating the boy's dialogue at the beginning of this sequence to uttering it in advance – and this establishes the clear link between the two characters and allows the unresolved information to fall into place. However, all this does is lock this sequence – Spider at the window – off from those other sequences that surround it and that con-tinue to problematize it. What is more important than deciding if Spider is still in his room, or if he last left it and is actually patrolling the dark-ened streets of London, is the fact that Spider, like Smith in *The Dead Zone*, is present in his own visions.

It is clear that this method of narrative delivery, with Spider as both the author of and the authorizing presence within his own memories, will provide an audience with an experience mirroring Spider's own move-ment towards self-discovery. The fact that both Spider and Smith appear as protagonists inside their own visions, be they prophetic or hallucin-atory, is explained diegetically by the fact that both men are 'abnormal'. We have seen how Smith's presence within his visions stops at the moment he acquiesces and rejoins civil society, which is to say, at the moment he is re-interpellated. Spider, in contrast, continues to feature in his own hallucinations and memories, although with significant absences. Thus Smith's visible presence in the visions, which only occurs twice, is designed to provide us with character information above and beyond the visions' narrative purpose; they are inserted into those parts of the film to elicit sympathy for Smith as we gain an ever deeper understanding of how much he is suffering and how, despite this personal cost, he continues to serve the greater good of his community. In comparison, *Spider* is much more complicated in its structuring of its diegesis, this being in order to more concretely represent Dennis' subjective experience and the manner with which it intrudes upon, colours and, ultimately, subverts his experience of a broader objective reality.

These films, then, posit a way of representing both subjective experience and the individual's degree of abnormality through the presence of the self-observer within the subjective experience. Thus *The Dead Zone*, which posits that Smith's particular abnormality is only abnormal for as long as it is withheld from use by society, may be usefully compared to *Spider*, which continues to represent Spider's abnormality by always including him in his own visions.

This is perfectly illustrated with the film's next hallucination/memory, which demonstrates the mechanism of conflation that makes Spider's own negotiation of his memories so treacherous. This sequence, based around Spider's recollection of having to fetch his father from the pub, stands out because of the presence of three women (Cronenberg refers to them as 'tarts') who are clearly coded as sexually promiscuous, if not prostitutes. This sequence features the young Boy Spider walking past adult Dennis, who is sitting at a table in the pub, writing notes in his diary. We see the boy pause, attracted to the loud laughter of the women, and when they notice him staring at them, the ringleader flashes her breast at the boy, to the raucous laughter of her colleagues. As Cronenberg comments, 'she's exposed herself to him, for fun, and he's taken aback by that' (Cronenberg, 2002b, director's commentary). At this stage, it is important to note that the woman who flashes young Spider has both a general look (a brassy blonde with a generally feral sexuality in her demeanour and clothing) and a specific presence (by which I mean she is clearly an individual – here played by Alison Egan[15]). This is important because the next time we encounter this woman at the pub, as the adult Spider oversees his father's attempts to collude with her, she is no longer this actress although she retains the same general look, which is a way of saying that for Spider she occupies a particular structural place in his memory of these events. What we might ordinarily miss on the first viewing, which becomes evident as the film progresses, is that the role of Yvonne, the pub tart, is now and hereafter played by Miranda Richardson, who now occupies two roles in Spider's memory: his mother, Mrs Cleg, and her doppelgänger, Yvonne. As Cronenberg comments, 'this woman we're seeing . . . is a creation of Spider. She's a fantasy. She's a fusion of Spider's imagination – of his mother and the prostitute in the pub' (Cronenberg, 1999, director's commentary). In this fashion the film, ever so slowly, reveals that Spider's role is not merely to report his memories :

> Dennis's participation in these scenes – he mouths their dialogue before it's spoken; he transcribes everything, after a fashion, in his diary – has its own justification. He is not just visiting these scenes, he is creating them, and it is purely through his spinning that the 'good' mother will come to be replaced by the 'bad' one, and that the motive for murder will arise. (Combs, 2002, 72)

While Dennis, like Johnny in *The Dead Zone*, is both participant in and witness to his visions, Dennis is implicated far more in the construction of that narrative he is subject to, as is made apparent from the shifting nature of his role in his own memories. The film continues to demonstrate the conflation that occurs in Spider's mind, primarily between the women that populate his memory (all of them bearing aspects of the mother/whore amalgam) but also going so far as to provide one notable example where Spider occupies the position of his father. This sequence, a brief interlude in the movement towards Spider's (self-) defining trauma, occurs as Bill enjoys a tryst with Yvonne near the canal. As they embrace, alone under a bridge, Yvonne masturbates Bill to orgasm and, as he hunches over, she flicks his semen into the water, before turning to walk back to the pub. At this moment, the hunched figure stands up, revealing it to be Spider, who continues what was Bill's dialogue with Yvonne, before we cut from this sequence back to Spider in his room recording these events in his notebook. This moment marks the point at which Spider appears to cross from reportage to participation, which is to say that his presence here in place of his father suggests not only his Oedipal anxieties and jealousies, as well as his attempts to fill in the various gaps in his memories with potential elaborations, but also the fact that this moment is a construction and therefore a fantasy.

A final example of Spider's involvement in the active creation of his fantasy-memories is provided with his understanding of his mother's death at Bill's hands. This sequence begins with Spider, seated again inside the Dog and Beggar, watching his father arriving and continuing his flirtation with Yvonne. The two arrange a tryst at Bill's allotment shed and make their way there independently, Bill arriving first and Yvonne, drunk and unsteady, coming some time later. Neither the adult nor child

Spider is present in this sequence, and again, the conventional unfolding of the narrative means that their absence goes unmarked. We cut
from a shot of Bill guiding Yvonne into his shed to one of the Cleg family
home and Mrs Cleg leaving Boy Spider as she goes out in search of Bill.
The adult Spider is at the pub and sees her arrive but is not present when
Mrs Cleg leaves and walks to the allotment. Indeed, his re-entry into this
sequence only occurs when Mrs Cleg, having surprised Bill and Yvonne,
is struck with a shovel and killed. At this moment we cut back to a shot of
Spider in his halfway house room, writing in his notebook and muttering
his narration of the events we have just seen. As Cronenberg explains it

> And now you can see that Spider is rewriting his memories here. He's
> not just recording things, he's actually inventing them and reshaping
> them and shuffling them for some purpose that he has. And one of the
> main purposes, of course, for doing that sort of thing is denial.
> (Cronenberg, 2002b, director's commentary)

Spider's work in these fantasies, and in the way in which he attempts to
generate a meaningful narrative from them, makes visible his attempts
to negotiate his own desires. His work, constitutive though it is, unsettles
the spectator as his memories, like Smith's visions, blur the boundaries
between what the film offers as objective reality and what we understand
as subjective. Indeed, as the film draws to its conclusion, we come to
understand that *Spider* actually has very little in the way of an objective
diegesis that avoids Dennis' interpretive touches.[16]

Attending the Visions

Spider's conclusion, where Spider appears to remember the moment
when the Yvonne he had killed was transformed into his mother, both
offers a resolution to the mystery of Spider's trauma and provides a
means for the narrative to remain unresolved. This second interpretive
avenue is one favoured by Cronenberg who, as the film concludes, notes
'[b]ut then we ask one question, which is – could this also be a fantasy of
Spider's? Could this feeling that he murdered his mother also be a fantasy?' (Cronenberg, 2002b, director's commentary). It is perfectly possible to entertain this wilful suspension of resolution, but the likelier
course of action is to see, as the film's resolving point, that the Boy Spider
has murdered his mother as a result of his conflation of Yvonne with

Mrs Cleg and that these events, repressed by the adult, are finally released with his obsessive revisiting of the places of his past. Cronenberg's preferred strategy views the entire film as essentially subjective, hence 'untrustworthy'; because we have little indication of when we segue between Spider's visions and memories, we can never be entirely certain of our relationship to any anchoring kernel of objectivity. In effect, Cronenberg suggests, because the film issues from Spider's unconsciousness and forms part of his 'working through' his repressed material, we can never really know when we might have reached the traumatic moment. He goes on to suggest, by way of illustrating this point, that 'perhaps Spider's mother left, perhaps he, as many children do, blamed himself for her leaving and invented this fantasy as a way of dealing with that guilt' (Cronenberg, 2002b, director's commentary).

In this fashion, *Spider*, like *The Dead Zone*, sneaks its heresy into the structures of characterization and narrative, into those facets of the film that we take seriously and which function invisibly. For example, one of the devices that give credence to this reading strategy is the eventual realization of the way in which Spider, both as boy and man, is conflating the women he encounters into a single dangerous amalgam. What marks this device as heretical (exactly as with Smith's visions) is the very nature of its seamlessness. As noted above, a seamless fictional diegesis '. . . provides a stable and continuous basis for the involvement of the viewer in the experience of the film' (Anderson, 1996, 124). Indeed, part of the power of *The Dead Zone* and *Spider* is their very seamlessness, and yet this is where their difficulties lie. As noted, Smith's presence in his own visions, which are formally similar to the film's objective diegesis, is used to undermine our empathetic attachment to his character and, especially, our attachment to and sympathy for his character's social position. Similarly, Cronenberg's elision of the formal markers of diegesis-shifting in *Spider* means that we miss the evolution of the Yvonne character as she overcomes the other female characterizations of the film, just as we have trouble coming to terms with the shifts between Spider's memories and fantasies. Both of these films deal with the collision between objective and subjective diegeses, and both absolutely recognize the power of a 'seamless fictional world'. What they both demonstrate is the fact that such a fictional world can be too seamless, with too little differentiation between its diegetic levels. For *Spider* this means that our experience of the film is altered and becomes far more open, in terms of interpretation and understanding, than we might otherwise expect. The result of this is that Cronenberg's evocation of Spider's interior state and the way this interiority fundamentally affects his experience of the film's objective world '. . . makes us feel his guilt before we know why he feels it, complicating our feelings towards him before we can opt out of our identification' (Hoover, 2002).

The manner in which the construction of a film's diegesis can take too seriously the requirements for a seamless fictional world is elaborated differently in *The Dead Zone* and *Spider*. What these films have in common is the fact that each of them deals with the relationship of a single protagonist to an objective diegesis that surrounds them. To a greater or lesser extent, the presence of that objective diegesis works to recuperate and therefore normalize the narrative (even if, as with *Spider*, we are never quite sure how far its boundaries extend). As well as this, the presence of visionary or hallucinatory states, within which the protagonists continue to feature, act as frames through which another (subjective) diegesis can be accessed. Each film establishes its own mechanisms for alerting the spectator to shifts in diegeses (and, hence, shifts in framing) and then, once this rhythm is established, further disrupts it in order to reveal and undermine the stability of the framed interpretation. The next move is to examine a film where all inhabitants of the diegesis suffer from *Spider*'s malaise – an uncertainty of reality's boundaries.

eXistenZ

eXistenZ, released in late 1998, had the great misfortune to arrive at the box office at a similar time as *The Matrix* (Larry and Andy Wachowski, 1999), that popularly definitive 'other' reality-bending science fiction film. It is to *The Matrix* that *eXistenZ* is most often compared, yet *eXistenZ* functions almost as the exact thematic, ideological and disciplinary obverse to *The Matrix*, deliberately eschewing the high spectacle, high-tech, body-transcendence route, in favour of a more contemplative and, in comparison, introspective approach. Indeed, the notion of a film as both functionally introspective and promoting a spectatorial condition echoing this is a useful way to consider the manner with which this film unfolds and attends to its heretical concerns.

Because of the nature of its central conceit, *eXistenZ* (1998) is a much more complicated film to summarize. In short, *eXistenZ* details the struggles of game designer Allegra Geller (Jennifer Jason Leigh) to keep her new game system, and herself, alive. Set in a deliberately indeterminate time period that might equally be the present or the near future, the world of *eXistenZ* is one in which video gaming is a high art and the game consoles plug directly into the player's spinal cord, via bioports. During the preview of her newest game, 'eXistenZ', Allegra survives an assassination attempt and goes on the run with her bodyguard, Ted Pikul (Jude Law). Because of the trauma of the event, Allegra is concerned that her gamepod, an organic technology constructed from amphibian organs, has suffered damage and decides that the only way to check her game's condition is to play 'eXistenZ'. When she discovers that Ted has no bioport (and, worse, is only a ring-in from marketing), Allegra seeks out Gas (Willem Dafoe), a mechanic at an isolated country petrol station who runs a sideline in installing illegal bioports, only to discover that he is prepared to kill her and, further, has installed a diseased bioport into Pikul. Gas is killed, but the diseased bioport has further damaged Geller's gamepod, and she finds refuge with Kiri Vinokur (Ian Holm), a gamepod designer and surgeon employed by Antenna Research, Geller's parent company.

Once the gamepod and Pikul's bioport have been repaired, the two port into 'eXistenZ' only to discover, as they attempt to proceed through the game narrative, that neither of them has any idea of what is happening or what they might be required to do. As they negotiate the game's narrative, which, at one point, involves them entering a game-within-a-game, Ted's increasing discomfort with the game leads him and Allegra to exit 'eXistenZ'. After assuring themselves as to the safety of their bodies in the real world, they re-enter 'eXistenZ' in order to rendezvous with a possible source of help at a local Chinese restaurant. After Ted, in response to what he considers game impulses, kills the waiter, the two find they are no closer to solving what increasingly appears to be a conspiracy at the heart of the game's narrative – one that mirrors the struggle in the real world between game companies and groups known as 'Realists', those who resent attempts to subvert lived reality. After Allegra ports, once more, into a diseased pod, the two exit 'eXistenZ' to discover that the Realists have launched an armed assault on Vinokur's complex. Escaping another assassination attempt, Allegra learns that Vinokur, too, has betrayed her, and she kills him. When Ted reveals that he has been a Realist all along, she finishes him off. At this point, we learn that everyone (and everything) we see has been part of another game, 'tranCendenZ' (with the accent on the last syllable), by Pilgrimage Research, and that Allegra and Ted are merely two of a group of game testers, with Allegra having 'won'. As they leave the testing area Ted and Allegra reveal, in conversation with the game's designer, Yevgeny Nourish (Don McKellar), that they are actually Realist assassins and shoot the designer and his assistant before turning to leave. As they exit the building they are stopped by the character who played 'the Chinese waiter' (Oscar Hsu) who, first, begs them not to kill him and then asks if they are not still in the game.

The Nested Diegesis

The seeds of the idea that would eventually become *eXistenZ* were planted when Cronenberg agreed to interview Salman Rushdie, at that stage still in hiding (and under twenty-four-hour police protection) as a result of the fatwa declared in response to Rushdie's *The Satanic Verses* (1988). What emerged from this interview were a series of important concerns, not least of which were long considerations of the possibility of video games constituting a form of art,[17] and the role of censorship in a contemporary society. As Cronenberg notes,

> We talked about games and about computers. He'd had to learn about computers because, being on the run, he needed to work on a laptop. He couldn't do things the way he used to. That meeting crystallised things for me, so I posited a time when games could be art and a games designer could be an artist. (Cronenberg, interviewed in Rodley, 1999)

Clearly Rushdie's situation finds its echoes with Allegra's various crises, on the run from shadowy forces because of her work of art and its disruptive effect on a putative status quo. In *eXistenZ*, the exact nature of this counter-force is never explicitly explored, but it is obvious, as we gain an understanding of the nature of this film's diegesis (although it would be more accurate to speak of this film's diegeses), that the Realists stand opposed to the games industry, at the very least. However, this binary is itself undone with the film's conclusion – the fact that we may still be 'in the game' renders all positions (ideological, ontological and hermeneutic) suspect.

It is in the film's efforts to upset or subvert the assumptions an audience might be led to develop that *eXistenZ* diverges from *The Matrix*, this schism occurring at the point where they most (albeit superficially) resemble each other: in the delivery of multiple or 'nested' diegeses. The concept of nested diegeses is usefully defined by Peter X. Feng as 'the worlds within worlds in the film's narrative' (Feng, 2002, 150) and accounts not only for the presence of distinct diegetic spaces situated (narratively and, for the characters, experientially) within each other, but also for the hierarchical nature of these spaces. Thus this provides us with an ideal way to explore the manner with which *eXistenZ* signals (or, more importantly, fails to signal) the characters' movements through, and their understanding of, the games and sub-games that form both the narrative and diegetic architecture of this film. As should be clear from the synopsis above, the film begins with the game already in motion (although the game is 'tranCendenZ', within which the game 'eXistenZ' is played), which means that as the characters on screen move through their diegesis, they are already subject to a 'game architecture' (to use Geller's phrase) that they, and we, must learn as the game progresses. At one point in *eXistenZ*, Pikul complains of the arbitrary nature of 'eXistenZ', and Geller's response echoes Cronenberg's oft-repeated comments[18] about the constitutive nature of experiential reality:

> **Pikul:** I don't like it here [in eXistenZ]. I don't know what's going on . . . we're both stumbling around together in this unformed world whose rules and objectives are largely unknown . . . seemingly undecipherable . . . or even possibly non-existent. Always on the verge of being killed by forces that we don't understand.
> **Geller:** Well, that sounds like my game alright.
> **Pikul:** If that sounds like a game, it's not going to be easy to market.
> **Geller:** But it's a game everybody's already playing. (Cronenberg, 1999)

Further, the nature of the technology in *eXistenZ*, which will be discussed in more detail below, means that as the various instruments plug directly into the characters' nervous systems and, literally, feed off their bodily energy, 'eXistenZ'

> . . . is a game interface and world whose particular gaming sessions or plots incorporate and hence manifest the individual players' preoccupations, in this instance, the vexed relationship between games, art, or fantasy and 'real life'. (Hotchkiss, 2003, 15)

Therefore where *eXistenZ* differs from *The Matrix* (and, hence, from other films utilizing Feng's concept of nested diegeses) is not in the way the nested diegeses are accessed. In both films, a narrativized intersection between the body and technology provides the means to usefully divorce the mind or intellect (that which 'travels' or engages with the game/

construct/programme) from the body (that which remains behind, painfully exposed).[19] The difference rather lies in the way an audience is allowed to locate, interpret and, hence, contain the diegeses and the movement between them. *The Matrix* is careful to provide each move-ment between the various diegetic 'levels' or spaces with a transitional period, and distinguishes each diegesis stylistically, formally, and with a mass of necessarily redundant mise-en-scène details, to ensure that we are never 'lost' between locations. Because *eXistenZ* is seeking to criticize exactly this kind of ontological framing and interpretive practice, these are precisely the kinds of disciplinary markers that are absent.

Thus *eXistenZ* provides a series of simultaneous epistemological and ontological analyses regarding the relationship of a constructed world to reality, however we decide to define it, and, indeed, regarding the rela-tionship of that world to those who inhabit it. As Hotchkiss rightly notes, both the film *eXistenZ* and the game(s) that feature within it are experi-ential structures based on the cumulative effects of mistakes and missed opportunities, meaning that *eXistenZ*, like 'eXistenZ', is designed to be 'played' more than once. Like other high-concept games, it is only through repetition and the making of mistakes that the narrative can be encompassed and understood. It is no surprise, then, that the narrative of *eXistenZ*, with its focus on the many 'mistakes' Pikul and Geller make in the game, mirrors gameplay (and, especially, video gameplay) in gen-eral, with each 'mistake' marking a narrative dead-end, at which point the character 'dies' in the game and must then renegotiate the task or obstacle that leads to the exit.

Playing the Game

A large part of Pikul's discomfort within 'eXistenZ' lies in the fact that there are clearly rules in place to govern gameplay – after all, the world of 'eXistenZ' is not chaotic – but they are unknown and can only be learnt 'the hard way'. After all, he effectively complains, why play a game that so closely mirrors reality as to be indistinguishable from it? At that moment, as Geller's response echoes comments Cronenberg has repeatedly made regarding his views about the experience of reality, we see Cronenberg at his most playful and, significantly, his most heretical. Pikul's complaints about 'eXistenZ' can equally be made about the experience of viewing and interpreting *eXistenZ*, as the same structural problems exist. Given that the entire narrative would appear to hinge on our being able to follow the characters through the various games and sub-games (each functioning as a nested diegesis, overlapping or sitting within the diegesis just exited), *eXistenZ* makes no effort to clarify our diegetic position, just as 'eXistenZ' needs to be played to be understood. Cronenberg clearly is not interested in providing a film that reports the experience of gameplay so much as he is concerned with replicating both the structure and experience of it. This provides a unique difficulty in that the game of 'eXistenZ' (like all games) is designed to be played, not merely watched. It is in how he attempts to overcome this difficulty that Cronenberg reveals the manner with which he pushes *eXistenZ* beyond the bounds of the other films that had, by this time, come to mark the 'virtual reality' sub-genre.

As noted in the introduction to this chapter, Anderson's comments about the relationship of play to the filmic experience allow us to comprehend the role of the framing device in structuring the information we encounter. These frames guide our experience of the narrative and, indeed, structure our play (in Anderson's terms) within the fictional diegesis. This play is rendered all the more effective with a seamless fictional world. However, the corollary to this is that the fictional world of the diegesis is expected to announce its very 'fictionality' even as it strives towards seamlessness. This announcement occurs through the use of the same mechanisms Anderson notes are used to constitute this diegesis and to mark our movement about and through it. Framing devices mark a pathway through the narrative, which means that their continued use within groups of films and across filmic traditions constitute exactly the rules of the game that Pikul complains are absent from 'eXistenZ' and which are missing from, or at least differently located within, *eXistenZ*. In discussing the film's relationship to the (then) emerging sub-genre of virtual reality films, Cronenberg comments that

> I knew people would want to categorize it as a virtual reality movie, and I felt that would be a big mistake for us to accept that category, because it will lead people to expect something they're not going to see. . . . So I was not being so innocent and naïve, because I was defining myself against the films which have been done about the techno-future. (Grunberg, 2006, 165)

Cronenberg's decision to set *eXistenZ* against the other films it would most obviously be compared with extends beyond the various omissions made in the film's mise-en-scène.[20] Indeed, what marks *eXistenZ* as distinct from these other films[21] is the fact that its frames are much harder to locate beyond the obvious framing device of game-playing, which sets up the narrative and is then undercut by the film's conclusion. By removing clearly marked (or demarcated) framing devices utilized in the movement between diegetic states or sites, Cronenberg places the audience in the same position as Pikul, aware that rules do exist to govern movement through this world but unsure of what they might be or how to recognize them. For example, the bioport seems to function as the most obvious indicator of gameplay. The first third of the film is spent getting Ted fitted with a port that actually works properly, and it is only when Allegra inserts the game's 'umby-cord' into his port that we see them formally announce that the game has begun. Other than that, our only other clues to the particular diegetic place we happen to be passing through come with minute (and easily missed) mise-en-scène details – the state of Ted and Allegra's hair being the most obvious. Once Ted has been fitted and 'eXistenZ' begun, every action involving the bioport could be seen to function as the introduction of a new level (or sub-level) of the game, meaning that we quickly learn to recognize the bioport as a diegetic framing device, with its use in the film signalling a shift in diegesis. However, the moment we see Allegra wearing the 'tranCendenZ' VR gear within 'eXistenZ' and then, upon exiting 'eXistenZ', see a group of players in the church hall all similarly equipped, we realize that the bioport was not a framing device at all and that, truth be told, we had no way of comprehending our movement through the diegesis of 'eXistenZ' because the 'real' framing device was missing. If anything, Cronenberg is taking both the premise of *eXistenZ* seriously and, at the same time, delivering far too much seamlessness in his diegesis.

eXistenZ, like *Spider* and *The Dead Zone*, is a film that deals with hermeneutics and ontology as constitutive practices: the characters of *eXistenZ* literally construct the narrative as they progress through the narrative they are busy constructing. The distinction between *eXistenZ* and the other two films discussed above is that there is no longer any kind of 'objective' diegesis to function as a recuperating mechanism or as a 'ground' at which interpretation can find stability of meaning. The moment we are asked if 'we are still in the game' (and we admit that the answer might be 'yes'), then the narrative of *eXistenZ* becomes provisional and certainly not resolved as *The Dead Zone* or even *Spider* resolve. In this fashion, the audience of *eXistenZ* is in the same interpretive position as Pikul (and, indeed, as Spider and Johnny Smith): attempting to fashion trustworthy meaning out of apparently meaningless events. But, more than this, the film functions as a broader comment on cinema itself. As Brian Johnson notes,

> In *eXistenZ*, however, the games industry also serves as a satirical meta-phor for the movie industry, with references to pre-release budgets and test previews. When Allegra declares that 'the world of games is in a kind of trance – people are programmed to accept so little, but the possibilities are so great,' the allusion is obvious. (Johnson, 1999, 63)

However, *eXistenZ*'s 'tongue-in-cheek metacinematic references' (Hotchkiss, 2003, 27) extend to more than a comment about the film industry; they represent an attempt to realize the possibilities offered by what Anderson correctly recognizes as the power of a seamless fictional world. What Cronenberg delivers, with these three films, are seamless worlds that become problematic precisely because the requisite 'seams' – the visible junctures between dieseses – are missing. Instead of the presence of various devices that ordinarily allow us to make sense of these films because their meaning accumulates through use and over time, what we have are their absences and/or their breakdown. This is not to say that framing devices are absent entirely from these three films. They are most certainly present, with the difference being that each of these films is so thoroughly self-contained and internally consistent as to generate its own framing devices which are specific to each fictional world alone and which do not recur from film to film. In this fashion, these three films render visible the various standard, ideologically invisible, disciplinary structures of framing at work in conventional cinema. This is done by choosing unique methods to indicate shifts in diegetic space and time, thereby highlighting the kinds of interpretive structures surrounding the representation of normal and abnormal subjective and objective states. In this fashion, an audience becomes aware of these frames even as they work to interpret the informa-tion that is being framed. This, then, is Cronenberg's specific heresy with these films: in recognizing the demand for a seamless fictional world, he exceeds this demand by delivering precisely what was asked for – films in which the diegesis is entirely consistent and self-contained – which turns out to be more than we were expecting.

Chapter 4

Functions of Failure

Escaping the Genre Bind

The three films of this chapter – *M. Butterfly* (1993), *Dead Ringers* (1988) and *Crash* (1996) – mark a significant development in the way Cronenberg's work continues his 'project'. This, as we have seen, consists of a career-long exploration of what the director has often referred to as the 'human condition': life, the experience of mutability and death. While these three films continue this exploration, Cronenberg's heretical activity shifts from a primarily formal focus to being articulated through these films' narrative and content. This means that the films' plots can address these issues expressly, foregrounding them as diegetic concerns and integrating them into the diegesis itself. Thus all aspects of these films – their narratives and their various contents (here defined as including characters and characterization and mise-en-scène details, and extending to the broader diegetic construction at work) – can now focus directly on attending to, and attempting to answer, these issues. As before, the same basic structure of heresy remains in play: in accord with Žižek's thought, a similar condition of 'taking too seriously' is at work in these narratives, but now this means that the characters, while freed from generic conventions in these films, can connect, become subject to and thereby critique more immediately the same kinds of disciplinary structures we have already seen discussed in his texts.

The previous films discussed take part to a greater or lesser extent in generic discourses that limit the kinds of narrative and thematic developments that can occur. Even *Spider*, perhaps the least 'generic' of the films thus far discussed, has a mystery at its centre and, for much of its length, is not so much a 'whodunnit' as a 'what happened', with all the concomitant elisions and caesurae. As evidenced by Cronenberg's other generic films, genre provides a template that is both a prison and a safety net. As he notes,

. . . genre does protect you in a lot of ways. . . . It kind of mothers you because it's a known quantity, . . . [a]nd you can make a lot of mistakes, and the momentum of the genre itself can carry you as well. (Cronenberg & Schwartz, 1992, 4–5)

The pressure of a disciplinary structure that controls the extent of experimentation a particular narrative may undergo reveals the tension faced by the heretical filmmaker. In effect, Cronenberg must succumb to these disciplinary structures (to some extent at least) if his films are to gain an audience, which they must do in order to render these hegemonic structures visible to someone and thereby affect their functioning. This tension plays out differently depending on each film's relationship to those structures that restrict or limit it, with the limitations of genre being the most visible and forceful of all. In his genre films, Cronenberg moves to extend the way in which each film meets that genre's requirements which, necessarily, can lead to extensions in the genres themselves. Nevertheless, it must be noted that his revisions (or additions) to these genres (e.g., his work in helping to develop the Body Horror genre) occur within clearly delineated structures that, to a large extent, pre-exist his work. Therefore while generic requirements mean that Cronenberg is required to fulfil particular narrative and content demands, he is free (again, relatively) to experiment with each film's form and, hence, the relationship of that form to an audience's experience of the film's content. This results in those situations where the form stands at odds with the narrative, working to undercut it (as in *The Dead Zone*, for example) or complicate it (as with *Spider* and *eXistenZ*). Once freed from overt generic requirements, however, Cronenberg's films are free to pursue overtly, as a series of central narrative concerns, what previously could only be referred to obliquely or buried beneath generic compliance.

The question then becomes, how is Cronenberg able to transcend genre, as *M. Butterfly*, *Dead Ringers* and *Crash* all appear to demonstrate? The answer is not at all straightforward and I am loathe to suggest a strictly teleological progression to Cronenberg's oeuvre. Nevertheless some trends do present themselves. As he notes, the horror genre is a particularly efficient way for young filmmakers to enter the industry, given that the genre's aforementioned structural limitations work to protect '. . . young filmmakers from their own ineptness and brashness and arrogance and so on . . .' (Cronenberg & Schwartz, 1992, 4). However, as each film built on the success (both financial and critical) of the ones that preceded it, Cronenberg gained access to increased budgets and, therefore, greater creative independence. So while Cronenberg's early films were lambasted by the critics, they were spectacularly successful at the box office, establishing a public fan base that has, subsequently, always supported his experiments.[1] As his work continues, critical attention has become more (although certainly not uniformly) favourable and this public, industrial, critical and academic support has provided, in turn, support for his continued artistic development. So it is that Cronenberg's work, fostered and supported by genre, is able – when he chooses – to transcend these limitations. Having gained this freedom he is able to bring into prominence the thematic concerns that were previously hidden inside their narrative events or themes. Similarly, once Cronenberg is able to move beyond the restrictions of genre, he is free to move his heretical notions forward in order to let them play out as narrative and character. It is important to note, however, that despite increasing budgets he is still subject to the disciplines of the industry and, not least, to the disciplines of film form. Nevertheless, success (both commercial and critical) and a proven track record gives Cronenberg literally more room to play.

With this freedom, the Cronenberg 'project' can now take centre stage and the three films of this chapter are all linked by a series of vital concerns involving the regulation of desire and the ideological function of failure. The regulation of desire has always been pivotal to any understanding of Cronenberg's work but it is the relationship of desire to satisfaction, legitimate and illegitimate, as it is evidenced in sexual practice that joins these three films and permits a more overt exploration. As we have seen, sex features throughout Cronenberg's films, but it is usually – and in the genre films especially – the means of the narrative instead of the overall purpose. Thus sex in *Shivers* and *Rabid* functions only as the vector for the various infections that are the films' central concerns. What issues emerge regarding the disciplining of the desiring body, and particularly the ways in which the desiring body seeks to satisfy its desire, are subsumed within a broader consideration of disciplining the body *per se*. Certainly sex can function as a narrative catalyst, as when Brundle begins to understand the 'craziness of the flesh', or Smith experiences, just once, the suburban idyll that fate will otherwise prevent him from possessing. But only in these later films does sex and the various discourses that surround it come to the fore in order to be taken, first, seriously, and then, too seriously. In this fashion, locating heresy at the level of narrative and protagonist means that these films all move to take the disciplinary discourses of sex absolutely at their word.

The Focus on Sex

As seen above, Cronenberg's desire to focus upon those issues of greatest interest to him were restrained by the same generic structures that supported his career from the outset. This is exactly the kind of tension the heretical filmmaker will face and, initially at least, Cronenberg's method of resolving this was to meet the demands of the genre with regards to the most obvious narrative and content issues, while utilizing his ever-increasing command of film form as the means to problematize, or provide counterpoint to, those same regulations and demands. What emerges from this period, regardless of the generic requirements, is his oft-repeated concern with the body. As noted, for Cronenberg the body is the first fact of human existence and, as such, is necessarily the most regulated object in culture. The body, then, becomes the site at which discipline must begin and any discussion of discipline will quickly encounter the various structures that serve to guide a population through their erotic lives.

As Cronenberg comments, once sex and childbearing are distinguished as separate activities, each with its own particular politics, then the field of erotic exchange becomes opened to an enormous potential for desire and satisfaction: 'sex as pleasure and energy and politics, and not childrearing and childbirth' (Simon, 2001, 45). In Cronenberg's view, this means that '[s]ex is a potent force all over the map right . . . ; it is reinventing itself, whether we want to accept it or not' (Simon, 2001, 45). Necessarily for Cronenberg, transformation of sexual practice and the manner with which sexual desire and satisfaction are achieved (and, especially, articulated) are linked to transformations in the body and, in this way, Cronenberg continues unabated to highlight various disciplinary activities that surround bodily behaviour. This is not, however, to suggest that Cronenberg is utopian in his imaginings, and it is here that the second aspect of these films comes into play: the ideological and disciplinary function of failure.

What links these films is the fact that they deal with desire as evidenced in sex, and that they all feature failure in some form as part of their narrative resolution. Indeed, it is in the relationship between the specific failure within the film and the manner with which an audience is led to assess and evaluate that failure which gives these films their particular edge. As a number of commentators have noted,[2] failure on the part of the protagonist, however failure is defined, has long been a staple of Cronenberg's work. Indeed, from the outset he has had made failure part of his films' strategies towards resolution, and as a way of providing narrative resolution (as demanded by the genre) without necessarily overwhelming his own expression within this film. Thus St. Luc in *Shivers* fails to contain the parasites and, at the film's close, joyfully leads the infected troupe out into the night. Yet Cronenberg considers this to be a happy ending and, if one assumes – as he asks us to – the position of the parasite, one can see that it is, indeed, a successful resolution where the parasite wins at the expense of the bourgeois system represented by Starliner Towers. In comparison Rose, in *Rabid*, fails to control her own surgically induced malaise and the successful resolution at the film's end is her death – the demise of the disease's vector represents a reassertion of the very hegemonic system disrupted in *Shivers*. This means that *Rabid* can be viewed as an effort to detail how a hegemonic system will respond (i.e., with the full force of the Repressive State Apparatus) to the kind of threat that erupts in *Shivers*.

So it continues: Smith's failure to assassinate Stillson in *The Dead Zone* can be interpreted as a partial success – Stillson, we presume, takes his own life – but, as discussed, we only have Smith's vision to support this claim and it must be weighed up against everything Smith has lost in the interim. Finally Brundle's failure at the close of *The Fly* comes as a result of a combination of scientific hubris and drunken oversight, with the success of his teleportation device giving way to the success of his mutated flesh in its bodily reassertion despite his attempts to maintain a solidly Cartesian control over his own transformation. Failure thus forms a noticeable part of Cronenberg's universe and it is interesting to note that in almost every case, and certainly more frequently in the latter films, failure emerges as a result of a partial success on the part of the protagonist.

As Cronenberg's oeuvre progresses, a distinctive narrative pattern emerges in which the protagonist enjoys, at least initially, the fruits of his (for the Cronenberg protagonist is almost always a man) labours only to have something go horribly wrong. Of course, such reversals are part and parcel of a restorative narrative structure that sees the world of the protagonist inverted in order to test him/her. Where Cronenberg's films differ is that the normal world of the film's first act is not restored in the third. Of course, the restorative narrative performs a clear ideological function, but Cronenberg's refusal of the restorative narrative is not merely a matter of authorial perversity. Rather, the presence of such failure suggests a disciplinary structure in operation, a training exercise in how *not* to desire, with failure functioning as a disciplinary mechanism that occurs in order to demonstrate what *must not occur.* Such narratives become training grounds (as are all narratives) specializing in demonstrating the penalties for transgression, for, in all of the films dealt with below, the subjects who fail, fail do so by attempting to transgress (or, in their eyes, transcend) their diegetic ideological restrictions. Thus their actions serve to demonstrate the penalties for failure and to demonstrate, further, that failure is inevitable. If this is the case, that the protagonist fails because of some transgressive element in his or her desiring behaviour, then the rest of the narrative begins to make retrospective sense: the success that marks the first third of the film is the act or site of transgression that is effectively legislated against by the film's remainder, and the reason the world of the film's first act cannot be restored in the third is because that is where the problem lies.

Of course, it is not nearly as simple as this, for with each of these narratives Cronenberg is at work to, at the very least, reveal these disciplinary structures and, in so doing, make obvious the ways they work to limit the very subjects they constitute. Thus the double articulation of discipline sees these three films in particular function as exemplars of how not to be, how not to behave and, especially, how not to desire, while at the same time working to render visible these same disciplinary structures. Yet at no point is Cronenberg doing any more than taking seriously these disciplinary requirements: as we shall see, each of these films proceeds from a very simple question that leads inevitably to the harrowing conclusion. Thus *M. Butterfly* asks us to consider if two men can have a heterosexual relationship, *Dead Ringers* queries the restriction of a monogamous relationship to just two people, and *Crash* explores the possibility of reaching the end of desire itself. In essence, this is Cronenberg's heretical gesture within these films; he provides space for an audience to question a narrative that does not resolve in such a way as to forestall such questioning. In this fashion, these films, which

> . . . seem at first sight to belong firmly within the [dominant] ideology and to be completely under its sway, . . . turn out to be so only in an ambiguous manner. (Comolli & Narboni, 1999, 757)

As a result of this, each film will

> . . . throw up obstacles in the way of ideology, causing it to swerve and
> get off course. Looking at the framework one can see two moments in
> it: one holding it back within certain limits, one transgressing them. An
> internal criticism is taking place which cracks the film at the seams. If
> one reads the film obliquely, looking for symptoms; if one looks beyond
> its apparent formal coherence, one can see that it is riddled with cracks;
> it is splitting under an internal tension which is simply not there in an
> ideologically innocuous film. (Comolli & Narboni, 1999, 757)

These three films therefore mark a shift in Cronenberg's presentation of
his interests – the aforementioned 'project'. The outcome of this shift
involves making visible the internal tension as the film works to resolve
its ideological and disciplinary critique. However, the moment these
issues (which are different for each film) become visible is the moment
when these films must confront and negotiate the hegemonic structures
that will govern and regulate their production and reception. In essence,
then, Cronenberg's protagonists fail because they must, because they are
required to acquiesce so thoroughly to the hegemonic structures that
Cronenberg reveals to be in operation.

M. Butterfly

M. Butterfly is Cronenberg's fourth adaptation and, of the work he had
adapted until this point, is usually considered the least successful.[3] As we
shall see, much of this negative critical response comes as the result of a
fundamental misreading of the film's narrative and themes, a fact necessarily compounded by the unhappy accident that this film was forced to
follow the extremely successful *The Crying Game* (Neil Jordan, 1992) into
the box office.

Cronenberg's *M. Butterfly* is based on David Hwang's successful
Broadway musical of the same name, itself based on true-life events.
Where the film and the play differ is in the way they deal with these
events. For Hwang, the true life story of a French diplomat who continues
a long-term affair with a Beijing opera singer, unaware that she is a man,
is meant to function as the means to deliver a blunt and forceful polemic
on Western imperialism, sexual identity and fantasy, and particularly on
the West's construction of the East within a broad Orientalist framework
(Hwang, 1989).[4] In the play, the diplomat Daniel Boursciot, now renamed

René Gallimard, moves as both a perpetrator of Western injustices and, equally, as a victim of a system of fantasy constructions that place him in a particular kind of role with regards to the other Asian members of the production. Within Hwang's play, it is not so much that Gallimard actively constructs his fantasy of the mysterious and feminine East to which his willing partner so readily conforms, as that he tacitly agrees not to question the structures of these Western cultural fantasies that place him in an unquestioned position of power. For all of this, Hwang's play makes no bones about its polemic and its narrative has a didactic function that Cronenberg sought to swiftly remove. What remains in the film is the skeletal outline of Hwang's play, but without the blunt, and at times crass, didacticism, leaving what drew Cronenberg to the project in the first place: the narrative of self-delusion and artistic creation, both of which work to draw attention to the mechanisms that control and regulate desire and fantasy.

The Film Itself

Within Cronenberg's *M. Butterfly*, the same basic plot points are retained, with French functionary René Gallimard (Jeremy Irons) falling inexorably in love with Beijing opera diva, Song Liling (John Lone) during a performance of *Madama Butterfly*. Their flirtation, initially antagonistic as Song taunts Gallimard with imperialist fantasies about the opera, quickly becomes a fully fledged affair. All the while Gallimard refuses to acknowledge what the audience have long since concluded: Song Liling is a man. As their relationship continues, Gallimard is promoted and gains access to sensitive diplomatic material, which Song seems to have no trouble in learning from him. In order to prevent Gallimard from learning the truth of her gender, Song claims to be pregnant and leaves Beijing in order to have their child, according to 'ancient Chinese custom'. During this period, Gallimard's hubris causes him to fall foul of his superiors, while the Chinese Cultural Revolution replaces Song's reasonably lenient superiors with the Red Guard, who are a great deal less sympathetic to the arts in general and to her sexual and gender orientation in particular. As Gallimard leaves China for France, Song is sentenced to serve time in the salt mines. Four years later, at the time of the student uprisings in France, Gallimard is again a minor functionary with the diplomatic service in Paris when Song reappears. At her urging, he becomes a dispatch rider, able to continue passing information to her, now in

order to help free their child, who is, Song claims, being held hostage by
the Red Guard. Eventually Gallimard is arrested and, at the public trial,
the fact of Song's sex and her deception emerges. Song is deported to
China, dressed as a man while Gallimard, now in prison, performs a
sequence from *Madama Butterfly* and, having made himself up as Butterfly, cuts his throat and dies.

The relationship between René and the opera *Madama Butterfly* is of
central importance to understanding the narrative of *M. Butterfly*.
Puccini's work and, especially, the construction of fantasy that it represents becomes the frame that the film uses to govern the roles that
Gallimard and Song must play in relation to each other. The opera provides Gallimard with the master narrative to which he must adhere, if his
fantasy is to be sustained. Gallimard's experience of the opera itself is
marked as a moment of transcendental pleasure, with his face framed in
a close-up that, as the aria begins to swell, moves slowly in to draw attention to his amazed features. He admits to never having seen it before,
and this ignorance of high culture serves to mark him as the perfect
(i.e., naïve or virginal) consumer of its ideological content. Without
prior knowledge of the opera's content, he is free to absorb it as a form
of 'truth-in-art', its narrative corresponding, we assume, to his already-
held assumptions about the 'mysterious' East and its relationship to the
paternal West. The tale of Butterfly, with all its sexual implications,
appeals to Gallimard because it conforms to and confirms the views of
China he has already established and which his position at the embassy
affirms.

Thus the narrative of the opera becomes the frame that regulates the
performance of the relationship between Gallimard and Song, although
their own roles within this highly regulated structure become somewhat
slippery as they negotiate each other's demands. Gallimard's first attempt
at flattery, a parroting back of the opera's ideological content, is quickly
undone by a much more astute Song:

Gallimard: I usually don't like *Butterfly*.
Song: I can't blame you in the least.
Gallimard: I mean, the story . . .
Song: Ridiculous.
Gallimard: I like the story, but . . . what?
Song: Oh, you like it?
Gallimard: I . . . what I mean is, I've always seen it played by huge
women in so much bad makeup.

Song: Bad makeup is not unique to the West.

Gallimard: But, who can believe them?

Song: And you believe me?

Gallimard: Absolutely. You were utterly convincing. It's the first time . . .

Song: Convincing? As a Japanese woman? The Japanese used hundreds of our people for medical experiments during the war, you know. But I gather such an irony is lost on you.

Gallimard: No! I was about to say, it's the first time I've seen the beauty of the story.

Song: Really?

Gallimard: Of her death. It's a . . . pure sacrifice. He's unworthy, but what can she do? She loves him . . . so much. It's a very beautiful story.

Song: Well, yes, to a Westerner.

Gallimard: Excuse me?

Song: It's one of your favourite fantasies, isn't it? The submissive Oriental woman and the cruel white man? (Cronenberg, 1993)

As Beard notes, Song, at this moment, ' . . . occupies the roles of both embodiment of the Oriental fantasy-female and the fantasy's chief critic . . .' (Beard, 2001, 350) Song's comments make it clear from the outset that she is aware that Gallimard's fascination is with the fantasy; her comments are designed not to pierce that vision but to render it more enticing. By causing Gallimard to consider the relationship between the fantasy of the opera-on-stage and some of its real-world implications, Song's complicity in performing the opera becomes, for Gallimard, proof of the opera's ultimate truth: that roles played out on stage have their real-world counterparts and that, having such counterparts, are therefore all the more truthful. Song, of course, is perfectly aware of this fact and plays, to perfection, the submissive Oriental who desires nothing more than a strong master to submit to. This performance reaches its apogee when she and Gallimard meet for the second time:

Song: We have always held a certain fascination for you Caucasian men, have we not?

Gallimard: Yes. But that fascination is imperialist, or so you tell me.

Song: Yes. It is always imperialist. But sometimes . . . sometimes it is also mutual. (Cronenberg, 1993)

Song's submission, her admission that, secretly, such domination is both highly demeaning and actively sought, renders her utterly desirable to

Gallimard, as Song's performance is orchestrated so as to place him in exactly the position of power unavailable to him otherwise.

Song's performance of the Butterfly role is designed to render the terms of the fantasy explicit to Gallimard by demonstrating that Puccini's opera is based on a clearly understood 'truth', with Song as both its arch critic and desiring victim. Of course, Song's admission that she is aware of the fantasy of Oriental submissiveness even as she succumbs to it – thereby revealing her 'secret' desire – is designed to ensnare Gallimard. In effect he has, however clumsily, dictated to her the terms of his own fantasy, which she refines and gives back to him. The irony here is that Gallimard is not schooled enough in the various cultural references he utilizes in constructing his own fantasy so that he must be assisted in its construction by the person who is to function as that fantasy's object. Of course, the complication comes with the knowledge (ours, not Gallimard's) that Song is a man. This fact demonstrates that what Gallimard desires is not Song in actuality, but a text upon which his various fantasies can be written out and played to the full.

Thus the opera's Orientalist narrative provides Gallimard with the framework to comprehend his attraction to Song as well as the means to overcome what would otherwise be an insurmountable obstacle: Song's sex. Here we see Cronenberg's heretical drive move his concerns towards the centre of the narrative, for the single issue that concerns *M. Butterfly* is, despite appearances, heterosexuality. For all of its Orientalist overtones and potentially paedophiliac narrative, *Madama Butterfly* is an opera that trades in clichés. Both the characters of Pinkerton, the American naval officer, and Butterfly, his Oriental child-bride, are circumscribed within a series of discourses. Hwang's play is particularly attuned to the ways in which sexual and gender politics coincide with issues of ethnic identity and construction, and Song carries this polemic forward into the film as she criticizes Gallimard for his naïve response to the opera. This, however, is to disguise the fact that what the film seeks to critique is not a politics of race or ethnicity, but the unquestioned nature of heterosexuality and, importantly for Gallimard, heteronormativity. In this fashion, the ready exchange of clichés and other truisms provide Gallimard with the means to wilfully ignore Song's sex. So long as the right clichés are exchanged in the right order, so long as the roles are performed in line with the requirements of the master narrative, then there can be no question of Song being anything other than what Gallimard assumes she is. This fact demonstrates the fragility of Gallimard's construction as it is ultimately based on his understanding of his own masculinity: if he is a man, the reasoning goes that he then must desire women. He is, after all, married. Women, the reasoning continues, act, speak and behave in a particular way. Oriental women, because of their Oriental 'natures' can therefore be understood as a rarefied form of 'women'. Thus, if a person performs a rarefied version of what Gallimard already understands to be true, then there can be no question of mistake, for an error would undo every piece of his construction as indeed the film makes clear. Here the heteronormativity that Gallimard subscribes to is in its first iteration (Gallimard desires women, Gallimard is heterosexual) functioning 'correctly', which is to say, is in line with its usual invisible processes. However, Gallimard's desire for his fantasy object forces the structure of heteronormativity into a second iteration, which runs along the lines of 'If I am a man and therefore heterosexual, the person I desire must therefore be a woman – and this is proved because the person I desire acts as I understand women to act'.

When a Woman Is Not

Of great interest to any examination of this film is the fact that nearly every review of *M. Butterfly* works to draw attention to John Lone's 'less than convincing' performance as Song. Kauffman notes that 'John Lone always looks like a man in drag, which kills the ambiguities in the Frenchman's mind . . .' (Kauffmann, 1993), while Corliss concludes that '. . . the opera singer's gender is never in question; his 5 o'clock shadow gives him away to everyone but the diplomat' (Corliss, 1993). Along the same lines, other critics conclude that Long's '. . . not-very-convincing drag act . . .' (Travers, 1993) 'wouldn't fool a baby . . .' (Ansen, 1993). The fact, as noted, that *M. Butterfly* had the great misfortune to follow *The Crying Game* into the box office meant that, as least as far as these critics were concerned, both films could be understood in the same way. However, the fact that Lone's performance as Song *is* that of a man performing a woman is exactly the point. After Song has left Gallimard in order to have their child, she has the following conversation with her Communist Party supervisor, Comrade Chin (Shizuko Hoshi):

Song: Comrade. Why in Beijing Opera are women's roles traditionally played by men?
Chin: I don't know. Most probably a remnant of the reactionary and patriarchal social structure . . .
Song: No. It's because only a man knows how a woman is supposed to act. (Cronenberg, 1993)

This, as much as anything, should alert us to the fact that this film is not interested in dealing with stable (i.e., convincing) identities, be they gender or ethnic. Instead, this film's function is to highlight and critique these categories *as* constructions, and this question continues into the film's form, which, while far more muted in terms of its drive to highlight interpretive and representational structures, still manages to draw attention to its own role in delivering the narrative.

A fine example of this occurs as Gallimard, at Song's urging, attends a performance of indigenous opera as a counterpoint to Puccini's polemic. Much is made, in the mise-en-scène and attending shots and reverse-shots, of Gallimard's uncomfortable presence as the sole European among an audience of Chinese. Though we see him visibly trying, the transcendent reverie that accompanied his experience of Puccini is absent here. However, it is as Gallimard moves backstage to meet Song that we see the film's form assert itself. As the sequence begins, Gallimard appears, in medium long-shot, at the backstage area's door, with the foreground filled with the chaos of performance preparation. As the camera tracks backwards, we see Gallimard walking through a series of miniature tableaux, each actor's dressing table providing us with scenes of make-up being applied, costumes donned and, essentially, identities constructed. Here, in what is a particularly unusual move for Cronenberg, we cut to a point-of-view shot, a fact confirmed when we cut out of this shot back to the backwards tracking shot of Gallimard, now in mid-shot, whose position exactly mirrors what was visible in the previous shot. There is nothing unusual in this juxtaposition of shots, nor in the fact that, from the shot of Gallimard (which functions as a re-establishing shot), we cut back to another point-of-view. This move from establishing shot, to point-of-view shot, to re-establishing shot and then back to another point-of-view shot is a rhythm that is entirely conventional. Its function and purpose is to allow us to experience what Gallimard sees, while at the same time allowing us to see him seeing. What is unusual, however, is the fact that this rhythm is interrupted when Cronenberg cuts from the second point-of-view shot to a third, without any re-establishing shot between them.

As noted, Cronenberg avoids point-of-view shots and so their occurrence should be treated carefully. Here I suspect that their presence, rendered visible by what is effectively a jumpcut between tracking shots, is designed to force our attention not towards what Gallimard sees but what he sees and misses: that this room is where performances are prepared. Gallimard is overcome by the strangeness of what he sees and the elision, the jumpcut, functions to draw us back to the narrative (and the film's conventional form for the rest of the sequence). In essence, the preceding shots have lulled us, as Gallimard has been lulled, into not exploring the idea of what he is seeing beyond the superficial experience of observing. Thus, what he misses here (and throughout the film) is that all performances are constructed, that even the 'natural' Oriental inhabits a position, a performative construction, exactly as Song does and, crucially, exactly as Gallimard himself.

Thus Cronenberg's decision not to overly disguise Lone's gender beyond the diegetic fact of his performance as Song necessarily draws our attention towards Gallimard's role in the construction and maintenance of Song both as a woman and as 'his Butterfly'. This is the point of *M. Butterfly*'s overall project, to draw attention to the construction of heterosexuality by taking it seriously, too seriously in fact, utilizing the figure of Gallimard, the man who so desperately wants to believe the version of heterosexuality made possible by his particular cultural position that he literally refuses to see what is in front of him. This is why Lone cannot be convincing as Song. A more convincing performance would turn the film into a tale of duplicitous activity and our relationship with Gallimard would alter as a result. It is important that we come to understand what Gallimard will not, as it is this that concentrates our attention on his role in the construction of his fantasy. This provides us with a meta-critical position in which an obvious ideological (and, hence, disciplinary) position which would posit Lone as the 'wrong' object of Gallimard's desire is undercut by Cronenberg's focus on Lone's performance as 'a man performing a woman' rather than as, for example, in *The Crying Game*, 'a man indistinguishable from a woman'.

Evidence of this process (both Gallimard's fantasy construction and Cronenberg's undermining of any hegemonic assessment of Gallimard's desire) accumulates through the film as Gallimard and Song trade various clichés of heterosexuality and Orientalism that are as banal as those from the opera they continue to enact. These moments would be laughable if it were not for the bloody-minded determination Gallimard displays in his desire to let nothing disrupt his fantasy. These clichés come in two forms: those that Song feeds Gallimard in order to sustain his fantasy and those Gallimard responds with as part of his fantasy construction. Prime evidence of both of these comes as the two picnic beneath the Great Wall:

Song: René, there is a mystery you must clarify for me.
Gallimard: What mystery?
Song: With your pick of Western women . . . why did you pick a poor Chinese with a chest like a boy?

Gallimard: Not like a boy, like . . . a girl. Like . . . a young, innocent school-girl . . . waiting for her lessons. (Cronenberg, 1993)

The black humour of this sequence marks the complexity of Cronenberg's take on Hwang's screenplay. Part of what is most disturbing about Puccini's opera is the fact that Butterfly is fifteen when Pinkerton marries and abandons her. That aspect of deviant Western sexuality, hidden beneath a discourse of Western paternalism, is here given a frisson of excitement with Gallimard's talk of guiding his schoolgirl protégé towards her sexual awakening. For him, Song's 'chest like a boy' works against the most obvious interpretation (Song is a man) to support a convoluted fantasy structure that, in turn, 'proves' that she is a girl. Her flat chest, once it is read through the heteronormative structure Gallimard subscribes to, is therefore not a signifier of gender but of sexual innocence. For Gallimard, Song's highly articulated sexual appeal further enhances his own role in the tryst by now placing him firmly – or, rather, providing him with the means to place himself – in the role of sexual educator. Thus Song, by drawing attention to the fact of her gender ('Look – I am a man'), causes Gallimard to maintain his fantasy of her as a woman even more rigorously.

This moment works well when compared to Gallimard's other sexual conquest: the distant, attractive and seemingly unconquerable Frau Baden (Annabel Leventon). After his promotion to vice-consul, Gallimard drunkenly pontificates about the Chinese people at a party, his confidence seemingly enough to convince Frau Baden to seduce him. At her hotel room, while Gallimard fusses in the bathroom and nervously wonders about the champagne he has ordered, Frau Baden waits, naked and confident on the bed. Gallimard pauses at the sight of her already undressed and exclaims, 'You look exactly as I imagined you would under your clothes' (Cronenberg, 1993). Frau Baden, nonplussed, replies 'What did you expect? So – come and get it' (Cronenberg, 1993). Gallimard's response, and the fact that he, in the next scene, rushes drunken and belligerent to Song's bed, makes perfectly clear that Gallimard in not interested in the plain and naked facts of women ('you look exactly as I imagined you would'). What Song provides him is more fulfiling precisely because the fantasy can never be confirmed (and therefore can never be completed). Song is, as she claims, a woman made by a man (or two men in complicity) and is therefore much more satisfying for a man to consume that a (mere) woman.

Gallimard's fantasy, supported by Song's faux-Chinese modesty (and endless supply of cod-aphorisms[5]), is based on never actually achieving the object of his fantasy. To continue this process, Song constructs an elaborate history of 'wisdom' to justify her never appearing naked before Gallimard. As noted, some of Song's clichés are designed to draw Gallimard into an ever more elaborate construction of his fantasy, while others seem designed simply to confirm for Gallimard what he already believes to be true of the Orient. These clichés are revealed as such at the trial when Song admits that Gallimard was '. . . very responsive to my ancient Oriental ways of love, all of which I invented just for him' (Cronenberg, 1993). The collapse of Gallimard's fantasy is complete by the time he and Song, now dressed as a man, must share a police van as they are transported after the trial. Song undresses, first to prove to Gallimard the truth he has so wilfully denied (proof which, due to framing and camera movement, is denied us also) and then, it would seem, to argue that their love was meaningful despite the deception perpetrated. However, Gallimard can only answer,

> You've shown me your true self when what I loved was the lie. The perfect lie, which has been destroyed. . . . I'm a man who loved a woman created by a man. Anything else falls . . . short. (Cronenberg, 1993)

Here the statement regarding the creation of women carries an ambiguity absent from Song's first mention of this fact, as it is unclear to whom Gallimard refers as the creator: Song or himself. Both are implicated in the construction of Song-as-woman, and it was essential for Gallimard's fantasy that Song *be* woman. As he notes, anything else falls short.

For Cronenberg, Gallimard is an artist, a man engaged in 'creating a reality for himself and, for her own reasons, Song is helping him' (Rodley, 1997, 174). The fact that the film becomes an exploration of fantasy and willing self-deception makes clear the reason why Lone is never meant to be entirely convincing as Song. As we have seen, Gallimard's active disavowal of Song's sex, even when Song draws attention to it, works to evidence his desire for the perfect fantasy of heterosexuality, so much so that Gallimard, as demonstrated, utilizes the disciplinary logic of heteronormativity to 'confirm' his heterosexual status. When compared to his startled reaction to Frau Baden's otherwise desirable body, it is obvious that rendering the fantasy literal (as Frau Baden's body is literalized) is enough to disrupt Gallimard's carefully preserved structures of desire. What remains is to consider Gallimard's reaction to the total destruction of his desiring edifice during and after his trial for treason.

As noted, even when finally confronted by Song's naked body in the police van, Gallimard refuses to let his fantasy dissolve, and his dialogue (quoted above) makes it clear that he continues to distinguish between the fact of Song's sex, finally revealed to him, and the fantasy which remains potent. What occurs, then, is his recognition of his fantasy as a fantasy. Thus the potential offered by Song-as-woman, having been jointly created by both Song and Gallimard, remains preferable to the fact of actual women as represented by Frau Baden. However, with this illusion of Song-as-woman and Song-as-Butterfly demolished by the unavoidable fact of Song's penis, all that remains for Gallimard is to retreat further into the fantasy, a route that leaves him with little alternative but self-destruction. Gallimard's final act of creation involves his performance in front of the massed prisoners he is incarcerated with. However it is important to note that Gallimard is not performing any part of *Madama Butterfly*: he is, instead, performing the act of transformation, the process by which one becomes the object of fantasy. Gallimard is finally aligned with the process of fantasy, demonstrating the lengths he is prepared to go to '. . . to keep desire alive by devising strategies to avoid its realization' (Feher-Gurewich, 2003, 192). As with considerations of Lone's performance, this sequence has also drawn criticism for its lack of realism, demonstrating the strength of resistance to Cronenberg's heretical movement.[6] As with Gallimard's disavowal of Song's gender, the point here is not so much about representative realism as it is about the construction and performance of fantasy, a process that Gallimard has clearly invested an enormous amount of energy into.

The sequence begins with Gallimard on a small stage, surrounded by serried ranks of prisoners. As the overture from *Madama Butterfly* plays on a cheap, portable cassette player, with all the resulting lack of clarity and perfection, Gallimard begins to apply the makeup that will transform him into Butterfly, or, more importantly, a version of Butterfly. The makeup Gallimard applies is of very poor quality and his skill is haphazard at best. This is entirely deliberate on Cronenberg's part and links directly to the speech Gallimard makes while donning the costume and makeup of Butterfly:

I, René Gallimard, have known and been loved by the perfect woman. There is a vision of the Orient that I have. Slender women, in jiamsangs and kimonos, who die for the love of unworthy foreign devils. Who are born, and raised, to be perfect women, and take whatever punishment we give them, and spring back, strengthened by love, unconditionally. It is a vision which has become my life. My mistake was simple, and absolute. The man I loved was not worth, he didn't even deserve, a second glance. Instead, I gave him my love . . . all of my love. Love warped my judgement. Blinded my eyes. So that now, when I look into the mirror, I see nothing but . . . I have a vision of the Orient. That deep within her almond eyes, there are still women. Women willing to sacrifice themselves for the love of a man. Even a man whose love is completely without worth. Death with honour is better than life with dishonour. And so at last, in a prison far from China, I have found her. My name is René Gallimard. Also known as Madame Butterfly. (Cronenberg, 1993)

Here Gallimard makes the hardest discovery of all: that no object will meet the requirements of his fantasy. As he says, 'there is a vision of the Orient that I have': his vision is, essentially, his projection, and is a compilation of his understanding of the processes and requirements of the disciplinary discourses of heterosexuality, rendered visible through their performance as an Orientalist discourse. Of course, the woman he seeks does not exist: his wife is 'disappeared' from the film once his affair with Song begins, and Frau Baden serves only to illustrate the reality of the flesh, which is a great deal less satisfying that the fantasy. Hence his discovery that, 'at last, in a prison far from China', he is able to find 'her', the 'real' object of his fantasy and the only woman (created by a man) who will ever completely meet the needs of his fantasy. It is no surprise, then, that having finally 'seen' her, the almond-eyed submissive construction, he uses the mirror to kill himself. In essence what Gallimard sees in the mirror is himself (obviously), but as both the source of, and end point for, his fantasy. Having constructed a heteronormative/heterosexual fantasy so rigorous in its pursuit of the fantasy object that Song could be removed entirely from it and the fantasy would remain in place (as evidenced by his final speech, which reaffirms his commitment to this 'vision of the Orient'), it is clear to Gallimard that he has nowhere left to go.

This also explains the deliberately tawdry costume Gallimard dons as he prepares to take his own life. Butterfly, his vision of the ideal 'woman created by man', is a collection of assorted signifiers which, together, function to indicate the correct (for him) construction of femininity: hence, for Gallimard, the Oriental is desirable not because of her 'otherness' but because of her passivity, a factor central to both the discourse of Orientalism and his understanding of heterosexual femininity. Gallimard's actions reveal that, beneath the naturalized (read: hegemonic) performance, heterosexuality is a text constructed by both partners. A final consideration of Cronenberg's meta-textual discourse is worth considering, for here, if we accept Gallimard's actions at face value, we will conclude that '[w]oman is she who is written, not she who writes' (Ricci, 1991, 309), that women are, indeed, made by men as objects to be consumed and utilized. What Gallimard demonstrates is that women are certainly written by men, yet the invisibility of masculinity as a similar site of discursive construction should not be read as an assessment of it as stable. Throughout Lone's performance as Song, and Song's performance as male and as female, the discursive traits of masculinity are raised through the very act of being erased and elided. Thus every time we are reminded that Song is a man, even and especially as Gallimard is not, masculinity is highlighted through its elision, absence and invisibility. As *M. Butterfly* confirms, so long as the roles are followed and the correct clichés traded at the right moments, not even the biological actuality of the participants need interrupt the ideological effects generated by the play.

Dead Ringers

With *Dead Ringers*, we see a continuation of Cronenberg's movement from a heresy of form towards the centrality of a heretical narrative. Unlike *M. Butterfly*, *Dead Ringers* is Cronenberg's project throughout and the handling of its central issue is much more coherent than Cronenberg's adaptation of Hwang's screenplay. As before, we find *Dead Ringers* addressing the invisibility of a central social-sexual structure and, through that examination – a taking-too-seriously – revealing the kinds of internal discontinuities working to demonstrate that these structures are far from being either natural or stable. The issues regarding the performance of heterosexuality are present in *Dead Ringers* but are not of key importance and, while the possibility of homosexual sex is certainly present, the film's central concern is to draw attention to the structures that govern, support and regulate monogamy. Whereas *M. Butterfly* sought to question heterosexuality by taking its demands literally, *Dead Ringers* extends the same drive to monogamy, utilizing the presence of identical twins as the means to achieve this.

Dead Ringers tells the story of the identical Mantle twins, Beverly and Elliot (both played by Jeremy Irons), who, as practicing gynaecologists, have earned fame and fortune through the invention of the Mantle Retractor, a unique surgical tool, and their successful practice specializing in infertility. Disruption of their perfectly attuned lives occurs when actress Claire Niveau (Geneviève Bujold) comes to them for help. Beverly discovers that she possesses a 'trifurcate' womb, a 'fabulously rare' mutation that renders her infertile and highly attractive to the twins. Claire is seduced by Elliot (whom she believes to be Beverly), who then passes her on to Beverly. Thus the twins' division of labour is made clear: Elliot, the more confident, is the showman, performer and fund-raiser, while studious Beverly is the skilled surgeon and researcher. Further, Elliot is the sexually aggressive one, without whom Beverly 'would never get laid' (Cronenberg, 1988). As Beverly continues the relationship with Claire, who has yet to discover that there are two Mantles, he finds himself falling in love with her, which manifests as a desire to keep the details of his liaison from Elliot. Soon enough, Claire is told of the 'wonderful Mantle twins' and, furious at the deception, ends her relationship with Beverly, who is distraught at the loss. Some time later, he and Claire meet by accident and begin their relationship again, which causes such anxiety in Beverly that, at Claire's urging, he begins to take tranquillizers to prevent nightmares in which he and Elliot are Siamese twins. As his addiction increases, Beverly's behaviour becomes more erratic: he becomes convinced that Claire is having an affair and he designs a series of highly ornate surgical instruments 'for operating on mutant women' (Cronenberg, 1988). Eventually he seriously injures a patient and the Mantles' surgical privileges are revoked. Elliot, convinced that, as twins, they literally share a single circulatory system, decides to become sympathetically addicted, in order that they may both come clean together. This drastic and doomed course of action climaxes on their birthday when, after sharing cake and orange pop, Beverly operates on Elliot with his gynaecological instruments. *Dead Ringers* closes with Beverly lying naked across the eviscerated body of his brother.

Given the various permutations of interpersonal contact that occur through *Dead Ringers*, it becomes obvious that monogamy, as a site upon which a series of disciplinary discourses converge, is central to any understanding of this film. These discourses are not at all unitary and this ambivalence means that the hegemonic concept of monogamy contains within it competing discourses, some of which necessarily run counter to the term's central ideological content. This concept thus contains the possibility for its own transgression. In its hegemonic definition, the term is seen to promote a stable, long-term heterosexual relationship between two people, a partnership that is granted both secular and religious recognition, but an entire alternate popular (and populist) discourse surrounds the 'unofficial' state of that union. This unofficial discourse is pervasive, the end result of which is to suggest that a monogamous union may well be less than satisfactory, particularly as far as sex is concerned. Therefore, these discourses seem to suggest that if a couple is to become, as required, monogamous, they will necessarily suffer the gradual diminishing of desire that comes as part and parcel of that decision.

In addition to the presence or absence of desire, another site of deep ambivalence that *Dead Ringers* contains and explores is revealed with the word's etymology. The word's two components, both of Greek origin – *mono* (single) and *gamos* (marriage) – clearly indicate the interpretive path that would generate 'monogamy' as a term used to indicate 'being married *to one* other'. However, *gamos* also provides the origin of the term *gamete*, the male or female haploid cell that is able to join with another of opposite sex in order to form the zygote, the diploid cell that is the fertilized ovum. As the *mono-gamus* refers also to the *mono-gamete*, the single cell which must undergo fierce multiplication in order to become a recognizable creature, we see in both cases that the term refers to two becoming one, and to the construction of singularity from multiplicity. Thus issues of singularity and bifurcation are central to both the term in its common ideological usage, and in its biological application wherein the Mantle twins (as identical twins) demonstrate how they are derived from the single zygote and therefore occupy this split position; the marriage of the two cells that would ordinarily produce one child here produces two. The intimacy of identical twins, that they emerge as a result of the marriage of two cells and that they are two instead of one (and yet, troublingly, seemingly singular as well), links the performance and regulation of monogamy strongly to its ideological obverse: the control and prevention of multiplicity.

It may, at first, seem like something of a leap to link monogamy as a social structure to the control of multiplicity, except for the fact that what monogamy enforces are structures of singularity: the singular relationship of a heterosexual pairing, each of whom is him- and herself, singular. The Mantles, as mirrors and marvels,[7] have already violated the tenets of monogamy by emerging as a bifurcation of the zygote; hence they are not entirely 'individual' – they occupy a liminal position between singular and multiple. They thus continue to problematize the broader ideological function of the monogamous unit by providing, through their relationships with each other and with the women they share, a series of alternative models for possible functioning relationships as well as the impossibility of a heterosexual monogamy entirely free of multiplicity. This fact, revealed through the film's initial moments prior to Claire's insertion into the Mantle dyad, allows us to grasp the inconsistency at the heart of monogamy: if the social structure – both secular and religious – is concerned with the formation of a *productive* unit (insofar as the unit contributes, in some way, to the broader social sphere), then we must consider productivity in the terms of monogamy's approved formulation. The film's first third details the Mantle's successes as surgeons, businessmen, academics – indeed, as socialized beings whose relationship utilizes the strengths of both twins in order to compensate for their weaknesses. Given that they appear to be both successfully productive and yet socially incomplete, the term 'monogamy' must therefore refer to a sanctioned heterosexual union within which the productivity required must necessarily be that of children. Yet if, as Cronenberg suggests, we strip sex of its association with childbirth and child rearing, then the monogamous unit – the couple – freed of the requirement to bear children, can be differently productive. Furthermore, if the onus on productivity remains in place (as would appear logical in a contemporary capitalist society) then *Dead Ringers* makes clear that the productive couple need not be either heterosexual or sexually linked at all: the fraternal union in *Dead Ringers* emerges as a monogamous possibility. Monogamy, which appears to be the bastion of heterosexual pairing, is now revealed a structure designed to limit social (or sexual) relationships within approved (i.e., hegemonically sanctioned) boundaries. It comes as no surprise, then, that *Dead Ringers* is full of instances where the approved singularities are multiplied in uncontrollable ways.

Multiple Monogamies

There are three different monogamies possible in *Dead Ringers*: Elliot and Beverly, Beverly and Claire and, most problematically, Elliot, Beverly and Claire. This last union is hinted at when, late in the film, Elliot and his current girlfriend Cary (Heidi von Palleske) dance while Beverly sits morosely ignoring them. At Elliot's urging, Cary pulls Beverly up to dance. Elliot soon joins them and, as we cut from close-ups of Elliot and Cary kissing, to medium shots of the three of them dancing, the two men sandwiching Cary between them, Elliot guides Cary's hands over Beverly's

FIGURE 4.1   *Dead Ringers'* multiple monogamies.

back (see Figure 4.1). As they continue to dance together, Elliot begins
to lead the other two towards the stairs to the bedroom. At this point
Beverly breaks away, muttering, 'No, I can't . . .' (Cronenberg, 1988), to
which Elliot responds 'Stay with us – stay with *me*' (Cronenberg, 1988).
We are left to wonder at the reason for Beverly's refusal of Elliot's offer:
does it occur because he will not have sex with his brother, or because
Cary is not Claire? The film does not linger on this issue, content as it is
to raise it and leave it hanging.

Superficially, Elliot's dialogue seems to suggest that the ménage à trois
that would result would provide the means for Beverly and Elliot to consummate their relationship, which, in its division of labour and clearly
defined active/passive roles, already resembles a stereotypical marriage.
However, this is one of only two suggestions the film provides of an erotic
bond beyond the perfunctory sharing of partners which, we are expressly
told, has more to do with Beverly's consummate shyness than anything
else. Indeed, given the narrative's prior events, attention should be paid
to the manner with which Elliot stresses the final word in his statement
'stay with *me*'. The sexual activity he proposes is his attempt at finding the
means to keep Beverly from leaving. While Cary might stand in for Claire,
so far as Elliot is concerned, his object is to provide Beverly with a reason
to stay, and a reason to remain faithful to him instead of to Claire. Thus

'stay with *me*' signals Elliot's recognition of the unique relationship the twins share, his wish to retain his brother as his companion, and, with Cary, his desire to demonstrate to his brother that while the women they share are interchangeable, the brothers themselves are unique as a *unit* rather than as two.

Elliot's concluding plea is an echo of an earlier statement that occurs in a sequence that serves to demonstrate the kind of relationship the twins have clearly negotiated for themselves. Immediately after Claire enters their lives, Beverly is forced to impersonate Elliot at a funding dinner while Elliot examines and then seduces (off-screen) Claire. Afterwards, as Beverly sits, working and sipping whiskey, Elliot enters and quizzes him about the funding dinner:

Elliot: How did it go with la bella Contessa? Did we get our grant?

Beverly: You were great . . . seductive and charming as usual. And I think you've got your grant.

Elliot: Hey! Wait a minute. What's this I hear? It's for *us*, not just for me. It's for Mantle Inc.

Beverly: Yes, yes. I know.

Elliot: Did she catch on?

Beverly: Hmm. 'Ah Contessa . . . you're looking so . . .', I don't know, 'So . . . Catherine Deneuve. And how is Marcello? Due cappuccini per favore . . . and quickly. . . . The Countess is a tigress until she's got her caffeine in the morning. . . .' . . . Hmmm.

Elliot: Hey . . . come on. I'm not that bad.

Beverly: You're a little bit smoother in real life. And the movie star? How was she?

Elliot: She's expecting me for lunch tomorrow. So you're going to find out for yourself.

Beverly: Oh no.

Elliot: Oh *yes*. It's all set up. The production's rented her this little apartment . . . in Rosedale . . . she'll just be getting out of bed . . . all cosy and warm.

Beverly: Look Elly . . . the clinic's booked to the hilt. We've got to pay the rent, you know.

Elliot: I'll take your patients . . .

Beverly: Oh yes . . .

Elliot: I want you to go. Bev, you've got to try the movie star. She's unbelievable. Don't worry . . . you'll be alright. Just *do* me. (Cronenberg, 1988)

Between these two lines of dialogue, 'just *do* me' and 'stay with *me*', lie the boundaries of the monogamous relationship the twins have, one which revolves around the indeterminacy of performance ('just *do* me') and the fact of total interdependence ('stay with *me*'). While Elliot and Beverly's relationship might be slightly more difficult to consider as a monogamous relationship, the film's first act, along with the sequence illustrated above, works to make it perfectly clear that the relationship these two have built up since childhood is, for all its difference from a 'norm', entirely practical and, better yet, entirely productive. Beverly's anxiety and ambivalence about his relationship with Claire is recognition of the fact that he is unable to maintain two competing types of monogamy. Here, as noted, the relationship that he and Elliot share is functionally like a marriage, their division of labour echoing, at least incidentally, a standard gender division. Certainly their relationship is not usual, but this is less important to note than the fact that, at least until the introduction of Claire, it works. In this manner Claire becomes the desirable third term that upsets the internally coherent relationship of the Mantles.

Thus the manner with which the twins initially deal with Claire (Beverly examining her, passing her on to Elliot, who seduces her and then passes her back to Beverly) is meant to represent the innumerable other times Elliot has seduced, and then passed on, his conquests to Beverly. This gives us an indication of the ways in which the twins are engaged in a bifurcated performance of masculine (and heterosexual) stereotypes, with Elliot's aggressive and self-confident manner working to win women over, and Beverly's softer, emotional intellectualism working to keep them. Nevertheless, the question arises, if their beginning moments with Claire replicate a pattern the twins have already established with no small amount of success (we surmise, given diegetic information in the first act to support this), then why does it go so horribly wrong this time?

The key, quite obviously, is Beverly. As stated above, he is unable to negotiate between his relationships with Elliot and Claire and cannot reconcile the quite different demands these relationships make on him. Yet the film makes it clear that he and Elliot have shared partners many times before, meaning that the answer lies specifically in Claire. There are three factors regarding Claire, and Beverly's connection to her, that we are led to believe are occurring for the first time. The first two are relatively banal and entirely in keeping with a superficial ideological interpretation of the film's intent. Cronenberg, when discussing the difference between the twins, comments that

Eliot has fucked more women, has a greater facility with the superficialities of everything, with the superficialities of sex. But in terms of ever establishing an emotional rapport with women, Elliot is totally unsuccessful. Beverly is successful, but he doesn't see this success as a positive thing. He sees that as another part of his weakness. (cited in Rodley, 1997, 147)

For Beverly, Elliot stands as an example of what a 'normal' man looks like and therefore to be a normal man one must be like Elliot, which is impossible while in a relationship *with* Elliot. In this fashion, Beverly has, in Cronenberg's words, '. . . been colonized; he's bought the imperialist's line about what is beautiful, proper and correct' (Rodley, 1997, 149). Therefore, for Cronenberg, a rivalry between the twins is brought into being through Beverly's assumption that Elliot represents the visible face of success. Here Cronenberg's notion of 'the imperialist's line about what is beautiful, proper and correct' indicates the imposition of an external disciplinary structure on the twins' relationship. Because Elliot conforms to this normative image of success, he represents – for Beverly – normality and the potential for success as a result of individuation and separation.

Beverly's anxieties at his own, as he views it, less-than-successful status – a fact he drunkenly laments at the awards dinner when he complains that 'I slave over the hot snatches and Elliot makes the speeches' (Cronenberg, 1988) – are only exacerbated by his deepening relationship with, and growing dependence on, Claire. As her dependence on drugs becomes clear, she begins to notice slight variations in Beverly's behaviour. This occurs after she learns that Beverly has a brother but before she discovers that they are identical twins:

Claire: You're subtly . . . I don't know . . . schizophrenic, or something. Sometimes I like you very much and sometimes you're an amusing lay . . . not much more. And I can't figure out why. (Cronenberg, 1988)

Her comment that there are subtle, yet observable differences between the twins, without further clarifying which twin it is that she 'likes very much', is a call for Beverly to attempt to further distinguish himself from Elliot in order to better emulate Elliot's model of success, since Elliot is the more obviously successful (and hence more desirable) twin.

By offering Beverly a means to individuate through being pulled into a heteronormative (monogamous) pairing, and thereby establishing himself as an externally ratified success (at least as he imagines success to

be ratified[8]), the conflict between the Mantles' own monogamous relationship and the external, socially sanctioned version that a relationship
with Claire offers is illustrated. Thus Claire's presence brings the Mantles
into conflict with each other, and their relationship with the social (and,
hence, disciplinary) structures that surround them. However, in his
effort to be successful and thus 'normal' – singular and individuated –
Beverly disrupts a fully functioning, if socially unusual, relationship in
order to attempt a socially acceptable, though diegetically doomed, version of the same.

Dead Ringers and Issues of Form

As with *M. Butterfly*, *Dead Ringers* utilizes conventional formal techniques
throughout, entirely in keeping with this chapter's overall thesis. There
are, however, a few moments when the form announces itself into prominence, demanding that it be paid attention to in its role of delivering
the narrative. A clear example of this occurs when Claire, having been
informed that there are, in fact, *two* Mantles instead of one, confronts
Beverly with this information. As the agitated Beverly, who is feeling the
effects of the narcotics he is now addicted to, paces in front of Claire, we
cut from a shot–reverse-shot sequence as Claire questions Beverly to a
long shot of the couple, which serves to also illustrate the relative geography of the room. The mid-shots that follow this assume an axis of
action that runs to Claire's right and is maintained until Claire asks to
meet Elliot. At this moment, as Beverly walks in front of her (and, since
the camera is focused on Claire, in front of us) we cut to a shot over
Claire's left shoulder in time to hear Beverly tell her that she can't meet
Elliot – 'You don't want to' (Cronenberg, 1988). Grant's reading of this
sequence posits this deliberate disruption of the 180-degree rule as
suggesting

> . . . very exactly the disruption that has already occurred in the rela-
> tion between them [Claire and Beverly], a disruption that later events
> (notably Claire's meeting with the twins . . .) are to exacerbate. (Grant,
> 1997)

While I certainly agree with this point, I would suggest that it is important to consider that the axis of action through which the 180-degree line
is oriented – both before and after this rupture of the form – runs

through Claire's body. She is the pivot around which the editing in this sequence is oriented, just as it is her introduction into the twins' lives that causes them to spiral into collapse: further it is her body around which the 'action' of the film, both literally and figuratively, occurs.

The particular shot in question is a relatively long one for contemporary film, at just over six seconds, but its length is entirely in keeping with a film which, like *Spider*, is edited at a pace that is both dictated by and reflects the actions and mental states of the protagonists themselves. The shot, then, does not immediately announce itself as different in any way from those that surround it, which means that the sense of unease this shot generates seems to emerge out of the interplay between the characters, rather than the fact that our viewing perspective has unexpectedly shifted. Thus while the focus of the action in the shot is on Beverly (i.e., he is in centre frame, and Claire is out of focus in the foreground) the fact remains that the geography of the shot, the architecture of the editing, and Beverly's diegetic unease are all generated by the presence of Claire. This nearly invisible rupture in conventional form goes some way to demonstrating how *Dead Ringers* marks the transition in Cronenberg's heretical articulation, from form through to content, with the understanding that, now, those disruptions in conventional form occur in order to support the content.

Without a doubt, though, the most spectacular formal technique in *Dead Ringers* is, perversely enough, the one that works hardest to avoid detection: the twinning effects that permit Jeremy Irons to play both twins. This, in and of itself, is not surprising, as the narrative itself hinges on the interchangeability of the twins. Only utilizing the same actor would provide Cronenberg with the 'same but different' performance required to deliver the identical twins as believable. The twinning effects mark a considerable advance on the then-standard practice of either masking the frame (and thus double exposing the negative) or utilizing an optical printer to the same general effect. These methods resulted in an often-visible division in the frame with the twinned images facing each other. This practice meant that

> . . . characters shown in images of this kind – unlike two characters in standard set-ups – were not able to spark off each other; the images were predicable and the camera placements static. (Grant, 1997, 7)

The technology utilized in *Dead Ringers* provided the means to substantially revitalize the possibilities for twinning effects. Cronenberg's effects supervisor, Lee Wilson (who had worked on *The Fly*) developed a series of techniques that, when coupled with motion control, would provide much more dynamic framing and movement possibilities. As Wilson notes,

> [w]ith careful choreography, that meant that two characters played by a single actor could be made to occupy the same space within a given shot – though obviously at somewhat different times. (Wilson, quoted in Grant, 1997, 7)

Nevertheless, Cronenberg's use of this technique, while impressive, '. . . is firmly kept in its place. Mere technology is never allowed to distract an audience from the film's ultimate subject' (Rodley, 1998). Thus the eleven twinning sequences in the film only occur in situations where two actors would ordinarily have appeared in the frame. Cronenberg's refusal '. . . to allow the technology to determine how he was going to shoot the film . . .' (Grant, 1997, 8) means that the twinning sequences, enormously elaborate and difficult though they are, never dominate the scenes in which they occur. As Ron Sanders, editor on *Dead Ringers* confirms,

> When we first discussed conceptually the twinning effects, the major thing we wanted to do was not draw attention to them as twinning effects. We wanted the coverage to be absolutely normal, the way it would be if they were two actors. We wanted just to cover the scene and make the scene look like any other scene with two actors. (Cronenberg, 1988, DVD commentary)

Thus, in order for the film's content to seem as realistic as possible, the spectacular twinning shots must be controlled, regulated and utilized exactly as ordinary two-shots, lest their presence draw attention to the fact that anything spectacular is happening.

The discipline of the two-shot, like all requirements of what is recognized as conventional film form, is taken up here in order to place greater stress on the heretical content of the narrative. This decision, which is consciously considered, means that Cronenberg is utilizing the standard interpretive weight of the two-shot, which involves prompting an audience to infer intimacy, relatedness (in a narrative, causal sense) and, with the addition of mise-en-scène details, issues of primacy, power and hierarchy. In this fashion, the interpretation of the significance of this shot occurs without difficulty and neither the shot itself, nor its spectacular content, stands as an obstacle to the narrative. Thus the marvels that bring the Mantles to the screen must be effaced in favour of the marvels that are the Mantles themselves.

Nevertheless, this example demonstrates, again, the manner with which Cronenberg is forced to choose between a heresy of form and one of content. Certainly, as noted previously, both are entirely possible but such films as would incorporate both heretical form and content are far less likely to succeed commercially, given the manner with which these films would generate obvious difficulties of interpretation. By shifting the heretical focus to issues of narrative, Cronenberg is able to utilize conventional form, and conventional interpretive practices, in order to direct his audiences towards considerations they might not have otherwise encountered. Thus if the twinning shots were rendered visibly spectacular – if they were not self-effacing – their presence would stand between the audience and the content of the narrative. Only by succumbing to the discipline of conventional form can Cronenberg slide these ideas into the popular consciousness.

Marvellous Mutations

Claire's disruption of the Mantles' relationship, as detailed above, illustrates a superficial understanding of her presence – as the desirable woman, she offers Beverly a chance for a more normal relationship and his failure to carry this opportunity through to fruition therefore represents the degree to which the Mantles' pre-Claire life was 'wrong'. Her function in the film is much more significant than this for the answer lies, specifically, *in* Claire. Her body throws Beverly into disarray, just as it forces the film to confront our desire to see with its inability to show. Furthermore, Claire's body, particularly her trifurcated – and hence monstrous – womb, forces an exploration of the fear of multiplicity and the various efforts made to suppress it.

Barbara Creed develops this notion of the monstrous womb in her discussion of Cronenberg's *The Brood* (1979), linking the womb directly to Julia Kristeva's concept of abjection (Kristeva, 1982). Here Kristeva's concept is utilized to discuss the way in which the (psychoanalytic) subject seeks to expel those things that trouble the boundary between 'me' and 'not-me', objects that include '. . . tears, faeces, urine, vomit, mucus . . .' (Brooker, 2002, 1), a task that is impossible given the fact that '. . . the body cannot cease to both take in and expel objects' (ibid., 1). The abject, as Kristeva states, is '. . . thus not lack of cleanliness or health . . . but what disturbs identity, system, order. What does not respect borders, positions, rules' (Kristeva, 1982, 4). Therefore, as Creed notes,

> The womb represents the utmost in abjection for it contains a new life form which will pass from inside to outside bringing with it traces of its contamination – blood, afterbirth, faeces. (Creed, 1993, 49)

Creed goes on to refer specifically to the 'womb problems' that haunt *The Brood* (which will be discussed in the next chapter) and it is worth noting that the womb she refers to, and which belongs to *The Brood*'s Nola Carveth, exists *outside* her body. In *Dead Ringers*, Claire's 'marvellous' womb is hidden from our gaze, and so we only have the comments of Elliot and Beverly to go on, but the important fact is that the womb, normally a site of monstrosity (for Creed) becomes a marvel for the Mantles and a symbol of their own marvellous presence. It should be noted, however, that the wombs that trouble Creed are monstrously fertile, whereas Claire's monstrosity (her trifurcation) renders her infertile. Nevertheless, Claire's trifurcate womb 'disturbs identity, system, order' by suggesting the possibility of a multiplication that would outdo even the Mantle twins.

Claire's body fascinates both Beverly and Elliot,[9] but for Beverly, Claire is a problem he cannot solve. This is not to say that Claire's body is a problem he cannot solve for, after the initial consultation, it is made clear that she is infertile. Instead, Beverly moves to link Claire's abnormal condition with her emotional effect on him and then, from this conclusion (itself reached as his mental condition is deteriorating), to further conclude that all women's bodies are 'wrong'. This moment marks the transition into the film's final act and incorporates Beverly's decision to commission a series of gynaecological instruments for 'operating on mutant women'. Yet, given the twins' occupation, it could be argued that the film is full of 'mutant' women (i.e., those with gynaecological difficulties) whose mutations are solved, which is to say healed. In seeking to explain Claire's effect on Beverly, Beard correctly draws attention to the ways in which Claire's mixture of health (she is easily the most 'normal' or 'adjusted' of the film's protagonists) and dysfunction (she is, nevertheless, 'mutant') makes her attractive to Beverly. This links their first sexual encounter, in which Beverly binds Claire with surgical tubing, to the film's first sequences of the twins as boys in which we see them discussing the 'problem' of sex over an eviscerated 'Visible Woman' model, itself bound with surgical tubing (Beard, 2001, 258–61). While Claire and Beverly make love, with her restrained, she responds to his actions by claiming, however ironically, 'Doctor, you've cured me' (Cronenberg, 1988). Then, as Beverly unties her and the two embrace, she confesses her pain at learning of her infertility:

> **Claire:** I'll never get pregnant. I'll never have children. When I'm dead, I'll just be dead. I will have really never been a woman at all – just a girl. A little girl.
> **Beverly:** You could always adopt a baby.
> **Claire:** It wouldn't be the same. It wouldn't be part of my body.
> **Beverly:** That's true.
> **Claire:** Don't tell, please don't tell anybody about me. Please don't tell. I'm so vulnerable. I'm slashed open.
> **Beverly:** Who would I tell, eh? Who would I tell? (Cronenberg, 1988)

Claire's paradox is revealed in this sequence: she is both potentially over-fertile (her womb has three openings) and yet entirely barren (the same potential for fertility renders her infertile). Similarly she appears to need Beverly's companionship and yet is fiercely independent and career- oriented, just as she offers him the opportunity to individuate (becoming the twin she 'likes very much') without any assurance that their relationship would offer the stability and security of his life with Elliot. Thus Beverly is drawn to Claire by her difference and her liminal multiplicity, only to discover that, unlike the other women the Mantles have 'cured', she cannot be resolved so neatly.

While no definitive critical statement appears to be made by *Dead Ringers*, the film nevertheless does function critically, insofar as it draws attention to the disciplinary discourses surrounding monogamy, individuation and subjecthood, as well as highlighting the problematic area of multiplicity and monstrosity. The 'marvellous' Mantle twins defy categorization insofar as they elude the ready-made definitions regarding twins and 'twinness' that popularly circulate. As high-functioning, socially adjusted and, crucially, productive subjects, their relationship – while unusual – is not necessarily 'wrong' except as it draws attention to the restrictive regulations that surround the central unit of capitalism, the monogamous heterosexual couple. Of the requirements for monogamy, as these circulate discursively, the only one the twins violate is that they be sexually involved with each other. This single violation, which they attempt to remedy through Claire, appears to be enough to warrant the dissolution of their relationship. What Claire brings to the Mantles' relationship is the ability to splinter their mutually dependant and self-sustaining structure by representing the introduction of external discursive demands. Interestingly, the discursive demand for sex between monogamous partners is reflected in the number of reviews and analyses that draw attention to the possibility for incestuous relations between the twins.[10] As explored above, this possibility is far less important than the concomitant suggestions of performance (where 'just do me' means 'just perform *as* me' rather than 'pretend you're having sex *with* me') and, importantly, a desire to prevent schism through the sharing of partners ('stay with us, stay with *me*').

Thus the Mantles are marvellous, just as the specific use of technology that permits Jeremy Irons to share the screen with himself is marvellous. Indeed, it can be argued that Cronenberg's use of the twinning effects, designed both to promote a naturalness of performance and to efface its own presence, works exactly as the twins work. Their marvel lies not in the fact that they are different – that they stand out – but that they are utterly the same (perhaps even more so than 'real' twins), and are all the more effective for that 'sameness'. Difference is therefore introduced with Claire; she is the third term that ruptures their too effective binary. Yet it appears obvious that what attracts Beverly to Claire is not just her difference (to him, to other women) but also her sameness (she, too, is a monster). Shaviro notes that the tragedy of the Mantles is that they can '. . . achieve neither absolute union nor complete differentiation' (Shaviro, 1993, 152), yet my point is that until the introduction of Claire there is no reason for them to want to achieve the 'secure corporeal identity' (Maher, 2002, 122) that is so often suggested should be their real goal. Instead of being seen as successful in their own terms (however different from a disciplinary norm they might be), the twins are viewed as '. . . contagious and compromised subjects' (Maher, 2002, 122). Thus the failure that ultimately occurs in *Dead Ringers* is not necessarily the Mantles', although they, too, fail. The primary failure is that of the disciplinary structures surrounding monogamy to cope with the possibility of productive extensions of its own discourse. Where the Mantles fail is in not maintaining their relationship in the face of the external pressures of individuation that Claire represents. Thus it can be argued that Claire's role is to introduce the mechanisms through which social disciplinary structures can regulate the twins, to provide some vehicle through which the productive fraternal monogamy can be split. Thus, after having introduced the spectre of 'real' (i.e., heterosexual) monogamy as the means to splinter the Mantles, Clair disappears unproblematically from the film. So it appears, given Cronenberg's heretical intentions, that it is Claire – who represents those discursive positions outside the Mantles' relationship, and whose own monstrosity is invisible – who ushers in the trajectory towards failure and who, in the end, fails to meet the possibilities the twins offer.

Crash

Crash, like *M. Butterfly*, is an adaptation (here of J. G. Ballard's controversial novel, first published in 1973) but, unlike *M. Butterfly*, *Crash* is arguably Cronenberg's most successful and certainly most controversial film. The specific controversy surrounding the release and reception of the film has been far more comprehensively handled elsewhere[11] and will not form a major part of this analysis. Instead this section will concentrate on the ways in which *Crash* demonstrates a continuation of Cronenberg's heretical 'project'. Of course, it must be acknowledged that the amount of controversy surrounding *Crash* is a perfect demonstration of this film's ability to highlight a potent intersection of disciplinary structures in action. Indeed, the ferocity of some responses reveals how deeply this film and its delicately crafted critique are able to penetrate into those structures and, in return, how desperately threatened by this film they were. To this end, this chapter continues with its specific focus: the manner with which *Crash* continues the movement of Cronenberg's heretical 'project' from film form into overt narrative content.

As will have been seen from the films previously discussed, sex for Cronenberg acts as a catalyst, a transcendent activity that pushes – or prompts – the individual into moving from their familiar world and into realms of the unknown. This movement is all too often fatal and with fatality comes the reassertion of a hegemonic structure threatened by the irruption of new possibilities for desiring offered by the films' doomed protagonists. While *M. Butterfly* and *Dead Ringers* offer the opportunity to examine the structures that govern the performance of the self as a sexual being in a social and cultural setting (according to heterosexuality, heteronormativity and monogamy), *Crash* allows for a discussion of sex itself, particularly with regard to the potential for sex to provide any kind of desiring satisfaction. Once sex is liberated from its conventional relationship to reproduction, as Cronenberg notes, it is potentially free to move into new, uncharted and as-yet-undisciplined

directions. Here *Crash* is at its most heretical when it suggests that
Ballard's warning about the 'death of affect'[12] stands as a logical result of
the continued search for satisfaction. As the film's narrative makes perfectly clear, those events that have been socially coded as providing the
most satisfying experiences (and that are therefore the most rigorously
disciplined) have their own particular points of exhaustion, a fact that
leads to an apocalyptic conclusion for those subjects caught up in these
events and experiences.

Crash details events in the lives of James (James Spader) and Catherine
Ballard[13] (Deborah Kara Unger), who, as the film begins, are caught in
some form of emotional and sexual ennui. We open with two sequences,
Catherine having sex with an anonymous mechanic in a deserted aeroplane hanger, and James having sex with a camera assistant while at work
as an advertising director and producer, before the two reconvene in
their high-rise apartment to discuss their various trysts and to use those
details as a way of stirring up some passion between them. Given their
state of exhaustion, the film's inciting incident is a considerable shock.
James, while driving home one evening, becomes distracted and allows
his car to cross the centre lane, colliding head-on with an oncoming car.
The other car's driver is killed by the impact, leaving James and the other
car's passenger, Dr Helen Remington (Holly Hunter) in shock, staring at
each other across the crumpled wreckage of their vehicles and the dis-
torted body of Remington's husband. Later, while in hospital, Ballard is
visited by a medical researcher he later discovers to be Vaughan (Elias
Koteas), a 'rogue scientist' with an abiding interest in car crashes and
their victims. As the film progresses, Ballard crosses paths with Helen
Remington again and, after they begin an affair, they attend a performance and reproduction of James Dean's fatal crash, orchestrated by and
starring Vaughan. Through Remington, Ballard becomes part of
Vaughan's cadre of car-crash enthusiasts, who include Colin Seagrave
(Peter Macneill), Vaughan's driver in the James Dean re-enactment, and
Gabrielle (Rosanna Arquette), a young crippled crash victim. Vaughan
increasingly becomes a powerful force in the Ballards' lives, first becoming a feature in their coital dialogue and, later, having sex with Catherine
and then James. After Seagrave dies while attempting to re-create the
Jayne Mansfield car crash, and James has sex with Gabrielle (in what is
the film's most famous and most controversial scene), Vaughan grows
increasingly erratic before finally dying by crashing into a fully loaded
bus. James claims Vaughan's car from the police and, in keeping with
Vaughan's wishes, fixes it up just enough to get it going, and then uses it
to continue Vaughan's project, pursuing Catherine across the city. The

film ends with James, in Vaughan's Lincoln, forcing Catherine from the road into a crash and, discovering her not too badly injured, makes love to her while murmuring to her, 'Maybe the next one . . . maybe the next one . . .' (Cronenberg, 1996a)

'Sex and Car Crashes . . .'

Crash, from its outset, examines the relationship between sex and the car crash, which Vaughan understands as a '. . . fertilizing rather than destructive event . . .' (Cronenberg, 1996b, 42). Thus it may appear that sex is the primary focus of *Crash* and, particularly, the ways in which various disciplinary structures govern the rituals and procedures that accumulate around this activity. Vaughan continues by noting that the car crash involves '. . . a liberation of sexual energy that mediates the sexuality of those who have died with an intensity impossible in any other form' (Cronenberg, 1996b, 42).[14] Deciphering Vaughan's intention becomes Ballard's objective (at least insofar as he is consciously aware of the shifting fields of desire that drive him through the film) and it remains deliberately unclear precisely what Vaughan intends with this statement.

As we encounter the Ballards, they are already running out of conventional options for sustaining their sexual relationship. They each pursue heterosexual affairs (although the book spends some time exploring Catherine's lesbian dalliances, the film leaves this out to focus on James) and, as noted, utilize these affairs as a kind of foreplay for their own lovemaking. Nowhere do either Cronenberg or Ballard suggest that the Ballards move beyond relatively normative sexual practices; *Crash* (both book and film) is no *Salo* or *120 Days of Sodom*, nor does *Crash* ever intend to be. Instead *Crash* details the movements of the Ballards (and others) as they cycle through a predictable routine of sexual liaisons that seems to offer each of them less and less of the satisfaction they crave. The film's first act, with its trio of sex scenes, makes it clear that something has to give; it appears as though the Ballard marriage is barely stable and this stopgap measure, we are led to believe, can only ever be temporary.

The film's third sex act, and the first between James and Catherine, demonstrates the ways in which this film will not be concerned with fleshing out the usual details of character. Nevertheless, much can be concluded from this sequence:

James: Where were you?
Catherine: In the private aircraft hanger. Anybody could have walked in.

James: Did you come?
Catherine: No. What about your camera girl? Did she come?
James: We were interrupted. I had to go back to the set . . .
Catherine: Poor darling. Maybe the next one . . . maybe the next one.
(Cronenberg, 1996a)

As the directions from the screenplay note,

> Their sex-making [not love-making] is disconnected and passionless,
> as though it would disappear if they noticed it. An urgent, uninter-
> rupted flow of cars streams below them. (Cronenberg, 1996b, 5)

The mise-en-scène of this sequence supports this general thesis; the Ballards' apartment, while contemporary, is empty of the kinds of specific details that would provide any more than a general sense of period or place. Similarly, the 'urgent, uninterrupted stream of cars' and the broad motorways they cruise could belong to any North American city.[15] Cronenberg, in this sequence, appears to be suggesting that the Ballards, as a ubiquitous Western heterosexual couple, are suffering from a version of the kind of affect-exhaustion that will eventually consume us all.[16]

James and Catherine's marriage represents an exhaustion of affect. Nothing thrills them or provides them with excitement any more, and this is Cronenberg's heretical impulse at work: sex is 'meant', according to the disciplinary discourses surrounding the practice of sex in a contemporary Western environment, to occupy a near-hallowed position as the apogee of experience, the most satisfying bodily experience available. When coupled with various other discourses regarding emotional 'completeness', sex should fulfil any number of desiring needs, from the base to the spiritual. Cronenberg's challenge, represented by the pre-crash lives of James and Catherine, is to take this hegemonic position at its word; if we take seriously that such fulfilment were possible, where would that leave us? Cronenberg's suggestion is that it would leave us in exactly the same position as the Ballards: bored, exhausted and barely stimulated.

Sexual Heresy

Crash takes sex very seriously indeed; so much so that the narrative of the film is effectively the movement from one sex scene to another. This provides us with the means to make sense of the ways in which the Ballards seek to redress their state of desiring-exhaustion and the ways also in which their attempts are, necessarily, limited. The Ballards seek to liven up their marriage with affairs, because the affair is the quintessential sexual event that rubs against the grain of marriage. As we have seen, the social discourses surrounding monogamy demand a stable, internally consistent partnership, and a monogamous relationship based on heterosexuality (unlike the Mantles', which is based on their productive commingled identities) is necessarily constrained by these structures. Thus the Ballards' attempt to liven up their relationship by violating the terms of monogamy remains initially within the constraints of heterosexuality, because for them their problems with achieving satisfaction appear to be a problem of monogamy (as a partnership and socially sanctioned union), not heterosexuality (as an invisibly restrictive sexual practice). Here, their condition is usefully illustrated by the Marquis de Sade when he comments that 'It is not the object of debauchery that excites us, rather the idea of evil' (Sade, 1987, 28). Leaving aside Sade's frisson of glee with his use of the term 'evil' (for no such moralizing exists in *Crash*), it is clear that Sade recognizes that excitement (which is a Sadean synonym for desire and the possibility of satisfaction) lies in the various discourses that surround the sex act, rather than the act itself. This means that far from being perpetrators of '. . . the most sickening display of brutality, perversion, sex and sadism ever to be shown on the screen . . .' (Coe, 1997), James and Catherine are the most disciplined of all of *Crash*'s characters and the most thoroughly conversant with (and hence unconsciously supportive of) the major discourses surrounding sex and its various institutions.

James and Catherine's activities, prior to James' crash and the introduction of entirely new experiences, consist of simply moving through the same few routines, and utilizing the same discourses, either through confirming them or transgressing them. While their various affairs work to transgress the discourses surrounding the monogamous marriage relationship, they fully support the disciplinary structures that offer sex as the apogee of experience. They are caught fast by the disciplinary discourses that surround the practice of sex, so much so that their every move to violate these bonds (in order to generate the 'excitement' they desperately crave) serves only to reconfirm the hold these discourses have over them. They are fully interpellated subjects of the discourses they seek to transcend, without realizing that every move they make is drawn from the very discourses that restrain them.

What James' crash and Vaughan's ability to interpret its potential offer the couple is the possibility of new experiential territory. This completes the first stage of Cronenberg's heretical contemplation of the sex act as the provider of such consummate satisfaction. As James convalesces in hospital after his accident, he is visited by Vaughan and, subsequently, finds himself drawn to the widow of the man he has killed. Here we see the burgeoning relationship between the sex act and the car crash. For Ballard, in the novel, the potential for death and injury offered by the car crash adds a level of excitement to intercourse that allows the couple to transcend the 'death of affect' they have previously suffered. Cronenberg's interpretation of Ballard's intention shifts this focus slightly in order to concentrate on the movement from sex towards the car crash, instead of marrying the two together. Under Cronenberg's direction, *Crash* becomes a text whose intention is to reveal sex as no longer entirely satisfying, as an act that can be exhausted like any other. This, in turn, reveals the legislation surrounding the performance and consumption of sex, and demonstrates that its application is designed not to preserve this most satisfying of acts but to prevent its exhaustion, the 'death of affect' Ballard warns us of.

The second stage of Cronenberg's heretical movement comes as James and, later, Catherine recognize that the possibility exists for other experiences to transcend sex, or, at least, transcend the kinds of highly legislated sexual routines they have, until this moment, been restricted to. As noted above, J.G Ballard's original book seeks to utilize the car crash as a means of adding excitement to the sex act, whereas Cronenberg's film offers a trajectory that begins with the routine sexual encounters of James and Catherine (and their various paramours), moves through the various permutations of sex-in-cars, before finally divesting itself of sex altogether. This deliberate movement is often missed in critical examinations of the film, which see Cronenberg as seeking to eroticize the car crash per se. This is plainly not the case. As Vaughan makes clear, the car crash offers 'a liberation of sexual energy', which can be understood as a kind of libidinal explosion that allows the subject to pierce the various disciplinary discourses that are designed to restrain the achievement of satisfaction. Thus the second stage of Cronenberg's exploration of sex is an attempt to understand whether other sites of intense experience can offer the kinds of satisfaction that the discourses surrounding sex lead us to believe are possible.

Vaughan's intrusion into James' life provides the means for the film to shift its focus from the death throes of a middle-class marriage towards something far more dangerous. Vaughan, as another of Ballard's famous 'rogue scientists', occupies a site where a series of competing discourses coalesce. Of greatest interest is the way in which Vaughan does not maintain any distance from his project, however he seeks to define it. Thus Vaughan is the furthest along Cronenberg's heretical trajectory and his own fate stands as a stark example of the results such a rigorous pursuit of satisfaction can have. These staged car crashes can be read as an attempt to locate and isolate the factor that generates the most excitement, which is to say the factor that generates the most desire and should be expected to provide the most satisfaction. Yet, conversely, the car crashes that punctuate *Crash* are deliberately unspectacular, in the same way that the sex is deliberately unerotic. The intention throughout *Crash* is therefore to force an examination of the fundamental discourses surrounding the achievement of satisfaction, both within the text as narrative, and among the people in the audience as they assess their responses to the film. Hence it should come as no surprise that the film works to draw its audience's attention to the mechanisms involved in the delivery of spectatorial pleasure, even as its primary focus remains on an examination of sex and sexual discourse. This fact is in keeping with the same drive to suppress the marvel of spectacle we have seen in *Dead Ringers*; here, in a film that specifically deals in '. . . sex and car crashes . . .' (Maslin, 1996, 11), these two on-screen activities are delivered as almost affectless events. In this fashion, the car crashes are rendered realistically, insofar as they occur without slow motion, multiple-sequence editing, point-of-view shots or any of the other conventional devices utilized to render the car crash as a spectacular intrusion into the narrative. This drive to deliberate un-spectacularity extends to the sex acts. As Shohini Chaudhuri comments,

> In *Crash*, where the central conceit is the connection between sex and the car crash, the characters appear detached from emotion in their sex acts. More precisely, they lack the clichéd exuberance of passion that the representation of sex in films has taught us to expect. (Chaudhuri, 2001, 64)

Thus we can conclude that the film is careful to distinguish between its characters' drive for pleasure and satisfaction and the audiences' own spectatorial expectations: we are expected to observe the actions of the film's protagonists, but this does not, it would appear, give us licence to take pleasure from them.

Crash and the End of Desire

The trajectory followed by Vaughan appears, then, to be one in which the libidinal charge of intercourse is linked explicitly with the car crash, which is then used as a way to jettison the exhausted sex act in favour of a new form of experience, and hence a new means to satisfaction. Sex is utilized because of the discursive disciplinary structures that surround it and which work to delimit it so as to foster an expectation of maximum experience, and hence maximum satisfaction. Thus the sex act, while exhausted, is the most readily familiar to the protagonists, especially given that their move towards new forms of desiring/satisfaction will necessarily involve the negotiation of new discursive forms. Vaughan's own sexual contact during the film always occurs in conjunction with the automobile, and his presence works to spur the other characters on towards new sexual exchanges, either in the hope that they will find a combination of acts and partners that works to provide some satisfaction, or that they will eventually exhaust sex entirely. Thus, as the film works towards its conclusion, Vaughan has sex with Helen Remington, Catherine and, finally, James before dying in his own spectacular (and yet, perversely, off-screen) crash.

What emerges through these acts is evidence of the second stage of Cronenberg's heretical supposition. The first stage leads us to ask, if sex is therefore *not* the site of consummate satisfaction, then what is? Ballard links the sex act with another event – the car crash – in the belief that the combination of eroticism and trauma will break the state of exhaustion and ennui that possesses his protagonists, but Cronenberg goes further to explore what happens when the sex is itself replaced. Thus the various connections that occur between the protagonists detail an exhaustion of the various possibilities for intercourse and mark, also, their movements towards the limits of the various discourses that restrain them. With James as the film's exemplar, his actions demonstrate his trajectory towards Vaughan's position. His sex with Helen Remington immediately after his release from hospital is the start of a series of encounters which includes a brief affair with Gabrielle (which, famously, sees him penetrate a vaginal wound on the back of her thigh) before he and Vaughan have anal sex in Vaughan's Lincoln Continental (the car Kennedy was assassinated in). Each of these combinations draws James through a decreasing series of combinations as he works towards the conclusion Vaughan appears to have reached some time before: that all articulations of desire will, eventually and inevitably, end in failure and disappointment.

While the Ballards' actions with Vaughan and his group result in a new series of combinations and partners, these too are limited and restrained by the disciplinary structures that surround them (both the protagonists and the acts they perform). Ironically (for the protagonists of *Crash* and for Cronenberg), the acts that are performed are only recognizable as perversions because they so closely resemble the discourses they seek to overcome. Thus Gabrielle's wound that James penetrates functions as a surrogate vagina (indeed, Cronenberg goes so far as to include a clitoral lump in the scar tissue), meaning that while the act may appear to be perverse, it remains another form of penetrative sex (between a man and woman) and, thus, subject to the same death of affect as all of the other sex acts performed in *Crash*. What remains is to jettison sex altogether in an attempt to carve out new pathways for desire and new modes of satisfaction. Yet what hope can there be if the same desiring structures remain in place? This is Vaughan's paradox, one that he can only overcome through the path of self-immolation. This is *Crash*'s concluding point – one of hopelessness in the face of our inability to satisfy our desires matched by the less-than-satisfying attempts to continue generating desire itself.

The final crash in *Crash* occurs as James, now driving Vaughan's Lincoln, hunts Catherine's much smaller sports car. Fulfiling Vaughan's wish regarding fixing up a car in which someone has died, James appears set to continue Vaughan's apocalyptic work and, upon discovering Catherine, sets about running her off the road. Her car soon spirals off the road and she is thrown clear of the wreckage, dazed but unhurt. It is at this moment that James throws himself upon her, entering her from behind while murmuring 'maybe the next one . . . maybe the next one' (Cronenberg, 1996a). At this point the camera cranes up and pans slowly away from the couple to reveal fast-moving traffic, freeways and an anonymous city skyline. This act demonstrates both the heretical notions Cronenberg is offering, as well as the hopelessness of the desiring individual. The two stages of Cronenberg's heretical thought – taking the discourses of sex so seriously as to exhaust the possibilities for satisfaction, and then seeking to replace sex altogether with a new set of satisfying experiences – leaves the film's protagonists rolling about in the mud beside a busy freeway. They may be still alive, the film is saying, but Vaughan's fate awaits them. What, then, can we conclude from this? There are four final points to be made.

First, *Crash* seeks to demonstrate that sex, as a means of providing satisfaction, is limited by its own cycle of exhaustion. Thus the highly charged disciplinary discourses that surround sex and both promote it as the most satisfying experience we can have and regulate how one might obtain it appear to be in place precisely to enable sex to retain its satisfactory potential. Second, as James and Catherine demonstrate (without appearing to be aware of it), the discourses of sex control our ability to transgress them. In exactly the same way that monogamy contains within it the form and possibility of its own transgression, the discourses of sex demand that the transgression of sex remain recognizably sexual. Thus the only way in which *Crash* can be labelled as perverse is through providing sexual alternatives that retain enough that is recognizably sexual so as to demonstrate their distance from a normative standard. In this fashion, Gabrielle's wound works to constantly remind James (and, hence, us) that it is *not* a vagina, meaning that, as Sade offers, it is not the act but the discourse surrounding the act that excites. Third, the film's conclusion (including Vaughan's death) demonstrates that replacing the object of satisfaction (here, sex for car crashes) without altering the discursive structures that surround the object will also lead to exhaustion. The manner of the film's ending works to suggest that the 'next one' the Ballards seek is their own death. For as long as they work to seek satisfaction from the crash in the same way they worked to seek satisfaction from sex, they are doomed. Finally, and most heretical of all, *Crash* tells us, in no uncertain terms, that all attempts to circumvent, break through or reinvent the circuit of desire/satisfaction will fail because one cannot escape the discursive structures that allow one to make meaning of the world. The fully interpellated individual (to use Althusser's term) cannot access the 'outside' of ideology in any meaningful meta-critical fashion, meaning that the disciplinary structures that govern one's attempts to find the satisfaction promised, but not delivered, by sex will fail. The discourses that surround the practice and performance of sex, that offer it as a particular kind of event that *should* provide spectacular amounts of satisfaction, are at work to limit sex in order to prevent the subjects of that discourse from discovering that this is not the case. The key word in James' final piece of dialogue, then, is 'maybe' – 'maybe the next one': maybe the next act, the next encounter, the next position. All iterations are governed by the discourses they seek to transgress and, as *Crash* seeks to demonstrate, though transgression may be discursively possible, discursive transgression is ultimately not possible.

Chapter 5

The Subject Under Examination

Shadow Texts

The three films of this chapter, *The Brood, Scanners* and *Naked Lunch,* all elaborate on the detailed analysis of disciplining discourses that we saw emerging from the films discussed in Chapter 4. Here, though, the focus is on the way in which the individual subject of discipline is either affected by his or her disciplinary contexts or, in some fashion, attempts to seize control over the disciplinary mechanisms that control him or her. Previously we saw how the films examined all sought to take a specific discourse – monogamy, heterosexuality, the possibility for satisfaction itself – to a logical, which is to say inherently absurd, conclusion. These absurdities contain within them the possibilities for resistance and for their own undoing or, at the very least, their own problematizing. What the three films of this chapter offer is a specific focus on the individuals that are subject to these disciplinary discourses and who undergo changes and alterations as a result of shifts in the disciplinary structures and contexts that surround them.

In a Foucauldian sense, these films explore the manner with which the individual emerges as a result of the activities of (disciplinary) discourse. Power which, in these films, circulates within a series of master discourses – medicine, the family, sexuality, addiction – constitutes the subjects it encounters as specific individuals. But, more than being merely passive objects to be passed between discourses, the protagonists of these films all attempt to articulate power as well: thus, as Foucault makes clear, '. . . not only do individuals circulate between its [discursive] threads; they are always in the position of simultaneously undergoing and exercising this power' (Foucault, 1980, 98). In this fashion, each film opens with its protagonist positioned by a particular institutionalized discourse: Nola, in *The Brood,* is a patient, Cameron, in *Scanners,* a vagrant and Bill, in *Naked Lunch,* an addict.

Thus, over the course of the narratives, our experience and understanding of each of these protagonists alter as they themselves alter in
relation to the discourses that have positioned them. This activity, as it
plays out across the bodies of the protagonists (and which is particularly
and literally visible in *The Brood* and *Scanners* while being metaphorically
referenced in *Naked Lunch*) means that these three films enter into a
reciprocal relationship with the three films of Chapter 4, functioning as
their thematic shadows. James' final dialogue in *Crash*, 'Maybe the next
one . . . maybe the next one . . .', resonates both with Catherine's comment from earlier in the film and with a moment in *The Brood* that establishes this film as its thematic shadow. In *The Brood*, after collecting
Candice from the police station following Juliana's death, Frank tries to
comfort his child. His explanation that Candice is safe turns out to be
patently false and his assurance that '. . . it'll be ok . . . it'll be ok' provides
us with a precursor to James' own wish that '. . . maybe the next one . . .'
will solve their problems. What Cronenberg reveals is that 'it' will certainly not be 'ok'; Candice carries within her the symptoms that, in Nola,
eventually produced the Brood. Similarly he reveals that the best one
can hope for from 'the next one' is, for *Crash*, a delaying of the eventual
exhaustion of satisfaction and, for *The Brood*, attempts to fulfil impossible
discursive demands. *Scanners* continues this trend by echoing the concerns of *Dead Ringers*, developing a focus on the Cartesian binary that
Cronenberg is so interested in. Within *Dead Ringers*, problematizing the
Cartesian binary occurs as a focus on the relationship between the disciplinary discourse of monogamy. This raises the possibility for an alterna-
tively productive dyad, represented by the Mantle twins. Further to this,
with its discussion of mutually imbricated selves and the possibility for a
form of 'sympathetic resonance' between the twins' physiologies, *Dead
Ringers* finds another route to question the stability of a mind/body distinction. *Scanners* shadows this discussion in its own argument for alter-
natively productive relationships and blurred subjective boundaries – here
occurring as a result of the psychic process of 'scanning'. Thus both of
these films explore the by now well-worn edges of the Cartesian binary,
permitting slippages and illicit entries between its previously hard and
impermeable discursive boundaries. Finally, *Naked Lunch* shadows the
territory of *M. Butterfly* by exploring the territory surrounding the *performance* of the subject as an individual. For Gallimard, Song's successful performance of the tropes of heterosexuality and femininity are enough to
'prove' (to him in his complex state of disavowal) that she is a woman.

Lee, similarly, encounters disciplinary discourses that 'demand' he perform in particular ways – as an addict, as a married heterosexual and as a homosexual. In both of these films the performance of discursive tropes are enough to 'prove' membership. Lee, however, is the obverse to Song's 'woman'. Lee *is* an addict and a homosexual but is forced to invent a complicated conspiracy that requires his performance of these discursive positions before he can begin to resolve, or at least understand, his positioning within them.

Lee's means of wresting control, however, demonstrates Cronenberg's point regarding the position of the individual within discipline: any control gained is illusory and any resolution – as evidenced by Lee's escape into Annexia – is a fantasy. Because the disciplinary discourses in these films pass through individuals but do not originate with them, there is nothing tangible or finite to take control of. Nola's assertion of her desires within the medical discourse of psychoplasmics results in the parthenogenetic production of a mute Brood who kill in response to her unconscious wishes, but she remains throughout a patient (and an hysteric). Similarly Cameron may (or may not) sacrifice his body in order to psychically join with his brother, but they remain – all of them – subjects of discipline. Yet the possibilities for some counter-version of discipline as a utopian ideal is not raised in these texts, because no such 'outside' or meta-disciplinary position exists. Each of these protagonists resists disciplinary placement, but in so doing they move from one discursive position to another. Thus the focus for this chapter is on the individual subjects of discourse themselves, the ways they seek to gain some mastery or control over the various disciplines that position them as individuals, and the ways in which whatever control is achieved is at best temporary and, at worst, entirely fictional.

The Brood

What is obvious upon viewing *The Brood* is its total difference in tone when compared with Cronenberg's preceding films. Those three films all combined a compliance with their various generic requirements with either a black humour (on the part of the two horror films, *Shivers* and *Rabid*) or a formal ability far in excess of narrative requirements (on the part of *Fast Company*). *The Brood*, in comparison, is unremittingly bleak both as a horror film (which it assuredly is) and as a narrative of familial collapse. Cronenberg is quick to link this severe shift in tone to his own circumstances at this time, as well as his desire to provide, as he puts it, a film to function as an antidote to the saccharine falsehood of that year's *Kramer vs. Kramer* (Robert Benton, 1979).[1] However, what emerges is a sense that *The Brood* is taking its generic responsibilities seriously. This distinguishes it from the previous films in that it does not extend its generic adherence to breaking point in order to reveal the disciplinary discourses of film form. Cronenberg's previous three films all, in their way, demonstrate that absolute adherence to the requirements of the genre works to draw attention to the moments when those generic structures (articulated in the film text as restrictions and prohibitions) break down under their own weight. *The Brood*, as a point of difference, has very little in the way of formal interruption to the delivery of the narrative, leading one to conclude that this film's purpose is to focus attention fully on the various disciplinary discourses at work in the film's content.

To be sure, *The Brood* continues Cronenberg's process of meta-commentary, with the primary point of distinction being that the formal processes at work in the film become invisible by being generically conventional. In this fashion, the interpretive and analytic gaze (of the audience and, eventually, the critic) is drawn to the narrative and what the narrative itself has to say about the various discursive structures it is demonstrating. This means that the requisite formal devices that permit generic identification appear without being cynically undercut with the black (or bleak) humour that so distinguishes the previous films. Like them, the film's ending does not provide a redemptive conclusion, but unlike them, there is no celebration, however perverse, at the success of the disease. Similarly, while the parasites in *Shivers* and the disease in *Rabid* may provide the means to highlight previously hidden (and therefore effective) disciplinary structures by pushing them to extremes (here one thinks of the way in which both films sexualize or render problematic the young, the old and the physically infirm), *The Brood* appears to be populated by people who are genuinely victims, all of whom suffer and none of whom is redeemed by the orgy of violence at the film's conclusion.

The Brood details the slow destruction of the Carveth family. As the film opens, Nola Carveth (Samantha Eggar) is in isolated therapy with Dr Hal Raglan (Oliver Reed), author of *The Shape of Rage* and inventor of the new therapeutic technique 'Psychoplasmics', which involves intensive role-playing in order to literalize the body's rage as psychosomatic symptoms, thereby cathecting the original impulses and leaving the patient cleansed and healthy. Nola's therapy permits visits from her daughter Candice (Cindy Hinds), and it is after one of these visits that Frank

Carveth (Art Hindle) discovers welts, bites and scratches on his daughter's body. Suspecting that Nola is abusing their daughter, Frank confronts Raglan but is unable to prevent Nola's access to Candice due to the terms of her therapy. Shortly after, Frank leaves Candice with her maternal grandmother Juliana (Nuala Fitzgerald), and as Candice sits alone in the lounge, Juliana is savagely beaten to death by a mysterious assailant. Frank is informed of Juliana's death while at work and collects Candice from the police station, where he is informed that the girl has been understandably traumatized by the event. Juliana's ex-husband, Barton (Henry Beckman), returns for his wife's funeral and, upon visiting Raglan's 'Somafree Institute', is told that Nola is unaware of her mother's death and that he is also denied access to her. Later, as Frank entertains Candice's schoolteacher, Ruth Mayer (Susan Hogan), he is interrupted by Barton, who drunkenly enlists Frank's help in freeing Nola from Raglan. While Frank is on his way to dissuade Barton, Ruth answers a phone call from Nola, and Barton is beaten to death by the same mysterious assailant who attacked Juliana. Frank discovers Barton's body and is himself attacked before the assailant, who is revealed to be a small, deformed child-like creature, dies, seemingly of natural causes. More of the creatures attack Ruth Mayer at school, killing her in front of a class of children, and abduct Candice. Frank, suspecting Raglan, returns to Somafree and discovers that the 'dwarf killers' are actually Nola's children

FIGURE 5.1 Producing *The Brood*.

or, as Raglan explains, the literalizations of Nola's immense rage at those she believes have abused her in the past. Raglan moves to free Candice from Nola's Brood while Frank confronts Nola, who reveals to him her external womb, the means by which she parthenogenetically produces the Brood (see Figure 5.1). While the Brood kill Raglan, Frank attacks and kills Nola and finally frees Candice. As the pair drive away, neither of them appear to notice two small lesions developing on Candice's arm.

Layers of Discourse

The narrative of *The Brood* is primarily concerned with two major discourses, the medical and the familial, and the film's plot concerns the manner with which these two discourses collide and/or combine. Of central concern is the individual who emerges as a result of the discourses that surround them, and *The Brood* explores how a shift in discursive position (from the familial to the medical in the case of Nola) will generate a new subject-position which appears to result in a variant performance of the self. Therefore, an obvious place to begin is with the institute that functions as the catalyst for the film's narrative: the Somafree Institute of Psychoplasmics. The word 'Somafree', another of Cronenberg's institutional neologisms, immediately draws attention to 'Soma', which can refer either to the parts of the body excluding the reproductive organs or to the body as distinct from the mind.[2] It is unclear if 'Soma-freedom' is freedom *of* the body or freedom *from* the body, but despite this assuredly deliberate ambiguity, both the Cartesian difficulty evidenced in the previous films and Cronenberg's own fascination with issues of reproduction and multiplication are made clear from the outset, along with the notion that the body might itself somehow be freed, or at least separated, from the restraints of the mind. Similarly, 'psychoplasmics' refers both literally to the plasticity of the psyche and analogically to psychoanalysis. Thus the institute and therapeutic practice at the heart of *The Brood* comments upon a particular kind of medical discourse as it intersects with the patient who succumbs to it and the social structures that surround it. However, psychoplasmics is not merely a mockery of psychoanalysis: part of its diegetic power and narrative purpose comes from the fact that it appears to work, if a little too well. *The Brood* therefore utilizes psychoplasmics in order to explore how any discourse, when taken to its extreme, will reveal its own inconsistencies and provide the means for a possible resistance. Psychoplasmics, as a form of psychiatric therapy, is the most visible discourse at work in *The Brood* and is utilized as a way of providing an explicit commentary on the specifically mind-focused (or, perhaps more accurately, body-ignoring) rhetoric of psychotherapy at large as it circulates as doxa. The bodily implications of psychoplasmics (as a way of rejoining the psycho- with the somato-) functions as a discursive pivot around which the other central disciplinary discourses of *The Brood* are wound and, as the film progresses, unwound.

There is, as noted, a second discursive thread running through *The Brood*, and it is with the intersection of the medical and familial discourses that the film begins to reveal the purpose of its critique. As Jacqueline Rose notes, any representation of a family in crisis, be it the Carveths or the Kramers, necessarily leads to '. . . the basic problem of family life. What are parents and children meant to do for, and to, each other?' (Rose, 2004, 20). The pivotal point in Rose's statement lies with the use of the past participle 'meant': the family is a site of requirements, obligations, responsibilities and, necessarily, restrictions. Failure to fulfil or comply with these, which, for *The Brood*, extends to the filial perception of failure, means that the individual who emerges as a result of the interplay of familial discourses carries the trace of failure. For *The Brood*, discursive failure is literally written into and onto the body. However, the familial discourse (or, more correctly, the discursive and disciplinary functioning of the family that is a collection of discourses) takes second place to the outright articulation of the medical discourse of psychoplasmics. In this fashion, the performance of familial discourses, including the manner with which an audience is led to interpret correct and incorrect familial behaviour, is naturalized by emerging as a result of the authoritative discourse of psychoplasmics. The film's first two therapeutic situations (with Mike and Nola) are designed to demonstrate not just how the patients believe they have been treated, but to reveal what their respective fathers *should* have done and said. In this fashion, the discourses of paternity are linked invisibly to the articulations of Raglan's therapy. Raglan's provocations therefore draw out of Mike and Nola a clear understanding of what they believe families are *meant* to do to and for each other.

By way of an example, *The Brood* opens, without warning, on a role-playing session between Raglan and another male patient, Mike (Gary McKeehan). On stage, in front of what seems to be a large audience, Raglan demands that Mike look at him, which Mike has trouble doing. As the sequence progresses, Raglan – who is performing the role of Mike's father – attacks Mike for his inability to return Raglan's look:

> I guess you're just a weak person. You must have got that from your mother. It would probably have been better for you if you'd been born

a girl. Then we could have named you Michelle. You see, weakness is more acceptable in a girl, Michelle . . . oh, I mean . . . Mike. I keep forgetting. Wait a minute. Why don't I call you Michelle all the time? That way I wouldn't have to be so goddamn fucking ashamed of you and your weaknesses. I could just think of you as a girl all the time, buy your frocks and your dresses and your frilly socks and your frilly scarves, and you could be . . . you could be daddy's little girl and I wouldn't have to be so . . . fucking . . . ashamed of being seen with you in public, would I, eh? (Cronenberg, 1979a)

It takes some time for the purpose of Raglan's outburst to become clear and it is only when Mike, finally responding in anger to Raglan-as-Daddy, rips open his shirt to show the welts and boils that appear to have emerged as a symptom (and thus a physicalization) of his anger, that the nature of Raglan's therapy and, hence, the role-playing performance is revealed. As the role-play continues, every cut back to Mike reveals his lesions to be a little more pronounced and, by the conclusion of the sequence, Mike's face appears to be damp with a mixture of sweat and mucous produced by his body in response to Raglan's provocation.

It is worth comparing this sequence to one later in the film in which Raglan performs a similar role with Nola in order to permit her to understand her husband's actions while coming to terms with her own father's behaviour.

Nola: Frank hates me, Daddy. He despises me. He thinks I'm trying to harm my little girl and I know that he's thinking of a way to take her away. And that's very unfair of him. That's very arrogant of him.
Raglan: You mustn't be too hard on him, Nola, sweetheart. He's just trying to be a good protective father.
Nola: No.
Raglan: Oh yes. He's just doing what a good father should do. He's protecting his little girl. Now there's nothing wrong with this, is there? He doesn't want to see her hurt. He doesn't want to see her hurt by anybody, not even her own mother. Now, is there anything wrong with that? Is there?
Nola: No.
Raglan: No there isn't. After all, it's just what I did for you, isn't it? Hmmm? Frank's protecting Candy the same way I protected you, isn't he? Isn't he?
Nola: No.

Raglan: 'No'? What do you mean 'no'? What do you mean when you say 'no'?
Nola: I love you Daddy.
Raglan: What do you *mean* when you say 'no'?
[. . . .]
Nola: You didn't protect me. You didn't. And you should have. You should have. You shouldn't have looked away when she hit me. And you shouldn't have walked away from the table when she twisted my words. You should have stopped her. You should have hit her when she hit me and you should have smacked her when she smacked me. Oh god – I love you. But you didn't protect me, and you should have.
(Cronenberg, 1979a)

In both sequences Raglan performs as the father in order to elicit responses regarding how the father should not have behaved, in Mike's case, and how he should have behaved, in Nola's. Three points emerge from these examples: the first of these is, as noted, the manner with which the medical discourse – these are, after all, transcripts of therapeutic sessions – naturalizes the performance of the familial discourses. With both examples we see patients in pain, suffering as a result of the perceived or actual (the film never distinguishes) actions of the fathers concerned. Our own conclusions of how the fathers in question *should* have behaved emerge 'naturally' as an extension of the performance, which is itself authorized by the presence of a medical master discourse – psychoplasmics. In these early examples, the naturalizing of the familial discourse, the way it is effectively rendered invisible by the function of the medical discourse, will be later problematized as we come to 'know' something of the patients who are performing in this manner and of the fathers who are so maligned. At this stage, though, what constitutes a 'good' or 'bad' father is unquestioned: the patients we see suffer because of 'bad' fathers, which, in turn, makes the performative requirements of a 'good' father obvious and 'natural'. The second point to emerge from these examples is the way both of them detail the manner with which the subject is positioned by the, in this case medical, discourses they are subject to. Whatever roles Nola and Mike might have played prior to their induction into psychoplasmics, they are now clearly identified as 'patients' and occupy that role entirely. The patient, brought into being under the glare of the medical gaze, is fully individuated and is entirely subject to the power of that discourse. As with the invisible function of the familial discourse, this facet of the medical discourse will be problematized by the narrative's momentum: here it appears to work and the visible extrusions on Mike's body seem to be symptoms of a successful therapy. Finally, psychoplasmics appears to rely entirely on an enforced transference between the analyst and the analysand. Of course, transference is both inevitable and necessary for psychoanalytic therapy to function, and Freud notes that as the transferential relationship between analyst and analysand comes to dominate the therapeutic session (and subsume the original illness), its newness and visibility renders it open to healing. Thus

> . . . the mastering of this new, artificial neurosis [the therapeutically induced transferential relationship] coincides with the getting rid of the illness which was originally brought to the treatment – with the accomplishment of our theraputic task. (Freud, 1973, 497)

However, the fact that it is enacted so forcefully, some might say aggressively, appears to be peculiar to psychoplasmics. Raglan utilizes his roleplay bullying to transform his participants into patients (specifically hysterics), literalizing their symptoms in and on their bodies. This allows him to occupy a range of subject-positions (as Mike's and Nola's 'Daddy', as Nola's husband, as her child and also as her rival Ruth), even as they are caught fast as 'patients', thereby forcing them into tightly framed discursive structures under the guise of 'lifting' their repression. This, in turn, gives them permission to experience their anger and to give an entirely somatic shape to their rage.

Producing the Brood

Frank's visit to another of Raglan's patients, Jan Hartog (Robert Silverman), demonstrates the danger of this kind of approach: Hartog is involved in suing Raglan and the Institute as his own therapy has left him with lymphosarcoma, a cancer of the lymphatic system. As Hartog bleakly comments, 'Raglan encouraged my body to revolt against me. And it did. Now I have a small revolution on my hands and I'm not putting it down very successfully' (Cronenberg, 1979a). What Jan is experiencing is nothing more or less than a 'correctly' functioning disciplinary discourse – in this case, the medical discourse of psychoplasmics. Here Cronenberg's deliberate pushing of these disciplinary and discursive structures to their logical ends is revealed with Jan's cancer and what the film's audience is in the process of discovering about Nola. The medical discourse of psychoplasmics involves, as noted, the systematic removal of the various repressive mechanisms that otherwise prevent the eruption of hysterical symptoms. By not only giving his patients permission to experience their rage but by demanding it (with some authority and menace), Raglan has generated a series of hysterics. The problem for all the inhabitants of *The Brood* comes with Raglan's success. The individual, transformed into a patient by the presence and requirements of the medical discourse, becomes subject to the demands of that discourse. That discourse, in this instance, makes very specific demands on the body of the individual and the way in which that body can be utilized to cathect the previously repressed rage of the patient. These new discursive requirements, which are disciplinary insofar as they involve the movement of power around and through the patient, supersede any prior discursive structures. There is nothing unusual about this, and the only difference between psychoplasmics and psychoanalysis at this level, at least, is the manner with which Raglan's therapy aggressively utilizes the body and its resources.

The point made above is that the individual, subject to a variety of discourses, alters in relation to those discourses, and *The Brood* literalizes those alterations in exactly the same way that Raglan's radical therapy literalizes symptoms as bodily extrusions. Thus Nola – wife, mother and daughter – becomes a patient as a result of Raglan's intervention, and this new role supersedes those previous ones. Nola, then, occupies an interstitial position insofar as her therapy provides a bridge between, and a way to understand, both her old and new subject positions. However, and crucially for *The Brood*, Raglan's therapy is literally playing out across the surface of her body, to the extent that Nola provides a shining example of how the disciplinary functions of these major discourses produce subjects in their image and aligned to their articulations of power. Taken to its logical extreme, the diegetic medical discourse of psychoplasmics itself stands in for a series of such extra-filmic authoritative discourses: the authority of science and medicine, the infallibility of such authority in comparison with the very fallible patients who are cured or solved by such discourses, the fact that such discourses present a more thorough knowledge of the patient's condition than they might have, and so on. In pushing such discourses to the extreme, Cronenberg reveals the hidden ambivalence inside these discursive structures. The body in psychoplasmics is permitted to manifest the ills of the psyche, and because Raglan encourages his patients to 'go all the way through', to push through their repression and give vent to their repressed rage and anger, the logical extension of this discourse concerns those symptoms that are so powerfully and hysterically motivated that they can escape the body altogether. In this fashion, psychoplasmics not only literalizes the hysteric's symptoms; its primary method towards therapeutic-resolution appears to be providing these symptoms with their own actualized presence in the world, enabling them to take revenge for the events that have brought them into being.

The generation of somatic symptoms as a result of psychological distress has a long history, and it may be this fact that generated Cronenberg's interest in it. Certainly Hartog's complaints about a self-motivated body acting in opposition to his consciousness echoes the earliest imaginings of the 'animal womb' and its self-propelled wanderings through the (female) hysterics' bodies.[3] Crucially, Didi-Huberman notes that

> ... hysteria is not only a sentimental event. In it, affects become bodily disasters, enigmatic and violent spatiality. . . . The body of the hysteric is even able to offer a total spectacle of all illnesses at once. And, contradictorily, it matters little to her. . . . This is the paradox of spectacular evidence: hysteria offers all symptoms, an extraordinary bounty of symptoms – but these symptoms issue from *nothing* (they have no organic basis). (Didi-Huberman, 2003, 73–4; italics in original)

This is a vital point for understanding the intersection of Raglan's medical discourse with Nola's and Mike's overdetermined version of the familial discourses they seek to critique. For all of their suffering (rendered visible as the 'bodily disasters' of psychoplasmics) there is no suggestion that they have suffered unduly or excessively. Their symptoms literally 'issue from nothing'. Whether such emotions (and their visceral productions) are justified, insofar as they might have some original basis in trauma, is never actually touched upon; what is important for Raglan is that the emotion is present. Further to this, Raglan's therapy provides a naturalized version of the various familial discourses: it is made obvious, through listening to Mike and Nola, what 'good' parents and children are 'meant to do for, and to, each other'. This is part of Cronenberg's heretical extension of these discourses. The film's actual fathers – Frank and Barton – both appear to behave entirely adequately, and while they may not be perfect, they both appear to be doing their best. However Barton's actual failure as a father to Nola is not important: what *is* important is Nola's perception of him as a failure, and of his having failed to meet her psychoplasmically inspired understanding of his disciplinary obligations. This structure leads us to imagine her perception of what, the film suggests, she will inevitably consider Frank's failure to adequately protect her. The film's conclusion, with the lesions on Candice's arm representing the daughter's continuation of the mother's therapeutic position, demonstrates that no matter how much Frank might have tried to protect his daughter, her move to occupy Nola's position of horror is inevitable. Therefore children, *The Brood* suggests, punish their parents for their various failings, without recognizing that the social function of 'parent', like all social functions, is an impossible condition. *The Brood*'s most heretical gesture, then, is to construct an inevitable circularity of discipline: one is caught by these structures which demand participation, yet are impossible to fulfil, and which will generate massive punishment for any imagined, let alone actual, failure.

Scanners

Scanners is widely regarded as Cronenberg's first fully fledged science fiction film and certainly stands as a mature development of the themes that are circulating in his student and independent pre-*Shivers* productions. As a shadow text to the concerns evidenced in *Dead Ringers*, *Scanners* foregrounds issues of permeability and subjectivity; thus Cronenberg's penchant for rendering bodily boundaries problematic is continued into the film's central issue, which pushes this exploration from bodily permeability towards psychic dissolution. Further to this, *Scanners* offers a comprehensive examination and extension of the panoptic mechanism. utilizing surveillance as a way of discussing the manner in which disciplinary structures must constantly address potential threats to their efficient functioning. It is worth noting that *Scanners* was, upon its release, Cronenberg's most successful film thus far, and it spent its first week of release at number one in the American box office, leading many to conclude that Cronenberg could at last take his place alongside others in the ' "new breed" category of filmmakers such as George Lucas, John Carpenter and Steven Spielberg' (Maronie, 1981, 26). This success is attributed to the film's confident mix of science fiction and action, with requisite car chases, explosions, gunfire and, crucially, cutting-edge special effects, and this generic hybridity can be seen as another strategy for successfully inserting these thematic concerns into a text that, superficially at least, conforms to its various generic requirements.

Scanners is the story of Cameron Vale (Stephen Lack), a 'Scanner', or telepathic psychic who, as the film opens, is living as a derelict and is unaware of the potential of his talent. Rescued by 'psychopharmacologist' Dr Paul Ruth (Patrick McGoohan), Vale is rehabilitated, provided with a drug, Ephemerol, which helps moderate the unwanted effects of his telepathy and recruited as an agent for Consec – the security and arms company Ruth works with. Vale's task is to penetrate a rival group of Scanners, led by the unpredictable Darryl Revok (Michael Ironside), and with much gunfire and supplementary explosions, Vale learns of another group of 'good' Scanners, led by Kim Obrist (Jennifer O'Neill). Infiltrating Revok's own pharmacological company, Biocarbon Amalgamate, Vale discovers that Revok intends to supply Ephemerol nationwide. The purpose of this is unclear until, again after much gunfire, Vale finally confronts Revok and learns that Ruth had initially invented Ephemerol as a drug to alleviate discomfort during pregnancy and that the drug's primary side effect is the production of Scanners. Revok's plan to supply Ephemerol is in order to create an army of Scanners. Further to this, it transpires that Dr Ruth tested the drug on his own wife, who produced two sons – Darryl and Cameron. The two brothers then engage in a 'scanning battle', during which Vale appears to die. *Scanners* ends with Revok, speaking with Vale's voice, exclaiming, 'Kim . . . it's me. Cameron. I'm here. We've won . . . we've won' (Cronenberg, 1981).

Scanning the Permeable Body

The permeable body – insofar as the body both becomes a site (from which scanning occurs) and a conduit (through which the never-identified power of scanning passes) – occupies the bulk of *Scanners'* narrative. Popular discourses surrounding psychic phenomena tend to trade on, and thereby support, a Cartesian distinction, wherein it is the mind alone that generates the effect. Cronenberg's own assessment of this Cartesian split is as ever sceptical, and *Scanners* continues his meditation on this discourse and its disciplinary effects. In this *Scanners* mines similar territory to that of all of his previous films (and particularly, with the focus on psychic phenomena, the early independent films *Stereo* and *Crimes of the Future*) and continues Cronenberg's thematic collapse of this Cartesian distinction in an effort to highlight the presence of the body in genres and narrative tropes most obviously dedicated to championing either a mind/body split or the mind in favour of the body.[4] As Dr Ruth explains to Vale, '[t]elepathy is not mind reading. It is the direct linking of nervous systems separated by space' (Cronenberg, 1981). Beard spends some time worrying about what scanning might actually be (Beard, 2001, 99–102), noting that what appears to be a type of sight in one sequence becomes a form of hearing in another, then a type of 'telepresence' or of communal experience and, finally, a means of exerting psychic influence. Perhaps the most important fact to take from this is that scanning appears to be a type of inhabiting, wherein the Scanner (in some never-explained fashion) inhabits the Scannee (sometimes with spectacular and devastating results). Cronenberg's point here seems to be less one of logical consistency and more one of suggesting a new permeability of the individual. Thus the direct physiological link between the scanning mind and body and, particularly, between individual Scanners is stressed and functions as a continuation of the somatic/psychological collapse witnessed in *The Brood*. This collapse of distinction is continued further in the film when Vale is required to scan Consec's computer system, an event made possible because, as Ruth explains, '. . . you do have a nervous system . . . and so does a computer. And you can scan the computer as you would another human being' (Cronenberg, 1981).

One of the mysteries of *Scanners* is the way in which Ephemerol, which is administered to Vale (and others) as a scan-suppressant can also work to produce in utero scanners, such as Vale experiences. By way of exploring this, it is worth considering the sequence in which Vale is scanned by an unborn foetus. Having followed the supply of Ephemerol from Revok's company out to various corrupt neighbourhood doctors, Vale learns that Revok's intentions are to supply Ephemerol to pregnant women resulting in, as he puts it, '. . . a whole generation of Scanner soldiers just a few months away from being born' (Cronenberg, 1981). While waiting in a doctor's lounge, Vale begins to experience the effects of a scan, which is transmitted to us as flinching and grimacing. Glancing around reveals no one obviously engaged in scanning, and it is only when Vale's gaze settles on a pregnant woman that he realizes that the woman's foetus is actively scanning him. This moment, as well as Revok's conspiracy to generate legions of Scanners as yet unborn, renders visible Foucault's considerations regarding the formation of the individual as an effect of the vacillations of power. As has been noted before, Foucault comments that '[t]he individual is an effect of power, and at the same time, or precisely to the extent to which it is that effect, it is the element of its articulation' (Foucault, 1980, 98). The Scanners (adults and babies alike) emerge as products of the drug that works to both generate *and* regulate them. Ephemerol, as a literalization of the film's medical discourse, works to continue that discourse's effects on the individuals it turns into subjects, insofar as, once 'medicalized' by Ephemerol, they are brought to the attention of, and therefore become subject to, the full extent of that medical discourse. Thus, the infant scan of Vale demonstrates a shift in the types of disciplinary discourses at work in the formation of the individual. Ephemerol, designed originally to 'manage' the 'difficulties' of childbirth (i.e., to intrude into the functioning of the pregnant woman's body), promotes permeability of bodily boundaries (a theme developed further in *Dead Ringers*), and the infant Scanner, we presume, marks the development of a new conception of subjectivity and a problematizing of the increasingly obsolete Cartesian model utilized by Consec.

Therefore scanning is a bodily process and, even when sympathetically done, is always presented as generating no small amount of distress for both the Scanner and the Scannee. In this, *Scanners* retains traces of Cronenberg's original 1974 screenplay *Telepathy 2000 (The Psychics)*, which features telepathic and psychic rape as a narrative mainstay. Nothing quite as abhorrent occurs in *Scanners*, but it is worth considering some of the scanning events that occur in order to better understand the manner with which Cronenberg uses scanning as a way of problematizing the Cartesian subject. While we see Vale using his scanning ability to induce a seizure in a woman in response to her insults – this act functioning as our introduction to his character – it is not until we first see Revok in action that the true maleficence of the scanning ability is made clear. This show of power occurs at a Consec-sponsored event, designed to demonstrate the potential of scanning as a surveillance tool. Consec's own Scanner (Louis del Grande) calls for a volunteer from the audience, reminding those gathered that the

> . . . scanning experience is usually a painful one, sometimes resulting in nosebleeds, earaches, stomach cramps, nausea. Sometimes other symptoms of a similar nature. (Cronenberg, 1981)

Revok volunteers and immediately responds to the Consec operative's tentative scan with one of his own. As with *The Dead Zone*,[5] the business of representing psychic process can be reduced to a series of grimaces, flinches and other symptoms of distress, but where *Scanners* distinguishes itself is with what occurs next as the film's special effects centrepiece: in direct response to the power of Revok's ability, the Consec Scanner's head literally explodes.

This moment forcefully demonstrates Ruth's point about the physiological nature of scanning, and demonstrates also the possibility for some kind of scanning feedback where Revok's scan (and, one presumes, some aspect of Revok himself) intrudes into the body of the Scanner. This process is explained later in the film as Vale undergoes training with Dr Ruth and Yoga Master Dieter Tautz (Fred Doederlein) in the art of the controlled scan.

> Dr Ruth: Mr Tautz has kindly consented to be your psychic sparring partner. He has publicly demonstrated on many occasions that by the power of his will, he can control his heart rate, his alpha-wave rhythm, and many other supposedly uncontrollable functions of the human body. Are we ready? . . . If you would be kind enough to sit facing this gentleman here, I want you to slowly release your scan. Slowly, with focus. I want it to touch his heart but not his brain. You understand? Telepathy is not mind reading. It is the direct linking of nervous systems separated by space. I want you to make a link from your brain to his heart. I want your brain to make his heart beat fast. Now, if his heart beats too quickly then he will take over control of his heart and slow it down. Don't worry about it. All you have to do is make his heart beat fast. (Cronenberg, 1981)

With generic inevitability, the experiment goes awry, and Vale appears to revel a little too much in the power to so directly control another person's physiology. Nevertheless, the point is made that the Scanner is able to physiologically influence Scannees in a way that goes beyond just 'reading' their mind or 'seeing' their thoughts. The commingling of consciousnesses that seems to occur forms the part of a later sequence when Vale, having contacted the 'good' Scanners, takes part in a group scan. Encouraged by Kim, Vale joins the group. They begin psychically 'chanting':

> Scan together. Scan together and our minds will begin to flow into each other until they become one. One nervous system. One soul. One experience. Beautiful. Beautiful. And frightening. So frightening to lose yourself. So frightening to lose yourself. To lose your will . . . to the group will. To lose yourself to the group self . . . to the group self. (Cronenberg, 1981)

Given the aggressive vitality demonstrated by Revok, these 'good' Scanners appear to be a trifle listless, and it is unclear what the purpose of their group scan is, especially since they are surprised and swiftly decimated by Revok's agents. Nevertheless, their psychic chanting[6] does make clear that the group scan fosters a form of group consciousness, such that when they are surprised and attacked, the entire group appears to suffer the effects of one of its members being shot.[7]

Similar evidence of the permeable subjectivity offered by the scanning relationship occurs when Vale visits Scanner artist Ben Pierce (Robert Silverman). Pierce is a disturbed man who had previously been incarcerated for killing his family while still a child. Now, through his sculpting, Pierce has found a degree of peace and a way to afford the isolation that Scanners require to prevent their being overwhelmed by the internal voices they are subject to.[8] Pierce's sculptures provide further metaphoric evidence of the interconnected status of Scanners: his refuge in his workshop is an enormous hollow head that he sits inside, while one of his sculptures features a patient in a hospital bed who is linked to a series of sculpted figures by a number of bright red threads that run from the patient's skull outwards. However, it is what Vale says when attempting to discover Revok's whereabouts that demonstrates the film's awareness of subjective mutability and permeability that *Scanners* is working towards:

Vale: I've heard you know a man named Darryl Revok.
Pierce: Who are you? I was told you were coming to pay me a visit, Mr Vale.
Vale: How did you know that? Well . . .
Pierce: I have friends. I don't want them . . . but I have them.
Vale: Scanner friends?
Pierce: What do you mean by that?
Vale: I am one of you.
Pierce: You're one of me?
Vale: Yes. (Cronenberg, 1981)

Crucially Vale's dialogue hinges on the phrase 'I'm one of you', which can certainly be interpreted as meaning 'I'm a Scanner like you', but which, given the evidence the film is gathering regarding scanning as the basis of a group entity, can equally mean that Vale considers himself a part of, or an extension of, Pierce. This clue is not developed further, and its implications are left hanging, as with the group scan, until the film's conclusion, which similarly hinges on an ambiguity of dialogue and which sees a return to the ambivalent ending that appeared to be absent from *The Brood*.

The final scanning battle between Revok and Vale is, alongside the exploding head, one of the film's special-effects set pieces, and it is certainly spectacular. Over the course of the battle, both participants experience their veins distending, and Vale begins to bleed and has large pieces of flesh come away from his face before his eyes appear to burst; finally, he spontaneously ignites while offering his arms up in a Christlike gesture of sacrifice. Beard summarizes this concluding sequence by commenting that '. . . Vale survives by destroying Revok's mind and inhabiting his body' (Beard, 2001, 96). Yet this decisive reading can only be reached by ignoring the deliberate ambivalence in Revok/Vale's final words. As the battle ends with Vale on fire, we cut to Obrist looking for Vale; seeing a figure hunched behind a sofa, Obrist approaches only to discover that it is Revok. It is at this point that Revok/Vale speaks, in Vale's voice, 'Kim . . . it's me. Cameron. I'm here. We've won . . . we've won' (Cronenberg, 1981). For Beard, Vale's exclamation 'it's me . . . Cameron . . . I'm here' can only mean that the singular entity of Revok has been overwhelmed by Vale's psychic presence and Vale's identity now inhabits Revok's body. Thus Beard concludes that *Scanners*

> . . . explores the fear of the collapse of boundaries of mental and corporeal self-containment, and the fear (experienced in different ways by both the scanner and the scannee) of losing one's self, being engulfed, taken over. (Beard, 2001, 99)

However, this summary of the film's conclusion misses Cronenberg's suggestion that such a state of subjective permeability may be positive in the same way that the conclusion of *Shivers* could be considered positive. Vale's deliberately ambiguous dialogue works to keep Cronenberg's exploration of individual permeability alive, and it is telling that many commentators work against the film's own material to provide a narrative resolution that does not occur. Thus Vale's claim that 'I'm here' can be equally interpreted as 'I'm here *instead* of Revok', or 'I'm here *as well as* Revok'. In a similar vein, the phrase 'We've won' leaves open not only the question of who 'we' are, but what exactly it is that we've 'won'. A cursory glance at the plot would suggest that the only 'we' who stand to 'win' anything are Revok and Vale, who have demonstrated that a competent Scanner is not limited by the frailties of the flesh, meaning that Vale has martyred his body in order to demonstrate the ways in which Revok's emerging 'Scanner army' will no longer be bound by the old Cartesian models, allowing a new permeable subjectivity to emerge.

Scanning and Surveillance

As will be clear, scanning is a bodily process and is, more importantly, an articulation of power. Throughout *Scanners* we are given ample evidence of this power in action, and, indeed, the film may be thought of as an attempt to demonstrate how disciplinary structures may be thrown into disarray with the introduction of new forms of articulation beyond Consec's ability to comprehend or incorporate.[9] Similarly, while Vale is positioned by the narrative as the 'good' scanner, in moral opposition to Revok's 'bad' status, this too is problematized by the power scanning makes available. Consec's demonstration reveals their intention to utilize scanning as a surveillance technology. The consternation generated by Revok's show of strength makes clear how scanning is perceived by them, and that Scanners are viewed as a threat, even by their employers. Therefore, the demonstration at Consec reveals that the hegemonic structure represented by them (and, by extension, the other institutions represented by the demonstration's hand-picked audience) views scanning both as a disciplinary tool and as the means to shift a balance of power by extending this corporation's ability to see – to perceive industrial or economic threat (although this is never actually explored in the film) and to act accordingly. How wrong they are is demonstrated by the fact that their show goes so spectacularly badly. Consec are applying an old disciplinary model to what is effectively a new technology, regardless of the fact that it is organic and evolutionary. Scanning, Consec believes, is a type of sight or hearing, a model that preserves the individuality of the one seeing or hearing. That the Scanner's head explodes demonstrates the possibility for feedback, meaning that the scan event runs both ways. That the Scanner becomes visible through the act of scanning can only lead us to conclude that scanning could never have worked effectively as a standard surveillance technique since it opens the way to being seen scanning.

The model of surveillance Consec adheres to is one that finds its origin in the Panoptic structure: the Scanner, for them, represents the invisible guard in the watchtower (Foucault, 1995, 200). At first glance, Revok's assault would appear to represent a fracture in the disciplinary mechanism represented by the Panopticon, wherein the efficacy of the hitherto invisible watcher is disrupted by the addition of another watcher, who is not so much involved in watching the watcher as she/he is in watching back. Foucault does touch on this when, in conversation, he comments that a panoptic structure of surveillance is '. . . a machine in which everyone is caught, those who exercise power just as much as those over whom it is exercised' (Foucault, 1980, 156). Yet the disruption represented by the new technology of scanning does more than simply construct '. . . an unbroken succession of observations recalling the motto: each comrade becomes an overseer' (Foucault, 1980, 157). The Scanner does not sur-veil the watcher in order to enforce productivity, efficiency or correct behaviour: here the Scanner is, potentially at least, in opposition to the power that surveils, and she/he disrupts the exercise of that power with the imposition of his/her own. This is rendered possible by the fact that scanning penetrates the body, whereas the panoptic model involves the play of the gaze (or its surrogates) across surfaces. The historically sur-veilling eye may see, or the ear hear, but neither of them presume to know the interior life of the subjects they patrol, though Foucault's point is that such an 'inner life' is brought self-consciously into control by the productive operation of surveillance itself. Even the invasive medical gaze (such as is represented in *The Brood* and, particularly, *Dead Ringers*) cannot provide the degree of intimacy that the Scanner achieves through the act of scanning. Thus by structuring and representing scanning as a kind of multivalent 'inhabiting' extended to incorporate all of the body's senses, the full intimacy of scanning can be suggested. *Scanners* therefore supplants the old technology of surveillance by taking the panoptic dis-course to its logical conclusion: if the model of the panopticon provides a particular kind of insight into the subjects it watches and controls, what aspects of their lives go unseen? This is the territory made available to the scanning individual. As Foucault eloquently explains, Bentham's panop-ticon sought to literally and figuratively attend

> [to] the fear of darkened spaces, of the pall of gloom which prevents the full visibility of things, men and truths. It sought to break up the patches of darkness that blocked the light, eliminate the shadowy areas of society, demolish the unlit chambers where arbitrary political acts, monarchical caprice, ... epidemics and the illusions of ignorance were fomented. (Foucault, 1980, 153)

By identifying those citizens who could potentially pose a threat, and by individuating them with a series of disciplinary discourses, those truculent groups could be splintered, held apart and thus divested of their power (to harm, to influence, to cause upset or unrest). However, the Scanner provides a means to evade this mechanism, as his or her physical location matters less than the ability to permeate other's bodies, thereby generat-ing a means of resistance founded on the fact that an old surveillance technology cannot arrest a new articulation of power. This is certainly not to say that Scanners could not constitute a new surveillance regime, or that the new penetrative gaze of scanning could not be incorporated into a new hegemonic structure; indeed, what Foucault suggests is that this incorporation is inevitable. This incorporation would not, however, be a recuperation of scanning by the existing power structure. As Foucault notes, the effects of power generate resistances that result not in a re-establishing of old orders, but in the evolution of new ones (Foucault, 1980, 56–8). The key then lies in the fact that scanning and Scanners would have to be incorporated into a *new* hegemonic structure; one that recognized and exploited the permeability of the body the Scanners represent and provide access to.

What remains of interest is the manner in which what *should* function as a liberatory experience – the ability to evade the panopticon by permeating corporeal boundaries – quickly becomes repressive, and the film's movement from the slightly facile (and possibly parodic) group scan to the scanning battle, with the various aggressive uses of scanning along the way, should leave us in no doubt as to Cronenberg's vision of the fate of scanning. Scanning opens the body up in a new and unique way, ensuring that whatever darkened corners of the psyche remained hidden from Bentham's gaze are revealed to Revok's and Vale's. Vale's specific trajectory throughout this narrative highlights the ambivalent articulation of power through the individual who emerges as an effect of its articulation, and Cronenberg's decision to play on Vale's ambiguous dialogue (as evidenced above) further demonstrates this. While Vale is positioned as the film's ostensible 'hero', there are moments when it is clear that his newly emerging control over his scanning ability is a temptation (although for what is unclear). Our first introduction to Vale, as a derelict not above using his nascent powers to punish disapproving onlookers, demonstrates that he is not as clear-cut a hero as the genre would ordinarily demand. Similarly the manner with which he manipulates his Yoga Master's heart during training (it is worth noting that it is never clear whether the man recovers or dies)[10] demonstrates that there is some degree of pleasure to be had both in controlling one's scan and in controlling another person by scanning. In the same fashion, the film's ambiguous ending – where it is unclear who inhabits Revok's body and what precisely it is they have (or he has) won – works to elaborate Foucault's point that '. . . individuals are the vehicles of power, not its points of application' (Foucault, 1980, 98). Power moves through Vale and Revok, and issues of their respective 'goodness' or 'badness' are, it appears to me, less important to Cronenberg than the fact that a new form of power demands the establishment of new hegemonic structures into which this power can be productively inserted. As Foucault makes clear, '[w]e are the very *material* of power, the thing through which it finds its expression' (Mansfield, 2000, 55; italics in original), and to consider Vale 'good' is merely to locate him (as the narrative does not) in a hegemonically orchestrated moral structure. The fact remains that Vale, throughout the film, is a cipher,[11] as capable of enjoying the effects of the power he has access to as Revok (the film's ostensible 'bad guy'). This, then, may be the film's final heretical point: that the articulation of power through individuals is ambivalent (insofar as power is amoral) and that the niceties of 'goodness' and 'badness', both as generic requirements and as ways of negotiating the pro-filmic world, are up for grabs.

Naked Lunch

Naked Lunch is Cronenberg's adaptation of William Burroughs' novel of the same name, although, to be fair, the film seeks to explore the writing of the book more than it attempts to simply reproduce the book's content. This is an entirely pragmatic decision; *Naked Lunch* is, as both Cronenberg and Burroughs attest, practically unfilmable.[12] Instead, what emerges is a fusion of both artists' sensibilities, and Cronenberg has often commented that this act of fusing through the process of interpreting a literary work for the screen produces a text that neither artist would be capable of alone. Thus, just as *Crash* emerges as the product of a hybrid 'Cronen-Ballard', *Naked Lunch* should, we are told, be considered the work of 'Cronen-Burroughs'.[13] Because of this, the congruence between the two men's work is highlighted in this fusion, as Cronenberg utilizes Burroughs' original concepts as a means to further explore his own fascinations, exactly as would occur with the later filming of *Crash*.

What we have seen emerge with the films thus far discussed in this chapter are ways in which, first, their narratives contain a thorough exploration of disciplinary discourses as highlighted by events and characters and, second, the manner with which alterations or extensions of those discourses will fundamentally affect the ways in which the individuals concerned are articulated within the text. *Naked Lunch* continues this trend, with the fundamental difference being that, for the first time, the processes of disciplinary and discursive articulation become the narrative's central concern rather than emerge as effects of the narrative. Thus *Naked Lunch* demonstrates attempts by the film's protagonist, Bill Lee, to take control of the production and articulation of those discourses that have the greatest disciplinary effect on his life and that limit and render illegal or immoral his activities as a writer, an addict and a homosexual. This shift in power would both explain the events that have happened to him and provide him with a means to make sense of his world. In this Lee is no different to any other subject of discipline, except for the fact that the discourses he sets about producing are required to make sense of random, meaningless or unpredictable events and, therefore, come to reflect and justify this irrationality. Rationality, in this sense, emerges as a result of one's compliance with, or adherence to, the hegemonic discourses that surround one. Lee, in accordance with Burroughs' dictates, 'exterminates all rational thought' and yet, equally, appears to seek recuperation from his position of extremity and isolation. This, then, necessitates the development of alternative discourses that enforce his productive reentry into the hegemony he has strayed from.

Thematic Accretion

As noted above, Cronenberg's film brings some narrative cohesion to Burroughs' novel, primarily by introducing biographical elements and pieces from other Burroughs texts. That said, *Naked Lunch* remains a film for which a linear plot is not a major requirement, concerned as it is with exploring what is a series of conflicting and conflicted hallucinatory states, real-life events and interwoven diegetic spaces. Therefore, despite the fact that the 'narrative' of *Naked Lunch* can be, somewhat tortuously, summarized, it might be more efficient to examine the narrative elements that combine to form the film. Clearly the film's characters are vital, with Bill Lee (Peter Weller) acting as a stand-in for Burroughs,[14] Joan Lee (Judy Davis) for Joan Vollmer (Burroughs' wife), Hank (Nicholas Campbell) and Martin (Michael Zelniker) for Jack Kerouac and Allan Ginsberg, Tom (Ian Holm) and Joan Frost (Judy Davis) for Paul and Jane Bowles, and so on. However it would be a mistake to decode the film as a veiled biopic – this was never Cronenberg's intention. Instead, the characters move in and out of the film's various diegetic spaces and are utilized in order to show Lee's movement through his hallucinatory states without necessarily providing any degree of diegetic certainty. A similar device is utilized in *eXistenZ*, where characters appear according to which game level they occupy, but without ever providing any degree of diegetic certainty.

To this end, Lee's movement through the diegetic spaces in *Naked Lunch* – which may or may not be hallucinatory constructions – can be read as representing his movement into and out of a state of crisis both triggered and solved by the accidental shooting of his wife.[15] The initial events of the film occur in New York in the 1950s. After the death of Joan, Lee escapes to 'Interzone', '. . . a notorious free port on the North African coast, a haven for the mongrel scum of the Earth . . . an engorged parasite on the underbelly of the West' (Cronenberg, 1991). Most of the film appears to take place in Interzone until the conclusion, when Lee and Joan Frost escape to Annexia. Just as Joan Lee's death prompts Bill's move to Interzone, Joan Frost's death signals the move from it and to Annexia. While in Interzone, occasional glimpses of an obviously Arabic diegesis can be seen through windows and balconies, but these are problematized as some of the windows in Interzone open onto views of New York skylines and spaces. Similarly, Hank and Martin – who are associated with the New York section of the film – visit Bill while in exile in Interzone, arriving and leaving this 'North African' port by bus and assisting Bill in the collection of reports and documents that will eventually become the diegetic book 'Naked Lunch'.[16] The film takes great care never to definitively locate Bill, preferring to focus instead on the way in which his internal condition bleeds through into his experience of the external world. This, too, forms part of the film's attempt to represent the manner with which our experience of the specific disciplinary discourses we are subject to affect the construction of the experiential reality that surrounds us. The primary disciplinary discourses at work in *Naked Lunch* concern Lee's status as an addict, a homosexual and a murderer, and it should therefore come as no surprise that each of the discursive sources he invents (the Clark Nova, the Mugwumps, the Mugwriter, and so on) work to provide alternative rationalizations for his placement within those subject positions.

Thus the narrative in *Naked Lunch* is never meant to be interpreted literally, and while the film never pretends to provide us with Lee's subjective experience, Cronenberg, as he has often done before, utilizes cinematic form in order to demonstrate how the protagonist's experience of the world he inhabits will necessarily impact on that world's construction. Because Lee's experience is so decisively affected by his addiction and by the death of Joan, it is inevitable that the world he experiences will lack the cohesion and linearity of a more normal (or normative) experience. In this manner, exactly as with a number of his other films – *The Dead Zone, Spider* and *eXistenZ*, for example – the film does not seek to represent the protagonist's experience but seeks to provide a spectatorial situation that locates our gaze with his. This process of locating the spectator within the same position as the protagonist with regards to diegetic experience and gradually accumulating diegetic knowledge renders this type of cinematic gaze perverse, as per Žižek's original schema. However, *Naked Lunch* works to complicate this further by aligning the spectator-rendered-perverse with the narrative, which is itself concerned with the recuperation of the (more ordinarily) perverse protagonist. It is in this interplay of perversities – the commonplace perversity within the narrative (Bill's homosexuality and addiction) with the spectatorial perversity of the audience – that *Naked Lunch* works to explore its heretical terrain.

Bugpowder Dust and Mugwump Jism

Perhaps more than any other Cronenberg film, *Naked Lunch* is a collection of metaphors, with nearly every character, object or piece of dialogue standing in for something else. The film itself provides a startling piece of meta-commentary that very clearly demonstrates this doubled relationship between the signs that *Naked Lunch* employs and their various referents. As Tom and Bill are walking through Interzone's Medina, on their way to a party, they begin to talk about Joan – both Joan Frost and Joan Lee (who are, of course, both played by Judy Davis):

Tom: They say you murdered your wife. Is that true?
Bill: Who told you that?
Tom: Word gets around.
Bill: It wasn't murder. It was an accident.
Tom: There are no accidents. For example . . . I've been killing my own wife slowly, over a period of years.
Bill: What?
Tom: Well, not intentionally. I mean, on the level of conscious intention, it's insane, monstrous.
Bill: But you do consciously know it. You just said it. We're discussing it.
Tom: Not consciously. This is all happening . . . telepathically. Nonconsciously.
Bill: What do you mean?
Tom: If you look carefully at my lips . . . you'll realize that I'm actually saying something else. I'm not actually telling you about the several ways I'm gradually murdering Joan, about the housekeeper Fadela, whom I've hired to make Joan deathly ill by witchcraft . . . about the medicines and drugs I've given her . . . about the constant nibbling

away at her self-esteem and sanity . . . that I've managed without being at all obvious about it. (Cronenberg, 1991)

In order to make perfectly clear the import of Tom's dialogue, at the moment when he asks Bill to look at his lips, the film's sound goes entirely out of sync so that the dialogue we hear (as written above) is plainly not what Tom appears to be saying at this point. After the phrase '. . . without being obvious about it' the sound and action sync back to continue a half-sentence about a much more innocuous topic, much to Bill's bemusement. However Cronenberg's intention is clear: as he notes on the DVD's commentary, 'Many things are understood that are never said' (Cronenberg, 1991, director's commentary). Tom is, so far as Lee is aware, involved in the exercise of power over Joan's life, and while we can never be sure if he is saying what Lee hears, our experience of Tom (which comes to us through Lee) is that of a man concerned with the movement of power through his world. Therefore we are told, in no uncertain terms, that this film is concerned with discourse, especially the disciplinary aspects of discourse. What is said and what is not, what is unsaid but effective nevertheless and, particularly, how to give voice to that which is never said are all issues at the heart of the film's narrative and Lee's struggle to understand both himself and the events that seem to occur around him. Here, in a film about creativity, what one writes fundamentally affects experiential reality; thus, the notion of discourse spills over its own boundaries, meaning that Tom's spoken discourse about Joan literalizes his exercise of power over her.

Central to Lee's struggle to understand is the concept of addiction. Addiction and the 'junk world' in which it occurs are, in Burroughs' texts, 'the image of the real world as a structure of addictions and controls' (Mottram, 1977, 34), for addiction is the abdication of control and the ceding of power from the 'mark' (the addict or target) to whatever the mark is addicted to and, necessarily, whoever it is that supplies the addict. Given Burroughs' biography, it is no surprise that drugs are central to *Naked Lunch*, but, in what Burroughs considers a stroke of genius (Burroughs, 1992), Cronenberg replaced Burroughs' references to the actual drugs of his addictions with new objects of addiction; hence the Bug Powder, the Black Meat and, finally, the hyper-addictive Mugwump jism that is Benway's masterstroke. Of course, none of these compounds exist outside the film, and their fictionality deliberately circumvents any mistaking of the film's intentions: *Naked Lunch* is never interested in discussing the process of addiction to a real drug, and the use of actual drug references in the text would distract from this aspect of the film's purpose. Instead *Naked Lunch* is vitally concerned with the movement of power that comes with addiction and uses the diegetic drugs as a means of forcing attention *into* the narrative (better considered as a network of discursive formations/articulations than a standard causal chain), rather than away from it and onto some other 'real world' concern. Thus while in *Naked Lunch* addiction is real and is treated as such, the interchange-ability of the various compounds Lee is addicted to stands in for a raft of other issues.

Issues of addiction very quickly lead us to consider issues of power and the ways in which these issues circulate through *Naked Lunch* as various discourses that seek to limit or permit some activities rather than others, some behaviours rather than others. Addiction is the film's primary disciplinary discourse, and its various permutations run through the film, are filtered through, and understood as, addictive experiences. Indeed, one of the ways in which this film is so effective as a commentary (and, indeed, meta-commentary) is that it examines how single discursive threads become, as it were, bundled – how discourses of addiction spill across into considerations of sexual behaviour and sexual identification, for example. Indeed, the permeability of disciplinary discourse seems to be one of the lessons Lee attempts to learn over the course of the narrative, and this is played out with the importance of the 'William Tell routine' and its relationship to his writing.

Discipline and Control

The activity of the addict, like that of the subject within hegemony, reveals a similar orchestrated 'handing over' of power: thus those institutions in *Naked Lunch* that administer addiction can be considered as analogies for the hegemonic conduits of discourse that Cronenberg has long been interested in highlighting. Lee's response, however, to the discourses of control and manipulation that are bundled within the master discourse of addiction is an attempt to both rationalize his position from within his addiction and wrest control of these discourses in order to gain some power of his own. The fact that, as the narrative demonstrates, this is not successful should come as no surprise, for the Cronenbergian protagonist is constantly thwarted by the machinations of disciplinary discourse. Nevertheless, Lee's attempt to discover the source of these discourses provides an interesting example of the kinds of rationalization that might occur from within the site of discipline.

Lee is forced by events to come up with some rationalization for the death of Joan, and this moment, when combined with the fact of his addiction, generates the Interzone conspiracy he spends much of the film unravelling. Here the film wrestles with a moment from Burroughs' own biography and with his realization that if it were not for the accidental death of his wife, Burroughs' might never have become a writer. This event is central to the film, as it marks Lee's entry into, and exit from, Interzone, which can be considered as a liminal space, or a point of transition from one state of being to the next; here Interzone serves as the territory Burroughs (fictionalized as Lee) must pass through on his way to self-recognition as an artist. However, prior to this moment (which in the film occurs at the conclusion with Lee's passage to Annexia) Joan's death makes no sense; it occurs as a random act. For Lee to resolve this event, he must come to understand it, and it is here that the Interzone conspiracy, with its issues of control, comes into play. However ludicrous Interzone might seem to those outside it (and we are given some sense of this with the figures of Hank and Martin, who 'visit' Lee in Interzone to assist him in assembling 'Naked Lunch'), it has an internally consistent logic, and it is this that permits Lee to find his way towards resolution.

Lee's first move in this attempt to rationalize his addiction, and subsequently Joan's death and his movement towards a career as an author, comes with the intervention of the insect controller that informs him of his status as an undercover operative. Crucially the insect 'speaks' from a large animated anus that sits between its wings and it is from this orifice that all of Lee's 'unspeakable' truths emerge. The insect's first order is to call for the death of Joan Lee. Later, once in Interzone, the insect controller – which has now taken the form of the part-insect / part-typewriter Clark Nova – tells Lee that the death of Joan was not his fault. As it says, 'I've been instructed to reveal to you that you were programmed to shoot your wife, Joan Lee. It was not an act of free will on your part' (Cronenberg, 1991). Thus the act is made bearable with the removal of Lee's control, and in this way blame for the act can be seen to lie elsewhere. Indeed, the Clark Nova's central purpose (aside from the requirements of the narrative) seems to be to say what Lee needs to hear, in order to make some semblance of sense from his life. This is vital, as those events that require rationalizing are those that contravene 'normal' disciplinary structures. Of course, first of these is Joan's death, and we have seen that the Clark Nova removes Lee's responsibility from this event. But this is not the only disciplinary transgression that Lee must come to terms with; his addiction and his emerging homosexuality similarly must be explained in such a way as to both make sense of events and provide Lee with a way

of reclaiming control over his own articulation rather than merely acqui-
escing to a higher power. After all, if Lee is simply following orders, then
he cannot be held responsible for the acts that are so demonstrably
transgressive.

Lee's emerging homosexuality is likewise explained away in a session
with the Clark Nova, where Lee is asked to type the following sentence
into a report to 'Control' about his activities in Interzone:

> 'Homosexuality is the best, all-around cover an agent ever had'. . . .
> These are words to live by, Bill. . . . I'm glad these words are going into
> your report. Our new management will be so pleased. We appreciate
> that you might find the thought of engaging in . . . homosexual acts
> morally and, ah, possibly even . . . physically repulsive . . . and, ah, we
> are encouraged . . . that you are able to overcome these personal, ah,
> barriers . . . to better serve the cause to which we are all so devoted.
> (Cronenberg, 1991)

Thus Lee's homosexuality becomes a cover, a way of better serving the
(always and necessarily unspecified) cause, which means that Lee is not
responsible for his actions and therefore cannot be held accountable.
This behaviour, which would have previously marked him as an aberrant
individual, here serves two functions: it is utilized to mark his dedication
to the controlling discourses he believes he is subject to; and further, the
act is removed from his conscious control, meaning that he is successfully absolved of any guilt he might suffer as a result of his actions. The
Clark Nova functions then as a device that permits Lee to project outward
an increasingly complicated rationale for his actions, precisely so that he
can receive back what he needs to hear in order to resolve his situation.
Although, at a naïve level, Lee is simply talking to himself, these utter-
ances need to be passed through some kind of disciplinary authority
(the Clark Nova is a conduit for an unnamed organization called 'Control') in order to carry any power. It is telling that the invention of the
Clark Nova (and its substitutes) occurs in order to provide Lee with the
means to gain some measure of control over the discourses he is subject
to. In the light of this discussion, Cronenberg's intention is clear: whatever discursive or disciplinary control one gains is phantasmatic, more
an effect of fictional narrative than an actual possibility. Real control and
real authority lie beyond the purview of the individual.

With Lee's movement through the narrative we see an example of the
Cronenbergian protagonist attempting to comprehend the disciplinary

discourses that seem unfathomable in their movements; thus Lee joins such figures as Johnny Smith from *The Dead Zone* and Dennis Cleg from *Spider* as a man searching for the means to explain his position and current state. Lee's actions, however, demonstrate that *Naked Lunch* functions as a shadow text to *M. Butterfly*, with its focus on the irrational continuation of disciplinary discourses beyond their point of logical extension. Gallimard's absolute adherence to the requirements of heterosexuality makes him blind to the fact that this disciplinary structure hinges on performance, and it is through this that he can successfully disavow Song's sex in favour of a literal reading of her performance of gender. Similarly Lee places absolute faith in the sources of disciplinary discourse, so much so that despite his contravention of them (as a murderer/addict/homosexual), he constructs new discursive sources that provide retrospective justification for his actions.

This movement through a variety of disciplinary discourses, which incorporates the invention of non-human sources to dispense these discourses, sees Lee move into, and then out of, Interzone. As noted, Interzone is a liminal space Lee passes through on his way towards Annexia – which is to be understood as the gateway to his artistic practice. As Lee moves through Interzone, the sources of disciplinary discourse shift and alter to reflect this movement. Thus the Clark Nova which he brings with him to Interzone is eventually damaged and destroyed and must be replaced with a new writing machine, the 'Mugwriter', which is effectively the head of a Mugwump with a typewriter keyboard in its mouth and which, as Lee comments, 'conveniently dispenses two types of intoxicating fluids when it likes what you've written' (Cronenberg, 1991). The destruction of the Clark Nova sends Lee out of control, and it is his young partner, Kiki (Joseph Scorsiani), who arranges for the creation of the 'Mugwriter', commenting that '[i]f we fix the typing machine, we also fix the life' (Cronenberg, 1991). From this moment, Lee's acknowledgement of his status as a writer seems to come more easily, and the movement out of Interzone and into Annexia begins.

Annexia

In an interview with David Schwartz, Cronenberg makes the point that the conclusion of *Naked Lunch*, with Lee's painful entry into Annexia, is to be understood as the movement of an artist into exile. Further to this, '. . . Annexia is Canada, of course . . .' (Cronenberg & Schwartz, 1992), which means that Annexia/Canada is a place of exile, a place of ambivalence and of definition through opposition. Thus the issue is raised, once again, of the place and status of the artist within a larger industrial structure, with the Annexia/Interzone opposition standing in for a Canada/America relationship. Lee must give up a great deal in order to be permitted entry to Annexia, and the mark of this comes with his having to shoot Joan again to prove to the Border Guards that he is a writer. Here, Cronenberg is negotiating this pivotal moment in Burroughs' own biography and utilizing it as a way of discussing what Lee must sacrifice in order to become a writer. This functions as a way of acknowledging Joan's death as the event that propels him forward from Interzone exactly as it propelled him into it.

While Cronenberg's comment about the Canadian nature of Annexia would tend to suggest a more autobiographical reading of the film than I am attempting, it is clear that the movement of the artist between these two very different disciplinary spaces (Interzone/America and Annexia/Canada) requires negotiation and sacrifice on both sides. The artist, I would suggest, goes into exile because of a failure of his or her homeland to comprehend the artist's work. Lee leaves New York, moves to Interzone (which may, actually, still be New York) and, from there, to Annexia. Burroughs leaves America only, eventually, to return to its very heartland, while Cronenberg famously resists every opportunity to film outside Canada unless absolutely necessary. What we find ourselves considering here is the status of the exile-at-home, the artist who is a stranger in his or her own land and whose art therefore functions as a dissenting voice from within the disciplinary structures that consistently fail, or only belatedly come, to recognize the artist's work. At a crucial moment in *Naked Lunch* Lee is told by his dying Clark Nova that

> [a]ll agents defect and all resisters sell out. That's the sad truth, Bill. And a writer – a writer lives the sad truth like everyone else. The only difference is he files a report on it. (Cronenberg, 1991)

Lee, like Gallimard, discovers the ambivalence of those disciplinary discourses they seek so vehemently to adhere to. That ambivalence is exposed when excessive compliance itself becomes heretical and demonstrates that Lee must take it upon himself to construct the means back into the hegemonic system that, in effect, leaves him without a place within it once he has violated (by exceeding) its demands. This is what makes the conclusion of *Naked Lunch* deeply affecting: the figure of the writer-as-resister begins as one whose actions define his exile, and eventually these same actions come to define his recuperation. Thus the accidental death of Joan forces Lee to flee New York for Interzone, and it is Lee's replaying of this act with the death of Joan Frost that promotes his entry into Annexia; both Joans must die for Lee's survival, and their deaths produce Lee as a writer. Exactly as the Clark Nova explains, the artist (represented by Lee) survives by turning his resistance into art (which, if one is slightly more cynically minded, can be considered a product), while that art, through being consumed, is defused in its ability to resist. This point about the trajectory from resistance to recuperation marks the distance Lee travels: his invention of a resistant discourse while in Interzone, represented by the dialogue that issues forth from the anuses of the various insects and writing machines he uses, serves the function of moving him from his state of absolute transgression to one where he is better able to integrate these aspects of his self into a coherent and functioning whole.

The insect, for Cronenberg, is the exemplar of an alien discourse; that is to say, a discourse that is so dissimilar to the hegemonic (hence rational) norm as to appear alien. As we saw with Seth Brundle, the 'politics of insects' is an acknowledgement both of disciplinary difference and of the possibility for hegemonic structures that are unrecognizable in their difference from the (human) norm. That the typewriter insects, the 'Bug Writers', are the ones to dispense and administer the disciplinary discourses is, therefore, vital. Each device represents a new source of discipline, and each works to adjust Lee's experience of his world, incorporating his various disciplinary failings (as addict, homosexual and murderer) into a structure that, as noted above, removes his conscious control from, and absolves him of guilt for, his transgression.

Chapter 6

'All Agents Defect . . .'

Can We Call for Meta-Heresy?

As should now be clear, throughout this volume I have sought to utilize Žižek's injunction about heresy as a means of exploring Cronenberg's cinematic activities. In each case, the actions of the heretic, in taking too seriously a specific disciplinary injunction, reveal the manner in which that demand functions ordinarily (and invisibly), rendering it visible by pushing it to its illogical extreme. The heretical action, specifically Cronenberg's heretical action, is therefore always political insofar as it aims to expose some form of disciplinary structure and, particularly, as it explores the ways in which power – the force utilized, preserved and expressed by the actions of any disciplinary structure – operates on the individuals who are subject to it. However there is a danger in overlooking the recuperative actions of the hegemony whose disciplinary structures are highlighted by this heretical activity. One possible outcome for Cronenberg's work, should it be recuperated, is for it to become what Terry Eagleton refers to as '. . . a *licensed* affair in every sense, a permissible rupture of hegemony, a contained popular blow-off' of potentially disruptive energies, ideas and concepts (Eagleton, quoted in Stallybrass and White, 1986, 13). Thus the central concern for this chapter is to examine the manner in which Cronenberg works to avoid this possible outcome, by meeting and adjusting to the shifting demands placed on him and his work by the same disciplinary structures that are rendered visible by his films.

While the specific disciplinary structures under examination alter, shift and change over the course of Cronenberg's career, the pool of concepts he is interested in exploring is coherent enough to support such authorial claims as have been made about his work. This means that while a teleological argument is avoided (by this author at least), authorial consistency between films allows one to explore their relationships to the shifting disciplinary contexts that surround them. These claims are based on three constants within Cronenberg's work. The first of these is a continued attempt to explore the possibilities for signification and meaningfulness outside the various structures that govern and control meaning. This is the impulse that finds expression in the ways his films push the limits of intelligibility into whatever possibilities for signification exist at these limits and beyond. This movement, identified as the push towards the establishment of a 'politics of insects', necessarily extends representational possibilities to their breaking point, beyond which, as noted in the first chapter, we pass from the signification of the human and into the alterant signification of the insect. As we have seen, Cronenberg's films are filled with moments at which the normal (which is to say normative) structures that govern the text, its content and the ways in which an audience might encounter and respond to it are subverted or disrupted. Throughout his career, then, Cronenberg suggests that experience can and does occur beyond the realm of the human, and his films can be seen not so much as attempts to report that experience – which, given his terms of reference, would be impossible and which is why so many of his films end as they do – but to indicate that the signification of the human (and, hence, the politics of the human) is merely one set of signifying/meaningful/disciplinary/ideological structures among a near-infinity of possibilities.

The second constant, which necessarily follows from the first, is Cronenberg's continued exploration of the relationship of film form to meaning and the ways in which the manipulation of a film's form will fundamentally affect the manner with which an audience will encounter, and make meaning of, the film's content. As we have seen, conventional interpretive strategies are often rerouted through the use of what might be best classed as 'aberrant form', formal techniques that either do not 'conventionally' fit, or on occasion exceed, the demands of the scene in which they occur and the narrative they would ordinarily, and invisibly, deliver. These events are entirely deliberate and equally political, for their use – and their effect – serves to draw attention not only to the specific instance of their occurrence (in the moment of de-suturing that occurs) but also to the interpretive devices of film form themselves. Thus the group of self-effacing formal techniques designed to act invisibly in the service of a narrative and its content are suddenly revealed in operation through moments when 'aberrant' techniques reveal the artifice in play. In turn the third constant involves the utilization of the diegesis and those who populate it as experimental subjects seeking to continually reinvent themselves in response to a variety of external forces. On most occasions, this reinvention leads either to the direct dissolution of the individual or individuals (as, e.g., in *The Fly*, *The Dead Zone*, *Rabid*, *M. Butterfly*, *Dead Ringers*, et al.) or to some other alteration of their being (as in *Shivers*, *Spider*, *Naked Lunch*, *Crash*, *eXistenZ*). In this fashion the films themselves explore, within their narratives (and, increasingly, *as* their narratives) the possibilities for change and alteration of the human subject either within, or in resistance to, the many varied disciplinary structures that regulate their lives.

These points, discussed in relation to the films thus far examined, demonstrate that Cronenberg is interested in exploring both the possibilities for new expression (however it might be articulated) and the limits to those possibilities. As a consequence, it is perhaps time to return to one of the first comments made about Cronenberg in this discussion and re-examine it in light of the territory covered. As has so often been noted, Cronenberg is fond of commenting that 'his project' is to '. . . show the unshowable, speak the unspeakable' (Rodley, 1997, xvi), and those commentaries that utilize this comment as a starting point (this document included) proceed on the understanding that to 'show the unshowable' and 'speak the unspeakable' mean to show and speak what *should not* be shown or spoken. Certainly Cronenberg's career is full of examples in which this occurs, films that contain material that extends their genre (for as long as he adheres to genre) or that brush up against, push through or overwhelm censorial restrictions and social mores. Equally certain is the effect that these moments have on the industry that must cope with them, the various civil authorities that oversee the distribution of them and the audiences that encounter and interpret them. The two most famous examples would be the Canadian parliamentary controversy that erupted over the tax-shelter funding of *Shivers* and, some time later, the cross-Atlantic furore that has become known as 'the Crash Controversy'.[1]

However, let us, as Žižek suggests, take Cronenberg's own statement and extend it to its limits. What if the drive to 'show the unshowable, speak the unspeakable' leads us not to what *should* not be shown, but what *can* not be shown? What does this mean for the films as discussed, and for those films – *Videodrome* (1983), *A History of Violence* (2005) and *Eastern Promises* (2007) – still to be discussed? With this in mind, Brundle's statements at the beginning of the exploration take on a new resonance. Now the politics of insects, which I suggested represented an attempt to explore and occupy new forms of discourse, falls into line with an attempt to speak the unspeakable in those instances where the unspeakable is framed off and hence constituted by varieties of discourse that lie beyond our ability to comprehend them. Žižek has written extensively on these facets of filmic discourse, and I draw particularly on his notions of the (Lacanian) Real and the pre-ontological in order to discuss the fate of the (Cronenbergian) flesh. However, before we turn to the very limits of representation, interpretation and intelligibility, it is important to consider the trajectory of perversion represented by Cronenberg's cinema. Of course, Cronenberg produces a cinema of perversion; indeed, it appears as though this has been part of his intention all along. The key is to examine exactly how that cinema is perverted and to what end he uses it, for its use is as politically motivated as are all of the discipline-revealing techniques I have thus far outlined. Further to this, when we examine the shift in perverse articulation that occurs between *Videodrome* and *A History of Violence*, and the subsequent alteration in practice and focus evident when we compare *A History of Violence* and *Eastern Promises*, what emerges is a trajectory of perversion – the mapping of which will provide us with the means to consider our final point: David Cronenberg as Agent.

Videodrome

The heretical content of *Videodrome* is writ large in its narrative and functions, in the first instance, as a very precise extension of a specific disciplinary structure: the discourse of censorship. As should already be clear, Cronenberg is no stranger to censorial pressure and controversy. From his first commercial feature, *Shivers*, he has attracted the attention of a variety of censorial factions, and in each instance, he has responded with works designed to slip underneath the screens of censorship while at the same time making his own political views perfectly visible. *Videodrome*, however, holds a special place in the Cronenberg canon. Not only, as I will argue, is the political content brought forward to function as the film's primary narrative motivation, but it is generally viewed as the quintessential Cronenbergian text, containing all the features that have become a recognizable part of the Cronenberg textual universe as well as pointing forward to his less generically located films. Thus in *Videodrome* we encounter a protagonist subject to forces beyond his control, a factor Cronenberg had been utilizing since *Shivers*. Here, as in *Shivers* and subsequent films, the powerless protagonist serves as a foil to the overly able and proactive protagonists of standard Western narratives and functions to generate discussion about the subject-of-discipline, rather than the mythical (even if spectatorially empowering) subject-as-arbiter-of-discipline. In recognizing that contemporary Western cinema is involved in a specific ideological and disciplinary exercise, Cronenberg's refusal to provide the latter kind of protagonist in any of his films points to the disciplinary function of this protagonist in a more 'conventional' text. Thus, in direct comparison to *Videodrome*, the resolution that restores the order of the conventional protagonist's world, and which is brought about by the exercise of power over the protagonist's own circumstances, provides a pleasure that blinds the audience to the manner with which it has been ideologically positioned by the disciplinary activity of the cinematic apparatus.

Similarly, the mutable flesh with all of its concomitant implications is very present in *Videodrome*. Here, the bodily alteration that Max undergoes as part of his exposure to the Videodrome signal involves the development of a highly sexualized slit in his abdomen which, while lacking the clitoral node of Gabrielle's 'neo-vaginal' wound on her thigh that James Ballard 'irrigates' in *Crash*, is clearly an orifice that invites a complex reading of the mutual implications of gender and power. Thus Max is rendered even more powerless once the slit has opened and videocassettes are inserted, and it is through this that he is programmed as an assassin by two distinct and opposing factions. The slit does become a weapon of sorts as the film moves towards its climax, but the fact that Max has been 'feminized' by Videodrome (and, thus, by *Videodrome*) is less important, for this discussion at least, than the fact that the irruption of flesh on Max's body (and the matching 'fleshy' hallucinations that accompany exposure to the Videodrome signal) mark Max's movement towards the condition of 'New Flesh'. The irruption of flesh in *Videodrome* occurs as a result of a technological innovation – the 'Videodrome signal' invented by Professor Brian O'Blivion – which is designed to induce a tumour (another of Cronenberg's neo-organs) that will lead our species to a new plateau of existence. As we have seen, the teleological imperative serves a particular function in the Cronenbergian universe, where such constructions (as they occur in narrative and *as* narrative) are to be critiqued and avoided. One is thus reminded of Hobbes' parasites in *Shivers*, Keloid's skin grafts in *Rabid*, Raglan's 'psychoplasmics' in *The Brood* and Dr Ruth's Ephemerol in *Scanners*. In each instance the 'object' is brought into being because it offers a promise of progress from a current position of 'stalled' evolution towards a transformation of the individual, as realized (and literalized) through a transformation of the flesh. This transformation therefore involves a movement towards some beneficial, species-wide goal, and in each, as in *Videodrome*, the experiment has unforeseen outcomes, overpowering the experimenter and spiraling out of control. Similarly, each of these films features a narrative whose conclusion is, to say the least, unexpected either in its deliberate aversion to successful (i.e., ideologically conservative) resolution or in its suggestion of the circularity and repetition of trauma.

Finally, as indicated above, *Videodrome* continues Cronenberg's tradition of highlighting the machinations of disciplinary discourses through the mobilization of a series of industrial-scientific complexes that are both ruthless and arbitrary in their actions. Hobbes, Keloid, Raglan, Ruth and, here, Convex and O'Blivion all stand as exemplars of, and representatives for, the kind of evolutionary (read: teleological) thought that Cronenberg seeks to critique. *Videodrome* is unique in that it details two distinct sets of disciplinary structures – O'Blivion's 'Cathode Ray Mission' and its efforts to bring about an evolutionary 'great leap forward' and Convex's 'Spectacular Optical' with its plans to use the Videodrome signal as a means of punishing those who, like Max, pursue their 'perverted' desires. The fact that both establishments use Max as their programmable assassin means that despite their political differences (broadly speaking, left and right wing, respectively), both institutions represent inverse articulations of the same kinds of disciplinary structures, resulting in the same kinds of restrictions on those subjects who must endure them.

Videodrome is the story of Max Renn (James Woods), director and operator of a small cable television station, Civic TV. Bored by the state of softcore porn, which appears to be Civic TV's staple fare, Renn complains that 'It's too soft. There's something too . . . soft about it. I'm looking for something that will break through. Something tough' (Cronenberg, 1982). Alerted to the presence of a rogue video broadcast by his resident satellite pirate, Harlan (Peter Dvorsky), Renn becomes aware of 'Videodrome' – a snuff television show that seems composed only of scenes of torture and murder. At the same time Renn begins an affair with local radio personality Nikki Brand (Deborah Harry), who is excited by the prospect of Videodrome and who introduces a sadomasochistic element to her relationship with Max. As he attempts to locate the source of the Videodrome signal, as well as deal with a series of sexually violent hallucinations, Max encounters Bianca O'Blivion (Sonja Smits), daughter of media prophet Professor Brian O'Blivion (Jack Creley) and chief publicist for her father's works. Through her he learns something of the secret of Videodrome: that it has been invented by Professor O'Blivion as the means to realize the next stage in human evolution and that the Videodrome signal is designed to induce a brain tumour that eventually transforms the viewer's experiences into a video hallucination indistinguishable from lived experience. O'Blivion's partners, having killed him, intend to utilize the Videodrome signal as the means to clean up a morally bankrupt society and have lured Max into acting on their behalf, with Civic TV providing access to a passive audience deserving of such a fate. Max, now under the thrall of the Videodrome signal, acts first as the assassin of Barry Convex (Les Carlson) and Harlan and then, after being reprogrammed, as the killer of Bianca O'Blivion. After having killed both Convex and Harlan, Max escapes to a deserted barge where Nikki appears to him on a broken television set, urging him to move into the next phase of his evolution, to become the 'new flesh' and do away with his 'old flesh'. After seeing images of himself committing suicide, Max puts his gun to his temple and utters the words 'Long live the new flesh' (Cronenberg, 1982). At this point the screen goes black as a shot is heard.

The 'Videodrome' Project

Formally, *Videodrome* is engaged in a project that Cronenberg increasingly explores from this point forwards: rather than simply utilizing the frame in order to report the experiences of the protagonist, he seeks to provide his audience with an experience that matches that of the protagonist. We see similar devices at work in *M. Butterfly*, *Naked Lunch*, *Spider* and *eXistenZ* – indeed, in every film where the structure of the diegetic reality is, somehow, rendered permeable and the boundary between objective and subjective experience is breached. As has been discussed, this project, with its variety of formal devices, is utilized in order to disrupt the positioning of those audience members in a stable ideological position, forcing them to become aware of the variety of devices at work in the production of the text they are consuming. This is never so simple as just revealing the apparatus at work, although the effect, a disruption of the conditions of suture, is similar. With *Videodrome*, however, we see the convenient fictions of narrative linearity, causality and full resolution dispensed with altogether, entirely in keeping with Max's own experience.

Through the film there is a subtle escalation in those instances of diegetic slippage such that by the time the pivotal moment comes and the film slides entirely into Max's experience, we hardly notice it. The Videodrome-induced hallucinations we encounter take a variety of forms; chief among these are the irruptions of the hallucination into the objective reality of the diegesis, including such examples as the breathing videocassette, the fleshy television that breathes and expands and, pivotally, Max's vaginal slit, into which objects are thrust and through which he is 'programmed'. The fact that other characters interact with some (but not all) of these hallucinatory events works to locate Max's experience of them as actual.

For example, the first appearance of the film's most famous special effect, the vaginal opening, occurs while Max is at home watching television. He is sitting on his couch, half undressed and with a small pistol that he is using, absent-mindedly, to scratch an irritation that seems to be developing on his abdomen. Noticing the irritation seemingly for the first time, Max looks down – an action that is accompanied with a matching close-up of his stomach – and we cut back to see him looking horrified at an opening in his abdomen that, as he watches, extends, opens and pulses. Almost without conscious control, Max inserts his hand, still holding the pistol, into the slit, which immediately closes around his wrist. After some horrified struggling, Max manages to pull his hand free and, as he leaps up from the couch and looks down, we cut back to a close-up of his stomach without the vaginal slit. This shot would ordinarily be enough to convince an audience of the fictional nature of the hallucination, except for the fact that the gun is gone. Thus the hallucinations, which had previously seemed to be Max's experience alone, begin to effect changes in the diegetic reality of the film. This collapsing of objective and subjective diegetic spaces both utilizes some markers of subjective experience (Max's reaction shot to the hallucinatory object followed by a cut-back to reveal that the object is unchanged) and denies others (when Max and Nikki first make love, we cut from languorous close-ups of their bodies to a very long shot in which we see that they are no longer in Max's apartment but are on the floor of the Videodrome set, without any framing shots to allow us to place this experience as either objective or subjective).

As these instances continue to occur, the various techniques used to locate and contain them as hallucinations are increasingly left aside, leaving the audience with an interpretive difficulty: are these events 'actually' (i.e., objectively) occurring, or are they Max's subjective experiences that are somehow straying into the objective diegesis? The film does not seek to answer this question but works hard to sustain the question as an interpretive difficulty, for the reason that this is exactly the difficulty Max is having within the narrative. Thus the film works to destabilize the viewer by removing those formal techniques that would locate, contain and solve the hallucinations. In this fashion *Videodrome* is at work to replicate the experiences of those suffering from the Videodrome signal. As O'Blivion warns Max,

> . . . massive doses of Videodrome signal will ultimately create a new outgrowth of the human brain, which will produce and control hallucination to the point that it will change human reality. . . . (Cronenberg, 1982)

Max is increasingly unable to distinguish between his hallucinations and his diegetic reality, exactly as the audience becomes unable to tell the two states apart. Indeed, part of Cronenberg's purpose in *Videodrome* seems to be to suggest that there is no appreciable difference, given that both the objective reality of the diegesis and the fantasy space of Max's hallucinations utilize the same kind of filmic language. Therefore through the judicious use, and absence, of particular filmic codings, the spectator of *Videodrome* is increasingly positioned alongside Max as an unwitting participant in a plot that remains unclear, even as it moves towards some kind of conclusion.

It should be clear, from these brief examples, that *Videodrome* does function perversely (in a Žižekian sense) through its utilization of the spectator (or, perhaps more accurately, the spectatorial position, inhabited or not) as a kind of co-protagonist. As will be recalled, for Žižek cinematic perversity occurs when the spectator is aligned with the *form* of the apparatus rather than with its apparatus, thereby rupturing Baudry's 'ideological effect' and revealing the spectator to be suddenly cast as the object of an Other's desire. However, the shifting structural positioning of the spectator that occurs in *Videodrome* is not of the same order as that in *Manhunter*. The audience for *Videodrome* occupies a different position to Graham in *Manhunter* and, it must be said, to Max in *Videodrome* also. Thus we are not just seeing Max seeing (although we do), just as we are not just seeing *what* Max sees, with the utilization of point-of-view shots (although we do that too): here we see *as* Max sees, which involves, essentially, experiencing the film's diegesis without the aid of those formal anchors[2] that work to locate and contain the diegetic experience. Our gaze is thus located, not just *with* the gaze of an other, but *as* that gaze, with all the concomitant gaps and elisions of knowledge that come from occupying such a flawed position. This is not to suggest that the Other, whose authoritative and all-penetrating gaze we can only ever partially and fleetingly occupy, is flawed; far from it. Instead, *Videodrome* posits a site of consummate authority (the site of the Other) as the point from which all conspiracies will be explained and all intrigues revealed. This position, which Max spends the entire film attempting to achieve, is constantly just out of reach; every revelation serves only to demonstrate that there are more intrigues yet, more conspiracies and no places from which all of the interlocking pieces are visible.

Thus *Videodrome*, by replicating the effects of the Videodrome signal on its protagonist with the elision or interruption of the various diegetic anchors usually expected (and, indeed, required) within a conventional film, actively performs its perversity by providing a spectatorial position that mirrors that of the protagonist (i.e., enacts a gaze that does not represent his but works alongside his). Issues of cinematic perversity will recur when this chapter moves to discuss *A History of Violence*, for while this film is, like *Videodrome*, perverse, the ways in which it locates and performs its perversity is markedly different, allowing one to suggest a trajectory in Cronenberg's articulation of the perverse and positioning of the spectator within it.

The Pre-ontological and the Real

The first of these concepts, which Žižek names 'the pre-ontological', has its correlations with Kristeva's 'abject' insofar as both terms are used to discuss situations and significations that threaten the unity and stability of the individual as an ontological subject. Thus, for Žižek, the pre-ontological is a place from which disruptive forces emerge, into which they descend and in which, so long as they remain there, they are contained. Žižek's examples, which occur primarily during his protracted discussions about Hitchcock,[3] equate the pre-ontological with the excremental, not so much in terms of content but in terms of the ways in which the excremental/pre-ontological is troubling only insofar as we must deal with it and only until such time as we can put it from our minds. Removing the excremental material renders its presence neatly invisible; thus the pre-ontological is offered as a site where such troubling, yet essential, material exists and to which it retreats (or is forced).

The second concept Žižek offers occurs as a result of his continued utilization, and extension, of the work of Jacques Lacan. Here the

Lacanian concept of the Real provides another way to approach that which cannot be spoken (drawn into the Symbolic), because it eludes the ability of the ontological subject to signify it. Žižek utilizes the Real throughout his work and it peppers his discussions about cinema in a way that sees it used as a term that can often be exchanged with the pre-ontological. However, a fundamental distinction emerges that allows us to further explore Cronenberg's own push towards the limits of signification and meaning. For Žižek, material contained or sited within the pre-ontological, like abject material, can and does emerge into the ontological sphere, and once there, however troubling or traumatic, it is made meaning of. Thus, utilizing Žižek's examples, the Mother Superior who emerges at the close of Hitchcock's *Vertigo* (1958) '. . . functions as a kind of negative deus ex machina, a sudden intrusion in no way properly grounded in the narrative logic, that prevents the happy ending . . .' (Žižek, 2001a, 208), while the swamp that Norman sinks Marion's car into, in *Psycho* (1960), '. . . is another in the series of entrance points to the pre-ontological netherworld' (Žižek, 2001a, 208). This is not to suggest that the pre-ontological realm is simply part of the diegesis, although if we follow Žižek's lead, it does open into the diegesis. It is, instead, a way of comprehending the relationship of diegetic and narrative material to the frames of reference that allow them to be made meaning of. Thus in *Psycho* the car that Norman disposes of is, for him, abject insofar as its continued presence threatens his stability (such as it is), as is the way he negotiates the demands of 'Mother', while the nun of *Vertigo* emerges from a site beyond the logic of the narrative at exactly the moment when her intrusion can have the greatest effect. So far as the narrative is concerned, she does not exist prior to that moment, just as, for Norman, the car ceases to exist (and, hence, trouble him) the moment it finally sinks into the swamp. The important point is that those elements that exist in the pre-ontological realm can intrude into the ontological space of the diegesis (often with devastating effects) and, once there, they can be made meaning of, even if that meaning is troubling or unsatisfying (to the audience, if not to the protagonists).

The Real, in comparison, resists every attempt to render it meaningful, and those elements that inhabit it continually elude signification. This is in keeping with Lacan's own utilization (and post-1953 refinement[4]) of the term that sees the Real being '. . . not simply opposed to the imaginary, but . . . also located beyond the symbolic' (Evans, 1996, 159). Žižek's extension of Lacan's thought sees him utilize the concept of the Real extensively, and for him, '[t]he real exists only in contradistinction to reality, and it corresponds to the limits, and limitations, of language' (Kay, 2003, 168). As Kay notes, Žižek's exploration of the term takes him some distance from Lacan and the term's '. . . Lacanian association with the split instituted in language by sexual difference' (ibid.). Crucially Žižek links the Real with the movements and articulations of ideology and, hence, of power and thus of discipline.

To draw this diversion back to Cronenberg, we now have two ways of conceiving of his demand to 'show the unshowable, speak the unspeakable'. The first of these utilizes Žižek's notion of the pre-ontological and can be thought of as a means of accounting for devices (be they diegetic or formal) that irrupt into the text from beyond its 'normal' boundaries. These irruptions, while unexpected, unwelcome and difficult to fathom, can nevertheless be made meaning of, regardless of how uncomfortable that meaning might be. The pre-ontological material is therefore political insofar as its appearance on-screen forces the spectator to forego pleasurable immersion (suture) and become aware (often painfully so) of the actions of the film apparatus that has positioned him or her as a spectator.

While pre-ontological material resists signification – insofar as it is unexpected or falls outside the immediate purview of the audience – it can be signified and made meaning of. Thus while part of this material's political purpose (for Cronenberg at least) might lie in its specific content (one thinks, for example, of the way Gabrielle's neo-vagina in *Crash* immediately fosters considerations of gender, sexuality and the possibility for erotic exchange outside the restrictions of hetero-normativity), it is clearly the effect of that content that provides the greatest political impulse. Thus it is not the neo-vagina, per se, that generates this effect but the fact that it must be made sense of, fitted into a pre-existing framework and thus rendered comprehensible. Hence, these interpretive frameworks are disciplinary, and it is these disciplinary structures Cronenberg challenges with the inclusion of pre-ontological material. Material from the Real, in contrast, cannot be signified and can only be approached obliquely. Yet the Real haunts the Cronenbergian text and, indeed, often functions as the point at which his narratives must close. Thus, for example, the bacchanal that marks the conclusion of *Shivers* marks also the film's need to conclude. Whatever happens to the world as the inhabitants of Starliner Towers spread their parasites cannot be shown – not because a post-apocalyptic world of lust-inducing vaginal and oral parasites *should* not be shown, but because the fundamental changes that would necessarily occur could never be adequately or comprehensively represented within the cinematic apparatus (and, hence, cinematic discourse) that currently exists. *Shivers* hits the limits of its representability with its end, and given its reception, it is no great surprise that *Rabid* concludes with the swift and brutal reassertion of civil and military control over the dark pre-ontological force that threatens it.

What traces of the pre-ontological exist in *Videodrome?* Žižek, in discussing Hitchcock's use of the pre-ontological makes it clear that such material, which occurs diegetically both as objects and events, are disruptive to the narrative and often traumatic to the characters who must work to respond to these irruptions. The key point, however, is that the pre-ontological material arrives from outside the previously charted diegetic universe. It is not so much that the objects cannot or do not exist within the diegesis, but that we have been given no reason to expect them. While *Videodrome* does not suggest that any of its specific characters emerge from the pre-ontological,[5] it does provide us with a gateway and access to this realm and forces us to shift our interpretation to meaningfully incorporate objects that emerge from it. Given Žižek's definition of the pre-ontological, the vaginal slit that opens on Max's chest provides a gateway to this underworld. The association of the vagina with the pre-ontological (and here we would do well to consider Žižek's linking of the pre-ontological to what is, essentially, the abject) has caused concern for a number of critics because of the gender correlation that appears to be occurring with this association. At first glance the film does indeed paint a troubling (albeit conventionally troubling) picture of the vagina, as it is into this orifice that videocassettes are thrust, through which Max receives his 'programming' as an assassin. Thus Max is, as Suzie Sau-Fong Young puts it, '. . . raped into unconsciousness or, more accurately, . . . raped in the Unconscious' (Young, 2002, 158). The association of power (masculine – it is Convex, originally, who induces the slit and programmes Max in this fashion, ordering him to 'open up') with gender (Max's slit, it is assumed, feminizes him[6]) is, however, troubled by the narrative as it continues to unfold. This conventional reading sees the introduction of a vagina into the abdomen of a pornographer as part of a degrading horror, in that Max is forced to become the object he has built a career on capitalizing. It is entirely possible, though, that Max's vagina is introduced precisely because it offers a problematic opening, and thus a problematic interpretation. With that in mind, it would be entirely pertinent to examine both what goes into and what comes out of Max's vagina.

The first object to move into Max's abdominal slit – and, hence, the pre-ontological – is the gun he loses inside himself. The key here is not just that the gun has been removed from the ontological reality of the diegesis (although this is important) but that the vaginal slit has the ability to function in this fashion. Thus the disappearance (and, as it turns out, storage) of the gun performs the function of inviting interpretation of the neo-vagina. The gun later reappears, although transformed into an organic weapon of some kind (a precursor of the flesh-gun that plays an equally pivotal role in *eXistenZ*), and, again, the vagina functions not just as a place of horror (cf. Creed, 1995) but as a site of transformation – of the object and, hence, of the interpretation that occurs around it. However, there are two other pivotal functions the neo-vagina has: as a receptacle of the programming orders of others, and as a weapon in its own right. As noted above, Max is in thrall to the Videodrome signal, itself Convex's politically oriented perversion of O'Blivion's original intention. The function of the Videodrome signal is to literalize the video-induced hallucination, and the vaginal slit appears as a result of that literalization.[7] The purpose of the slit, at least so far as Convex and his associate Harlan seem concerned, is to provide them with direct visceral access to Max. Thus, once Max is 'opened up' by Convex and Convex's video-flesh-cassette inserted into Max's (pre-ontological) cavity, Max is programmed to act as Convex's assassin. Once programmed, Max 'plays out' (we presume) the content of Convex's cassette, thereby demonstrating the worst fears of the censorial moral majority Convex claims to represent: that media content will have a direct impact on the minds (and hence actions) of those that consume it. The fact that Max is forced to consume this content by Convex makes no difference.

The second assault on Max's neo-vagina comes when, acting on Convex's orders, he attempts to assassinate Bianca O'Blivion. It would appear that she, like Convex, has power over Max's hallucination-made-real and is also able to insert programming material into Max's cavity. This action would appear to defuse a straightforward gender critique (that would see the feminized Max, bearer of the slit, suffering solely at the hands of powerful men) and, as before, appears to suggest a focus more on interpreting the function of the neo-vagina than on discussing gender politics. Finally, the neo-vagina appears to offer a transformative potential that Max utilizes as a weapon. The gun which vanishes into Max's abdomen during the first vaginal hallucination reappears, melded to his forearm, once he has been programmed by Convex. Once Max has been de-/re-programmed by Bianca, this weapon appears to become a vehicle for transformation in its own right – so much so that when Max uses it to kill Convex, it fires cancerous tumours into his body that literally turn him inside-out. More important, however, is the way in which Max uses the neo-vagina to deal with Harlan's duplicity in acting as Max's 'good pirate' while actually being the one to steer Max towards the Videodrome signal. After being de-/re-programmed by Bianca, Max returns to Harlan and Convex, effectively as a double agent. With Convex absent, Harlan approaches Max to insert another cassette. However, as Harlan inserts his arm into Max, the slit closes around his wrist, trapping him inside a grinning Max. With some screaming, Harlan finally pulls his arm loose to discover that his hand has been transformed into some kind of explosive (literally a hand grenade) that detonates, killing him.

While the neo-vagina has offered its transformative potential before this moment, turning Max's gun into some kind of prosthetic, Harlan's hand grenade is the first 'new' object to emerge from the slit (which appears to enjoy puns and wordplay). Just as the Mother Superior in *Vertigo* must be made sense of in a diegetic framework that had given no previous indication as to her existence, so too must Harlan's transformed hand. It emerges from a place beyond signification, but, once within the diegesis, it can be made sense of (however tenuous that sense might be); once interpreted, its role in the narrative is transformative and, for Harlan at least, disruptive. Indeed, a case can be made that Max's hallucinations all draw from the pre-ontological realm, with the irruptions of fleshy technology that overcome various items in his diegesis. However, while the pre-ontological realm provides a force for disrupting the diegesis and the narrative that occurs within it, the realm of the Real remains forever beyond the diegesis and hence beyond any attempt to represent its aspect. Yet, as I claim, the Real haunts the periphery of *Videodrome* and provides the means to comprehend the film's deliberately ambiguous conclusion.

In contrast to my own decision to support an ambiguous conclusion, many commentators favour a more decisive ending in which Max's suicide is unquestioned, while also supporting the plain fact that, as Rodley makes clear,

> *Videodrome* all but abandons a complex and fascinating conspiratorial plot some forty minutes in, for a relentlessly first-person point of view – never to return. As Max begins to lose any sense of reality or the ability to control his situation, so the movie wilfully disintegrates along with its confused protagonist. (Rodley, 1997, 94)

It seems to me that such a negotiation – locking the film into a decisive conclusion despite the increasingly ambiguous narrative that leads to

Max's supposed suicide – works to limit what is truly disruptive about this film: the fact that it forces its audience to the very limits of interpretation and intelligibility, confronting them with the possibility for transformation beyond the ability of discourse to recount and, hence, contain. We have seen how Cronenberg resists the easy (spectatorial and commercial) satisfaction of full narrative resolution and closure, preferring to provoke discussion rather than close it off. The ambiguities inherent in *Videodrome* are certainly part of this provocative structure, especially since Max 'abandons' his 'old flesh' in order to continue some kind of metaphysical struggle against the forces of Videodrome. As Nikki instructs him,

> Videodrome still exists. It's very big, very complex. You've hurt them, but you haven't destroyed them. To do that you have to go on to the next phase. . . . You have to go all the way now. Total transformation. . . . To become the new flesh, you have to kill the old flesh. (Cronenberg, 1982)

To assume that Max has died effectively locks out any other interpretation, including any discussion of what the 'new flesh' might be and how it fits into what we have seen. If Max commits suicide, then his hallucinations are reduced to being merely that, when the formal devices utilized to deliver them to us indicate that they have a far greater importance. What is at stake, then, in supporting an ambiguous ending, is the film's own political (and, for this discussion, heretical) content.

The Trajectory of Perversity (I)

Given Žižek's careful elaboration of the manner in which the cinematic gaze can position the spectator in a perverse position (with all the concomitant discomfort this generates), there can be no question that *Videodrome*'s replication of the effect of the 'Videodrome' signal functions in this fashion. With the deletion of those formal techniques that work to anchor interpretation, the spectator has no choice but to experience the film exactly as Max experiences his diegesis. Thus Cronenberg's use of this perverse positioning works to collapse interpretive distance between his audience and his protagonists. What *Videodrome* demonstrates is that this positioning is never so simple as just revealing the apparatus in action. Cronenberg's increasingly sophisticated utilization of cinematic (by which I mean 'Žižekian') perversion works to align the spectators not simply with the protagonist but alongside him or her, ensuring that they see and encounter the diegesis as the protagonist does. This does not necessarily mean a reliance on point-of-view shots; instead, it incorporates into the spectatorial experience the same kinds of diegetic knowledge and, crucially for *Videodrome,* assumptions about diegetic knowledge that are developed as the protagonist works through some comprehension of the same narrative material.

What renders this perverse, as Žižek makes clear, is the fact that the audience experiences Max's desire – the desire of the other – which is linked strongly to the desire to gain mastery over the events of the plot. Given that this is a Cronenberg film, the protagonist will only ever gain partial control over his or her own articulation (such is the fate of the Cronenbergian protagonist), meaning that the usual spectatorial pleasure at having utter control over the interpretive process is thwarted. What is offered, instead, is a powerlessness that, when coupled with the irruptions of pre-ontological material into the diegesis and thereby into the narrative, makes the experience of encountering a Cronenberg film a unique one.

The development of this perverse structuring in relation to the gaze, though it has its strongest and clearest articulation in *Videodrome,* has been a factor in Cronenberg's films from the beginning. What is most interesting is that it does not appear to be simply an attempt to represent 'difficult' material, as one might expect. Thus *Fast Company* (perhaps the least 'difficult' of Cronenberg's films) contains moments when the spectator becomes forcefully identified with the apparatus of the cinema (as discussed in Chapter 1), wrenched from the spectatorial pleasures of suture and forced to confront the possibility that the specific delivery of the narrative occurs as a result of the desires of an Other, regardless of the fact that this potential Other is never located. Increasingly, however, Cronenberg's use of perverse structuring becomes associated with the presentation of those Cronenbergian themes, resulting in spectatorial difficulties (lack of resolution; identification with a powerless protagonist; irruptions of pre-ontological material into the diegesis, etc.). This is important for my discussion insofar as it alerts us, not only to Cronenberg's increasingly sophisticated criticism of disciplinary structures (as evidenced within his films), but also to the fact that his developing auteurial status itself begins to function as a kind of disciplinary mechanism.

Throughout Cronenberg's career, a stable set of themes is established such that one is able to recognize the Cronenbergian text by both the areas of interest it expresses and the manner in which it attends to those interests. It is no coincidence, then, that I chose *Videodrome* to function as the ideal example of such a text, and the list of features provided serves to demonstrate how this text neatly contains all of Cronenberg's oft-stated concerns; it also serves as a transition from the grossly physical explorations of his early period to the largely psychic transformations of his middle and later period. Of course there are exceptions to this generalization, and given that Cronenberg emerges as an anti-teleological philosopher, it is no surprise that a hard-and-fast evolutionary schema is impossible to place against his work. Nevertheless, the previous chapters have sought to explore the ways in which his works all attend to a now-familiar set of concerns and the ways in which these explorations shift and alter as the contexts of their production and reception similarly change.

With this movement through his career, based on the exploration of a relatively stable set of concerns but with refined techniques and, of course, different generic and narrative structures to frame and deliver this information, it becomes possible to refer to the Cronenbergian film as an identifiable auteurist object, distinguishable from other texts and other auteurist productions. Given the fact that, as I explore his work, Cronenberg emerges as a filmmaker fundamentally concerned with the articulation of discipline over the body (both physical and psychic) of the individual, it is of crucial importance to consider, even if only briefly, the ways in which the Cronenbergian text – a tool utilized in the criticism of discipline – becomes itself a tool for discipline. This should come as no surprise, for the act of recognizing an auteur's oeuvre necessarily means responding to the work's inherent structures of meaning (and meaningfulness), which, as disciplinary mechanisms, train the spectator in the art of recognizing them. The fact that a text is recognizable as coming from a particular director therefore means that his or her work has a consistency – both of its content (and here I am referring to formal techniques as well as narrative content) and of the demands it makes upon its audience. Here the reciprocal nature of the disciplinary structure is made clear; as Foucault details, the Panopticon functions not just because of the anonymity and presumed constancy of the surveillance it offers, but because the prisoners/workers/students *respond* to those disciplinary features.

As I suggested in the Introduction, film functions as a disciplinary mechanism because of the manner with which it demands and requires particular kinds of responses from its audience. These are fundamental to the operation of cinema. As with his specific collection of themes, the manner with which Cronenberg critiques disciplinary structures as functions of social hegemony displays a continuity that allows one to explore them as a body of work. To identify Cronenberg's work (or, indeed, any auteur's) is, therefore, to recognize that these works function as disciplinary structures in and of themselves, training their audience in the means of recognizing them and, crucially, responding to them. By this I mean that recognition and response to a Cronenberg text is fundamentally tied into the manner with which a spectator might take pleasure from the cinematic experience. Thus as the spectator becomes familiar with the Cronenbergian text qua structured text, the spectator is trained in the process of recognizing this text as such and interpreting it in line with previous encounters. In this way, the spectator is able to recognize the presence of the auteur's hand in the text under examination, as well as extend that recognition to other, similar texts (which is to say, other texts which similarly discipline their audiences).

It is for this reason that *A History of Violence* and *Eastern Promises* are offered in direct comparison with *Videodrome*. These two most recent films break, almost entirely, with the formal and narrativizing disciplinary structures that are identifiably Cronenbergian (and which might be, however arguably, best exemplified in *Videodrome*). Having spent the better part of thirty-four years[8] producing commercial works that have all sought to critique and draw attention to the functioning of disciplinary structures in contemporary Western society, Cronenberg has himself become established as a force for cinematic discipline. To be recognized as an auteur is, as I argue above, to function as a disciplinarian, producing works that not only require audiences to respond in particular (and repetitively similar) ways but also train these audiences in the ways the texts are to be most pleasurably understood. Thus, as I argue, *A History of Violence* offers us the first non-Cronenbergian text by Cronenberg, a film in which (apart from a single instance) all attempts at utilizing the film's form to heretically provoke the audience have been reigned in, and in which all of the recognizably Cronenbergian themes (see *Videodrome*) have been so refined as to be only obliquely visible. That *Eastern Promises* continues this developmental trend allows one to posit these two films as representing a coherent shift in Cronenberg's focus and in the manner with which he might now continue to explore the themes central to his oeuvre.

A History of Violence

What *A History of Violence* offers us, more than anything else, is a closely wrought exploration of the ways in which the interpellated individual might come to both comprehend his position within that ideological structure and seek to affect it. Thus far I have utilized each Cronenberg film as a way of exploring a different aspect of the complex interrelationship between the text and a specific disciplinary context, one which contains and responds to those texts and offers possible readings along the lines I have suggested. Throughout this discussion, the individual (both as a narrativized character in the film and as a spectator watching the text) appears to be relatively powerless to do anything about the post-panoptic structure that surrounds him or her. Much of this has to do with Cronenberg's own particular will to either construct characters that are rendered powerless by the disciplinary structures that overwhelm them or be drawn towards those films, written by another, which provide opportunities to continue this exploration.

A History of Violence is both the story of Tom Stall (Viggo Mortensen) and the story of the possibility of forgiveness and change. As the film opens, Tom, who owns and operates a small-town diner in Millbrook, Indiana, is happily married to Edie (Maria Bello) with two children, teenaged Jack (Ashton Holmes) and younger Sarah (Heidi Hayes). Their lives appear to be both settled and loving, and this routine is only changed with the entry of two killers who come to town as part of their cross-country rampage. After they threaten the customers and staff of Tom's diner, Tom leaps into action and disarms and kills both men, becoming an instant celebrity in the process. The media attention, generated by the actions of this unlikely small-town hero, brings Carl Fogarty (Ed Harris), a Philadelphia mobster, to town looking for Tom and claiming that Tom is, in fact, 'Crazy' Joey Cusack, '. . . a dangerous mad-dog killer and member of a criminal dynasty' (Nayman, 2006, 29) who has a history of unsettled debts to account for. Tom denies these accusations, but Edie's suspicions are aroused with Fogarty's continued presence. Eventually Tom is forced to confront Fogarty after he and his mobster cronies kidnap Tom's son. During the ensuing fight, Tom efficiently kills two of Fogarty's men and, as he lies wounded by Fogarty, reveals that he is, after all, Joey. Before Fogarty can kill Tom, Jack shoots Fogarty in the back. While recovering in hospital from his injuries, Tom explains to Edie that while he was, once, Joey Cusack, he disposed of that identity as a means of escaping his life as a murderer, becoming Tom Stall in the process. However, recognizing that the death of Fogarty will not end the continued interference of people from his past, Tom sets off to Philadelphia to meet with his estranged brother Richie (William Hurt), another gangster and one, clearly, of some repute. After Richie reveals something of his and Joey's past together, as well as admitting that Joey's actions have cost him dearly, another confrontation occurs during which Joey kills a number of Richie's henchmen and, finally, Richie himself. The film finishes with Tom/Joey returning to Millbrook and home, entering as the family are having dinner and sitting wordlessly at the table.

Millbrook, Indiana

The small town is the perfect place to consider the ways in which disciplinary structures operate and affect the manner in which contemporary subjects become and remain interpellated. Unlike the city, the small town provides a different disciplinary framework and, consequently, a series of different interpellative goals that, while necessarily aligned to those of the dominant hegemony, are focused more tightly upon the individual. Millbrook, however fictional it might be, is a 'nice' town, and this niceness is enforced through the mise-en-scène and, particularly, through the characterization of its inhabitants. The Stalls are perfectly placed in this environment, and in turn, the Stall family both reflects and continues this disciplinary situation. This is exactly what one would expect of any (Western nuclear) family unit, and it is for this reason that Althusser calls the family an Ideological State Apparatus (ISA): the family is one of the sites where hegemonic control is articulated and expressed. While Althusser distinguishes between the largely public operations of the Repressive State Apparatus (RSA) and the private operations of the ISA, he does go on to comment that regardless of this distinction (which, as he clarifies, may very well be false), the distinguishing factor in terms of operation lies in the relationship of ideological action and activity to repressive actions and activity (Althusser, 1994, 110–12). The family unit, Althusser suggests, by being classified as an ISA, is only ever secondarily repressive. Because the film is focused on the Stall family, with only a glancing mention of the other inhabitants,

the Stalls therefore function as both an idealized family unit and a representative of the other inhabitants of Millbrook; we are therefore justified
in reading back through the Stalls to our assessment of the town's 'good
and proper' inhabitants. It should be noted, also, that there is no 'Lynchian'
irony present in Cronenberg's representation of small-town America, no
Frank Booth set to explode out and reveal the dark heart that beats
beneath the white picket fences. Indeed, Millbrook seems to be entirely
without a 'heart of darkness'. Instead, Millbrook is entirely seriously constructed, as it has to be if it is to function as a platform for Cronenberg's
heretical exploration.[9]

Millbrook therefore functions as an idealized set of introspective cir-
cles, with almost the entirety of the film's ideological concern focused on
the Stalls. They, in turn, represent the inhabitants of the town, and the
town serves as an idealized version of the kind of hegemonic structure
offered as a template for the United States (and, hence, the Western
world). It is important that the trouble Millbrook experiences comes
from outside. While it might be stretching the case to utilize as parochi-
ally focused a film as *A History of Violence* as a means of discussing broader
(by which I mean international) social and moral issues, it does seem
clear that there is an insularity about Millbrook that extends beyond the
ability of a small town to sustain itself. This has implications for under-
stating the kind of heretical discussion Cronenberg is entering into. The
question, then – as central now as it was when this project began with *Fast
Company* – is, where is the heresy? Answering that question involves
exploring the role and function of Tom Stall, just as it involves attending
to Cronenberg's sophisticated and, for the most part, entirely conventional use of form.

As noted, Millbrook is, as we first encounter it, an enclosed space
where whatever disciplinary difficulty the town suffers is represented by
the bullies Jack must endure at school, and the three pieces of rubbish
Tom collects as he opens his diner. These two events are the sum total of
the town's disciplinary violations; thus, the town's status as a well-
functioning hegemonic institution is confirmed, which necessarily means
that all of the town's smaller sub-units – families and so forth – also 'correctly' function. This observation is important as, once it is revealed that
Tom Stall is actually Joey Cusack, the film draws attention to the function
of Millbrook as a hegemonic cluster of ideological structures that do not
function 'naturally' but which are performed and enacted by the interpellated inhabitants. At some point Joey, in the process of becoming
Tom, has arrived in Millbrook and set about seeking interpellation as

part and parcel of becoming a member of that society. Indeed, as Richie comments during his confrontation with Joey,

> So you like that farm life? Milking cows and shit? . . . You're living the American dream. You really bought into it, didn't you? You've been this other guy almost as long as you've been yourself. Hey, when you dream . . . are you still Joey? (Cronenberg, 2005)

Tom is therefore important as his performance of the town's specific hegemonic, ideological (and, hence, disciplinary) requirements is knowingly and consciously enacted. His activities as Tom and his performance as a citizen of Millbrook may be naturalized, but they are certainly not 'natural', which therefore demonstrates that the only difference between his performance of himself as a correctly functioning member of Millbrook's civil society and that of, for example, his wife (who, as a lawyer, is a perfect example) is that Tom is aware that he is performing.

Necessarily, however, for the town and its inhabitants to define themselves as 'good', there is a concomitant necessity for 'bad' to exist. As noted, whatever 'badness' the town can generate is minor and inconsequential. Badness must enter the town, and, ideologically, this fact generates a series of conclusions. First of these is that because the criminal events that occur in Tom's diner are generated by 'out-of-towners', the town's own sense of itself as a correctly functioning civil society is confirmed. The violence that these two men bring to town could therefore never be generated by local inhabitants, and this sense of self-assured insularity is confirmed with the sheer inability of the town's sheriff to cope with the fast-escalating events, once Tom has dispatched the two criminals in his diner. Second of these is that Tom's response is both entirely in accordance with the disciplinary dictates of the society he is a member of (both, at a local level, Millbrook and, at a much larger level, the United States), and also entirely in excess of those dictates. On the one hand Tom is required, by the fact of his membership in Millbrook's community, to act in order to save his fellow citizens; on the other hand, Tom both takes two lives and, more importantly, acts too efficiently. It is at this point we confront the first of Cronenberg's heretical points: the opening scenes of *A History of Violence* make it clear that some violence is justified, so that when Tom acts in order to save the staff and customers of his diner, he does so in contrast to the kind of men who murder simply for the pleasure of the act. As a result, Tom is considered an 'American hero' by the media types that flock to cover this situation, and initially,

Tom's reticence in the face of this attention works to confirm these assessments of his actions. However, the fact that Tom acts so readily and efficiently reveals his own history of violence, a fact that cannot be reconciled with his performance as an interpellated citizen of Millbrook. One is forced, entirely as the film intends, to confront both the violence itself (including its bloody aftermath) and the fact of violence. This includes the difficulty in resolving the notion that, while some violence may be justified by the hegemonic system in which it occurs, the performance of that violence cannot occur too readily or be enacted too efficiently. To do so demonstrates that the perpetrator is too familiar with the ways of violence, meaning that another series of difficulties emerge. Chief among these is the impossible-to-resolve ambiguity that catches Tom out: his role demands that he act, but in acting he reveals his willingness to act. Certainly, this first violent irruption results in Tom's being lauded as an 'all-American' hero who had acted as he was required to, in order to safeguard the lives of others. Yet, as Fogarty comments in conversation with Edie, '. . . how is it that [her] husband is so good at killing people?' (Cronenberg, 2005).

The hegemonic structure that Tom has escaped from, and which Joey is still a participant in, stands as the heretical and, Žižek would argue, hysterical obverse to that which governs the citizens of Millbrook. It is while discussing David Lynch's *Lost Highway* (1996) that Žižek makes the following observation about the film's Mr Eddy, an obscene father figure whose most spectacular sequence involves him running another motorist off the road and then pistol-whipping him for not following the rules of the road:

> It is crucial not to misread this scene whose shockingly comical character can easily deceive us: one should risk taking the figure of Eddy thoroughly *seriously*, as someone who is desperately trying to maintain a minimum of order, to enforce some elementary 'fucking rules' in this otherwise crazy universe. (Žižek, 2000a, 18)

Again we find Žižek asking us to take seriously a figure of extremity, and while, as I note, *A History of Violence* does not have the same Lynchian intention as *Lost Highway*, the same heretical impulse is present, and similar figures of extremity are presented. Tom's dilemma – he must act violently to prevent violence, but in so doing reveals himself to be more familiar with violence than he 'should' be – is resolved utterly with the heretical underside to the dominant hegemonic structure, the world of organized crime that Joey has, for whatever reason, escaped from and, in escaping, has become Tom. The world of organized crime, as represented both by Fogarty and Joey's brother Richie, is, perversely, far more clear-cut than the ambiguous ideological and disciplinary terrain of Millbrook (and, hence, civil society). There, among the criminals, the 'fucking rules', as Mr Eddy puts it, are entirely clear and perfectly visible.

The ideological structure of the world Joey which leaves behind in order to become Tom and which Richie still inhabits (successfully, if his house is anything to go by) is clear both about the demands it makes on its interpellated subjects and on the reason for those demands. This stands in contrast with the hegemonic structures that discipline life in Millbrook – their ambivalence makes negotiating civil society much more fraught, even if the stakes, so to speak, are not quite as high. Jack, for example, is clearly an intelligent teenager and yet must suffer at the hands of the school bully – a jock – for no clear reason at all. When Jack acts to assert himself, in exactly the way that Tom has done, he is punished. Thus the decidedly ambiguous presence of violence in society is brought into relief: Tom's use of violence to defend himself, his business and his staff and customers is justified (even if his expertise draws attention to his actions), while Jack's decision to meet the bully's latest attack with some violence of his own oversteps a boundary that was (and is) never clear to begin with. However, it must be noted that Cronenberg's criticism of the interpellative structures that govern Millbrook (and, hence, civil society at large), including the deeply ambivalent disciplinary injunctions that Tom, in responding to, both meets and contravenes, is not the most explicit site of heresy. These points, as discussed above, are important, but it is with the construction of *A History of Violence* as a Cronenbergian text that we see the clearest articulation of this film's heretical role.

The Trajectory of Perversity (II)

As noted above, *A History of Violence* might be the first of what could be a series of non-Cronenbergian texts,[10] at least insofar as the flesh – previously Cronenberg's de facto marker of the mutability of the subject – appears to be entirely normalized. Thus there are no irruptions from the Žižekian pre-ontological, and in this *A History of Violence* marks a shift in the constitution of Cronenberg's oeuvre, in the same way that *Videodrome* functioned as its exemplar. As the amount of pre-ontological material appears to decrease over the course of his career (meaning that, to put it bluntly, his films become less 'fleshy') the drive towards the Real, towards narrative irresolution and the limits of meaningfulness and interpretation, appears to increase. Thus, in *A History of Violence* there is the narrative irresolution to be dealt with – do Tom's family accept him back as Tom? – and, as well as this, there is a single moment that provides a glimpse of the Real beyond the film's ability to signify[11].

This occurs at the end of the third explosion of violence, when Tom, now Joey, returns to Philadelphia to confront his brother Richie and end the disruption of his life at Millbrook. During their conversation, where some small hints are provided as to Tom's prior life as Joey, Richie's henchmen attempt to kill Tom. They, in turn are swiftly dispatched, and the sequence ends with Tom/Joey shooting Richie in the forehead, killing him outright. This sequence occurs at night – Tom having driven non-stop from Millbrook to Philadelphia – and ends with Richie dead on his own front doorstep, lit by the house lights. The next shot is of Tom at dawn (presumably, given the quality of light) washing blood from his body in Richie's boating lake. Obviously some considerable time has passed during which any number of important events may have occurred – disposing of the bodies, for example. Yet we are not provided with these moments, and the jarring cut from pitch-black to the frosty light of a cold Philadelphia morning stands out for its disjunction and for the elision it represents. It is pointless to fantasize about what events might fill this elided moment, for the simple fact that no possible narrative is adequate to filling this gap. There is, of course, an important reason for this: we are never given enough information about either Tom or Joey to be able to confidently assume his or their actions during this period. What remains, then, is an uncomfortable lack. Something has occurred during this period that the film is unable to represent, and we spectators, for all our assumed advantages over the characters and their diegesis, do not have the requisite information to fill in this space. It remains unfathomable, not so much meaningless (indeed, it is consummately meaningful) as unable to be made meaning of.

What makes this single elision uncomfortable is the fact that it appears to be so meaningful. The film's narrative trajectory has led towards this moment, towards Joey's confrontation with Richie and their face-to-face sparring. Thus the film's deliberate move to *not* give us specific historical or contextual details (to, in effect leave out or thwart the interpretive frame we would ordinarily expect) delays the resolution that the film's narrative content leads us to expect. This means that by the time Joey confronts Richie, this sequence gains a significance in that it appears to be the final point at which comprehensive resolution is possible. This sense of impending resolution occurs, necessarily, because an audience has been thoroughly trained by these very cinematic structures to expect such resolutions. Joey/Tom is, after all, a mystery, and every moment in the film that might have provided some (however temporary or minor) insight into his history and rationale has been elided. Thus, this final violent dénouement would appear to be our last opportunity to explore what actually constitutes Joey/Tom's 'history of violence' and, more importantly, what his life will hold now. One can certainly imagine alternate scenarios in which the mystery of this man is solved – through flashback, through voice-over, through the insertion of some other sequence to bridge the elided time between killing Richie, leaving Philadelphia and returning to Millbrook – and yet, equally, one can see that all of these options (and more) do not work because they *are not satisfactory*. Why? Because this film, which does not appear to be a Cronenberg film, *should* be offering us the explanation and resolution (hence the interpretive security) we expect, based on the manner with which this film looks and behaves conventionally. Yet none of these conventional devices for resolution are up to the job of providing a resolution worthy of the mystery that has been constructed over the course of the film. In essence, then, this film becomes Cronenbergian the moment it leaves out the vital piece of information we have been led to believe will 'explain everything' – the piece of information that would grant us the standard spectatorial satisfaction and pleasure, that would allow us to occupy a position of authority over the text's interpretation.

Surprising the Non-Duped, or The Emperor's New Clothes

Proof of this critical position, which is necessarily proof of the manner with which disciplinary structures have been either threatened or contravened, comes in the general response to the film. Exactly as we have seen with all of Cronenberg's films, the degree and manner of the ensuing criticism demonstrates which disciplinary structures have been highlighted and violated. Of the negative comments that have accumulated around *A History of Violence*, the most revealing come from committed 'Cronenbergians' who feel betrayed by this film and its refusal to accommodate what might be ordinarily expected from a Cronenberg film.

These are people who demonstrate a familiarity with his work and have clearly defined positions regarding 'the Cronenberg project'. What these comments have in common is the notion that this film somehow contravenes 'expectations', which is enough for them to consider it a failure. Thus *A History of Violence* is considered Cronenberg's 'most 'mainstream' movie ever' (Eggers, 2005), a 'quasi-attempt at mainstream moviemaking' (Vernucci, 2006) that is 'easily the most "mainstream" of his films' (S. Wilson, 2006). These reviews (and there are an enormous number of them accumulating on the internet) for the most part begin by noting how much of a fan of Cronenberg's work that person *used* to be (or, at best, still is despite this film). This position is best summed up by one self-described committed Cronenbergian who writes,

> I never believed I would be writing a negative review of a David Cronenburg [*sic*] film. As someone who firmly, and still, believes that this director is truly original and has an extraordinary vision, this film was a crashing disappointment. . . . I will never trust the Cronenburg brand again and I suggest anyone considering watching this film not waste their time and watch one of the many superb Cronenburg films out there. (Nixon, 2007)[12]

These critics, who all admit to being fans of Cronenberg's work, recognize that the consistency across his texts that allowed them to be grouped together is missing from this film. They are experiencing an interpretive crisis as the expected authorial frame (a Cronenberg film is expected to be 'stylized, interesting, and special' [PolarisDiB, 2005]) is absent, leaving them bereft of the familiar structures that would guide them through the text and make sense of (i.e., account for) the elisions this film contains. What one fan identifies as belonging to the typical Cronenberg film – 'viral contamination, sex as monstrosity, the evolution of a "new flesh," a lust-driven car crash' (Westcott, 2006) – becomes, then, the expected content for all Cronenberg films. Across these comments and reviews, different reasons are proposed for this film's fundamental difference to the rest of Cronenberg's canon. The result, however, is the same: for these people (and therefore for the disciplinary position they represent – as people trained by Cronenberg's oeuvre in the art of pleasurably interpreting the Cronenbergian text) *A History of Violence* has failed them.

Yet there is more to be made from these responses than simply the grumblings of disappointed fans. Throughout this volume I have argued

that the heretic's actions are radical insofar as they work towards revealing the ways in which disciplinary structures discipline the subjects who
are constituted by them. Thus, as noted above, the presence of such critiques reveals the contravention of the disciplinary mechanisms that
Cronenberg has come to represent. Yet it is possible that more is occurring within these responses than merely that. Mark Andrejevic, in exploring a similar territory within the viewing practices of Reality Television,
makes the valuable point that perverse spectatorship and perverse spectatorial positioning can itself come to function as a fully recuperated tool
for disciplinary activity within the aegis of a dominant hegemony. As he
notes, the utilization of a perverse spectatorial position, and the deliberate structuring of texts to achieve this among an audience, means that

> [p]erversion . . . is to be viewed not as a (subversive) expression of the
> unconscious desire repressed by the dominant order, but rather as the
> expression of this order's *inherent* transgression: its 'obscene, super-
> egotistical reverse'. (Andrejevic, 2004, 176)

Thus the perverse spectatorial position becomes a part of the very disciplinary structure rather than a tool for the subversion of these mechanisms. Those subjects who have been fully inculcated by their viewing
practices into accepting the perverse position of the gaze of the other
are referred to by Andrejevic (utilizing work by Žižek) as the 'non-duped'
who practice a form of 'savvy voyeurism that is a form of surrender'
(Andrejevic, 2004, 173). The 'non-duped' spectators are those who recognize, from their position as perverse spectators, their own powerlessness before the image. However, rather than preventing the possibility of
deriving conventional pleasure from the text (as would the duped spectator), the non-duped spectator utilizes their identification with the form
of the text as a way of occupying a position of authority over the text,
allowing them to derive pleasure from that positioning. What is crucial is
that the non-duped spectator does not, through this perverse position,
occupy the position of the Other (although part of the pleasure derived
comes from assuming that one has achieved this). The non-duped spectator remains in a thoroughly disciplined (although differently positioned) relation to the text. Thus

> [t]his attitude of savviness is properly perverse insofar as it sacrifices
> the possibility of social struggle in order to claim the status of the 'non-
> duped' – so as to recognize behind every social ideal the way in which

it is deployed as a ruse of power (and thus deriving satisfaction from the knowledge of one's own impotence. (Andrejevic, 2004, 178)

The savvy non-duped viewer of Cronenberg's work is, as evidenced by the brief collection of critical responses above, familiar with his oeuvre, is conversant with some form of the 'Cronenberg project' and has come to accept the irrational, illogical and inarticulable (as represented by the irruption of the pre-ontological and the constant movement towards the Real) as markers of his auteur status. Crucially, the very ways in which Cronenberg's films thwart conventional viewing practices (unlikable and powerless protagonists, absence of resolution, interruption of conventional formal practices) become sites of pleasure for these spectators. They become non-duped, first, once they recognize that a Cronenberg film will provide pleasure through eluding conventional mechanisms of interpretation and, hence, of information/satisfaction/pleasure delivery, and second, because they take pleasure in the exposure of the disciplinary mechanisms revealed by his heresy.

Yet, as Andrejevic notes, the position of the perverse non-duped spectator is one from which no critical activity will issue, for within the non-duped position pleasure comes from inactivity, from the recognition that all political or critical gestures are 'always already' accounted for by the disciplinary mechanisms that position them as perverse spectators. Stephen Turner notes that this is a form of cynicism, the product of 'polite but cynical modern society' (Turner, 2007, 86); it means that '[p]eople are well off yet miserable, rational yet disillusioned, pessimistic yet still functioning' (Turner, 2007, 86). Thus the question, given Cronenberg's interruption of this circuitous self-justification regarding critical inactivity, becomes, 'how does one interrupt the non-duped spectator?' Žižek comments about exactly this process when he notes that

[p]erhaps one should read Hans Christian Andersen's 'The Emperor's New Clothes' along these lines: of course everybody knew that the emperor was naked, yet it was precisely the disavowal of this fact that held the subjects together – by stating this reality, the unfortunate child dissolved the social link. (Žižek, 1994, 58)

What the child's actions do, in commenting loudly that the emperor is naked, is to draw attention not to the fact of his nakedness, but to the disciplinary structures that work to prevent comment on this (obvious) fact. By dissolving the mechanism that links the community together in their ability to avoid commenting, the child forces the population into action, mobilizes them, not against the person of the emperor (who, in his nakedness, requires the support and complicity of the population to remain powerful), but against the mechanism that maintains their docility before the structural position of 'emperor'. The non-duped spectators who are aware of the emperor's nakedness and yet do not comment (because such comment is pointless since all present are aware of his nakedness) are surprised by the child's actions which reveal the manner in which they have been positioned. As Žižek concludes,

> [t]he fundamental pact uniting the actors of the social game is that the Other [in this instance, the emperor] must not know all. . . . For this reason, the social game (the rules of etiquette, etc.), in the very stupidity of the ritual, is never simply superficial. We can indulge in our secret wars only as long as the Other does not take cognizance of them, for at the moment the Other can no longer ignore them, the social bond dissolves itself. (Žižek, 1992, 72–3)

I have noted above that the rationale for Cronenberg's shift in position with *A History of Violence*, which is expressed as an alteration of thematic content and formal style, occurs because he recognizes that his films have become as disciplinary in their functioning as the structures he seeks to critique. This movement which, as we shall see, may very well be cast as a 'selling out' reveals that a great deal is at stake in his heretical process. The response of his non-duped fans, in particular the anger they all demonstrate, lies in the fact that they have been surprised, in effect thwarted in their attempts to gain pleasure and satisfaction from their own non-duped status. In Žižek's terms, this means that their social bond dissolves and renders their non-duped complicity visible. Thus *A History of Violence*'s own history (it is a Cronenberg text) appears poised to offer particular kinds of spectatorial engagements and yet frustrates these immediately. It then appears to be another kind of text (i.e., a standard genre film, evidence of Cronenberg's selling out to a mainstream), only to frustrate that, too. Thus the non-duped spectators have two separate sets of interpretive mechanisms thwarted by the text and, in this situation, are forced to respond critically, which is to say, both politically and actively. The fact that their critical reactions are directed against the text that has thwarted them is beside the point. What is important is that Cronenberg's text has ruptured the easy stability of the non-duped spectator and, through that rupture, has generated a response by stirring the non-duped into action. *A History of Violence* utilizes its very difference from the Cronenberg canon to demonstrate how thoroughly disciplinary those texts were in danger of becoming and, as a consequence, how thoroughly disciplined his audience has become.

Eastern Promises

Eastern Promises (2007) continues the shifts in focus, style and assumed-audience made clear in *A History of Violence* without giving up, in the least, on the overall trajectory of the thus identified and continuously evolving 'Cronenberg-project'. This film contains the same explorations, the same attention to detail (both narrative and formal) and the same problematizing of the interpretive possibilities inherent in the presence of the director's name as a guide to our encounter with this film. However with *Eastern Promises* it would seem that the shift from art-house auteur to multiplex maestro is complete. *Eastern Promises*, as Koehler notes, marks a decided move '. . . from his ongoing preoccupations with the body towards the ways the mind – particularly the imaginative mind – can alter reality' (2007, 76), resulting in a far more favourable response from the same fan quarters that had derided *A History of Violence*, and a concomitant lessening in support from those who had previously supported the director for his very difficulty and incomprehensibility (cf. *Sight and Sound*, November 2007). This pivotal schism reveals the ways in which *Eastern Promises* functions as the result of a new arc on Cronenberg's work and demonstrates the claims made earlier for the ways in which the disciplinary activities of cinema work continuously towards specifically articulated interpretations.

Like *Spider*, *Eastern Promises* is played out against an expressionistic London cityscape populated by only the figures required to give the diegesis the valence needed for spectatorial engagement to occur. The streets are certainly more crowded than we have ever seen in a Cronenberg film before, but these scenes are utilized in order to isolate individuals who feature in them, rather than link them to their brethren. Indeed, for all the discussion of family and familial obligation, this film is populated by individuals at odds with each other and themselves, distinguished from what passers-by exist by their own comings and goings. Here, again, we encounter a selection of bifurcated protagonists who, like Tom in *A History of Violence*, have depths only partially revealed by the story unfolding before us.

Ostensibly, *Eastern Promises* tells a story of the Russian mafia, white slavery, prostitution and internecine power struggles within a crime family.

Anna (Naomi Watts), a midwife in a London hospital, is on hand to assist when young Tatiana (Sarah Jeanne Labrosse) has a miscarriage which leaves the girl dead and her infant an orphan. With only the young girl's diary to guide her, Anna asks her émigré uncle to translate the diary, using an old business card to link the dead girl to a plush local Russian restaurant. Immediately suspecting the truths inherent in the diary, the restaurant owner Semyon (Armin Mueller-Stahl) seeks to insinuate himself into Anna's life in order to contain the danger to himself as a leader in the *Vory V Zakone* (literally 'thieves in honour'), the Russian mafia involved, among other things, in the importing of illegal immigrants to serve in local brothels. Semyon's son, Kirill (Vincent Cassel), named throughout the diary as one of Tatiana's abusers, is saved from feckless ineptitude by the family's driver and 'fixer' Nikolai (Viggo Mortensen), and with generic inevitability, the paths of these characters cross and intertwine as we discover that Semyon is the father of the baby, having raped the girl in disgust at Kirill's inability to do the same, that Kirill is himself being forced towards increasingly erratic acts of violence as his lack of criminal ability (and possible homosexuality) becomes known within the criminal community at large and, finally, that Nikolai is a Russian police plant working deep undercover within the *Vory V Zakone*.

Anna is, herself, of Russian émigré stock, and her uncle Stepan (Jerzy Skolimowski), whom she originally asks to translate the diary, provides what Nikolai refers to as an 'old school' link to the Russian criminal traditions of the past, where one either died or was exiled, itself a kind of cultural death. Thus *Eastern Promises* establishes a set of conflicting positions regarding emigration and disappointment, the law and its obscene underside, the vanishing past of a lost homeland and the new, violent traditions of a contemporary existence. Through all of these, as with *A History of Violence*, are woven complex discussions of family and obligation, power and the possibilities for redemption. However, unlike *A History of Violence*, where the lies and subterfuge inherent in Tom Stall's attempts to create a new life for himself exist in evanescent dialogue before they are played out as action, *Eastern Promises* plays these factors out in full view using the marked bodies of the protagonists as a canvas. Where we only have Tom's word for the changes he has sought to make, which must be then weighed against the actions we see him commit, for Nikolai, as the film's visible focal point, the body becomes its own site of discourse, replicating in the prison and gang tattoos his history leading up to his full initiation into the *Vory V Zakone*.

The Mark of Cain

Of the film's many arresting sequences, the initiation of Nikolai into the *Vory V Zakone* stands as the one most clearly linked to the progression of Cronenberg's exploration of the body as the 'first fact of existence'. Here, though, the final possibility of this fact ever being linked to any kind of ontological certainty is removed. Nikolai, in this sequence of familial initiation, is seated stripped to his shorts in front of a group of older men, all patresfamilias within the organization (see Figure 6.1). For these men, the tattoos on Nikolai's body reveal his criminal history, his prison terms and time in solitary ('I was called "The Stump" because they couldn't move me'), and there remain empty spaces destined to eventually hold the marks of the *Vory V Zakone*: twin stars on his chest and knees (because he will never kneel before anyone). Amid the deception and lies of the Western promises (the better life which Tatiana, Semyon, Stepan and all émigrés hope to find and which is revealed as a fraudulent deception), the Eastern promises made by the tattoos of the *Vory V Zakone* are designed to speak to the truth of a life actually lived, crimes committed and punishments actually undertaken. By these marks, a man (for this is an entirely homosocial discourse) might be known in advance of acts committed by the traces of those events already known to be truth.[13] Indeed, as the sequence progresses, Nikolai is forced to renounce

FIGURE 6.1   Nikolai's demarcated body (*Eastern Promises*).

his mother and father and acknowledge that he belongs now and forever to the *Vory V Zakone*. This rebirth, which retrospectively removes any history outside the narrative of the tattoos, confirms his belonging to this new family structure, with its rites and obligations. Therefore, as Mark Fisher accurately notes:

> The surface of the body becomes a site for a semiotic struggle between free will and pre-determination, with tattoos functioning as both a physical signification of the persistence of the past and a symbolic rejection of personal and family history. (2007, 58)

Yet this rebirth and concomitant mutual obligation means nothing. The event that opens the film – the assassination of a rival Chechen gang member by the nephew of one of Semyon's associates – is organized by Kirill in retaliation for the man's slander. In return for this, the man's Chechen brothers seek revenge and, after slitting the throat of the original assassin, come after Kirill. Semyon, learning of this from his associate, offers to substitute Nikolai for Kirill, certain that the Chechens do not know Kirill by sight. This leads to the film's most shocking sequence; the close-quarter knife fight in the bathhouse, with Nikolai, naked and defenceless, forced to fight two fully clothed thugs. That Nikolai survives, although badly wounded and hospitalized, proves once and for all that he is no simple 'driver'. It proves also that the familial linkages of the *Vory V Zakone* are an entirely utilitarian bond and that for Semyon, one 'son' (the initiate) can replace another (the legitimate, if substandard, heir to Semyon's throne). Thus the bond offered by membership of the *Vory V Zakone* is a fabrication, a promise that works only for as long as all members require it to.

More forcefully, if under-expressed given the above treachery, Nikolai's role as a police plant, and his ability to defend himself revealed in the bathhouse sequence, demonstrate that the story of this man's life, written on the surface of his skin, is itself a fabrication. Here, though, the agency of the flesh is different to the unknowable processes at work in the generation of the Brundlefly. Instead, Nikolai posits an agency determined in advance by the proof demonstrated in his body's ability to hold a specific record, which functions as a screen for some kind of more 'authentic' agency beneath that screen. Thus the inauthentic biological family is undone by the *Vory V Zakone* ('your father was a coward . . . your mother was a whore') and replaced by the authentic family of the gang (whose authenticity lies in the truth of the stories told on the screens of their bodies). But with Nikolai's duplicity, we are thus led to question the legitimacy of the tattoos themselves, used here as markers of a truth to those who would read them as such. The Eastern promises ring as hollow as their Western counterparts.

'Family Is Important to You People . . .'

Eastern Promises is full of families. Indeed, one is hard pressed to think of another Cronenberg film since *The Brood* that spends as long exploring the family as a site of anguish and anxiety instead of the safety and fulfilment it is usually supposed to offer. And while the Stall family in *A History of Violence*, as temporary exemplars of the success of the American Dream, are gradually undone by the history Tom fails to hide, none of the families in *Eastern Promises* are complete to begin with. Anna lives with her mother Helen (Sinéad Cusack), and the pair play frequent host to Anna's uncle Stepan, whose 'old school' beliefs reveal much about the old country. His comments about Anna's estranged (and never-seen) partner Oliver ('. . . black men always run away') culminate in his opinion that Oliver's race is the reason for Anna's miscarriage. They are, as Helen notes, 'ordinary people' who struggle against the dark and cold metropolis that is Cronenberg's London. Anna's family, for all their difficulties, function in entirely appropriate ways, offering support and assistance despite their growing horror at the situation unfolding around them. In direct comparison (a comparison the film asks us to make) Semyon's families – both actual and criminal – are flawed and compromised, rife with internecine rivalry and home to the undercover agent Nikolai. Vitally, and in keeping with the exploration of family undertaken in *A History of Violence*, what both families in *Eastern Promises* reveal is the fact of family as a performance, one that can be faked with the requisite amount of training and the right props.

Most obviously, Nikolai's use of the *Vory V Zakone* tattoos as the means to ensure the certainty of his cover story demonstrates the ways in which any language system can be used both to give people what they expect and to use those facts against them. But, more than this, Nikolai's deceptions reveal the ways in which any family is as arbitrarily constructed as the various rituals used to hide that very fact from all those involved in the performance. The old men of the *Vory V Zakone* expect to see what Nikolai reveals to them; as his reward, Nikolai is given his badge of office and further access to the inner recesses of the family. This, however, renders Nikolai as dispensable as any other member of the *Vory V Zakone* family, a fact that nearly costs him his life. Kirill might very well be Semyon's son, but the old man has no hesitation in promoting Nikolai as the more able soldier or in replacing Kirill with Nikolai in the hope that the Chechens will mistake one for the other. Thus, at the film's conclusion, Nikolai has arranged with Scotland Yard for Semyon to be removed and imprisoned and finishes the film as the ostensible head of that family behind Kirill as the titular successor to Semyon's crown.

Anna's family is without a head, a fact Stepan alludes to when carving the Christmas chicken. Into this family without a father comes an infant without a family: Tatiana's miscarried child, named Christine by Anna. Within a more traditional cinematic narrative, Nikolai and Anna would each find ways to incorporate the other into their lives. Thankfully *Eastern Promises* does not fall prey to this restorative impetus, and while the film ends with both partial families restored – Anna with Christine, safely enjoying a spring day in the suburban home; Nikolai now de facto head of the London *Vory V Zakone* – neither Anna nor Nikolai, we are led to believe, will ever encounter the other. Thus, *Eastern Promises*, continuing the criticism of this most ideologically invisible of structures, concludes that families come and go, that every position can presumably be occupied by any appropriate member given access to the correct performance and that, while families might find ways to make sense and meaning out of their situation, this is often at the expense of the restorative version so beloved of cinema usually.

'Now I Live in the Zone All the Time . . .'

These words, uttered by Nikolai during his initiation into the *Vory V Zakone*, are meant to indicate the fact that he is fully a part of the organization, absolutely contributing to and benefitting from the distinct ontological enterprise undertaken by any para- or extra-legal organization. But this phrase, which rings strangely as a piece of dialogue – for there is no mention of life as a *Vor* (the Russian equivalent of a Mafia 'made man') as being part of this 'zone' before or after this mention – links this film concretely to *Naked Lunch* (via Bill Lee's retreat into, and then exile from, Interzone) and more obliquely to the entire Cronenberg corpus, wherein troubles with ontology generate the trauma that lies at the centre of all of his narratives. Nikolai, as another deeply flawed Cronenberg hero, can here be usefully compared to Tom Stall, as Anna can to Edie. For Edie, an unthought-of realm intrudes on the orderly manner of the world previously thought to be so stable, and her growing horror at this intrusion is reflected in the way she responds to Tom with an appalled fascination. In the same way Anna, motivated by her desire to see the orphaned infant restored to her biological family, is drawn into the orbit of the *Vory V Zakone* and finds herself in a position where none of the previously workable strategies for survival are possible. In the face of this alternate system, this zone, the entire meaningful struc-ture of any 'ordinary' person's life is powerless. Once Kirill, in order to protect his father, steals the infant from the hospital, Anna's only recourse is to Nikolai who is able to talk Kirill around by promising him the keys to Semyon's kingdom once the old man is removed and replaced. When Anna later asks him why he has helped her, knowing nothing of his dual role, Nikolai can only reply, 'How can I become king if king is still in place?' The compassion of his actions, which Anna might recognize (and which might suggest the restorative meeting of unlikely lovers), must be hidden beneath the performance of the utilitarian gangster. This ambiva-lence is further indicated by the final shot of Nikolai sitting alone in what was Semyon's restaurant while Tatiana's voice-over details the bitter truth discovered by so many émigrés to the West, leaving us to wonder as to Nikolai's own future.

The zone of the *Vor*, an ontological substratum, becomes, then, another example of the ways in which Cronenberg seeks to continuously explore the possibilities for resistance to, and survival within, any form of dom-inant system. As he comments:

> . . . I realized I'm not interested in the mechanics of the mob . . . how they get the drugs, how they launder the money, how things are shipped. I'm not a fan of heist movies, where the mechanics of the heist are lov-ingly detailed. But criminality and people who live in a state of perpet-ual transgression – that is interesting to me. (Nayman, 2007)

As noted, the increasingly less 'fleshy' films offer, instead, narrative irreso-lution, and in *Eastern Promises* we finally see the full and comprehensive use of a consistent and coherent (which is to say, conventional) Western cinema form. Unlike *A History of Violence*, there are no suspicious elisions. Instead, what is absent from the film is what *should* be missing – material of no narrative importance, the general messiness of life that editing con-veniently removes for us. This may result in *Eastern Promises* looking increas-ingly like the conventional multiplex fare it has been exhibited alongside and with which it must compete for box office profits, but it need not necessarily result in a diluting of the 'project' itself, the attempt to explore the possibilities for a 'politics of insects', a 'deep, penetrating dive into the plasma pool'. All of these desires are coexistent with the developments, noted above, in Cronenberg's career, which, for all of the shifts and alterations, continues to offer a hard and consistent exploration of the 'brutal, essential malleability of the human vessel' (Nayman, 2007).

. . . All Resistors Sell Out – a Conclusion

As noted above, Cronenberg's continuing exploration of the disciplinary functions that, at times arbitrarily, govern and regulate the lives of the film's inhabitants reveals his heretical intent: Tom's failure to meet the demands (however impossible) of the disciplinary forces at work in civil society meets some of these heretical requirements; Nikolai, at the film's end, seems entirely in danger of being subsumed into the lifestyle, ideologies and ontological structures of the systems he, as a police officer, would ordinarily be expected to disrupt. Of more interest, however, are the ways in which these later films, as textual objects, function heretically when compared to the operation standard established by *Videodrome*. This allows us to explore the trajectory of perversity and the way in which Cronenberg's increasingly sophisticated texts shift the articulation of the perverse spectatorial position. Given that both *A History of Violence* and *Eastern Promises* utilize an entirely conventional construction,[14] it becomes obvious that neither film will demonstrate the representation of a perverse position (as with Žižek's example from *Manhunter*) nor construct a perverse position for its audience (as *Videodrome* so fluently does). Instead *A History of Violence* first recognizes its own position in the Cronenberg canon and works to undermine and subvert all that is implied through its membership, establishing a revised public perception of Cronenberg himself that, then, prefigures the reception of the more recent film. Therefore, and despite the appearance of cinematic conventionality that surrounds this film, it would appear as though *A History of Violence* is the most heretical of all of his texts, insofar as it extends its heresy outwards into *Eastern Promises* (and whatever follows that film), implicating its audience in the disciplinary activities they willingly agree to be a party to.

Videodrome demonstrates the manner with which Cronenberg is prepared to construct texts that perform their perversity at a formal level, positioning the spectator alongside the protagonist in a similarly powerless position, subject, in this instance, to the whims of a never clearly articulated third party (the ultimate source of the Videodrome signal and program). What *Videodrome* makes clear is the extent to which Cronenberg's filmic output becomes associated with this form of spectatorial positioning, so much so that the expectation of a perverse spectatorial position is accepted as part of what it means to encounter and interpret a Cronenberg film. In this fashion, the notion of the Cronenbergian film comes to function as a form of disciplinary discourse as much as the films themselves critique such discourse. I am suggesting, therefore, that the Cronenbergian text – prior to *A History of Violence* – does more than simply explore a coherent and stable set of thematic concerns. It articulates those concerns with the use of specific formal devices and, more importantly, works to position the spectator perversely in relation to those mechanisms. However, by the time we come to examine *A History of Violence*, Cronenberg's texts are functioning in exactly the same way as those disciplinary structures he seeks to critique. It is for this reason that there is no perverse spectatorial positioning in either *A History of Violence* or *Eastern Promises*. Such a positioning is anticipated by those audience members who have come to expect certain things from the Cronenbergian text, hence Cronenberg's decision to refuse to deliver on those expectations. In this fashion, and in direct comparison to those films that have preceded them, *A History of Violence* and *Eastern Promises* remain focused on exploring and highlighting the functioning of disciplinary structures – here by highlighting the audience's own complicity with these structures and demonstrating their own expectations based on the prior knowledge they bring to the cinematic experience. By subverting spectatorial expectations and thereby thwarting the recuperation of his heretical articulations, Cronenberg's films continue to explore the disciplinary fields that intersect with, and overlay, the production of cinematic texts.

With the above points in mind, it is clear that Cronenberg is, to utilize ideas from *Naked Lunch*, an 'agent' at work within, and resistant towards, the broader operations of 'control'. However, it should now be clear that 'control' is not simply equivalent to any single political force, censorial impulse, social or cultural mores. Here 'control' means, literally, those disciplinary structures that provide meaning and within which meaning must be made. Cronenberg has a clear political position, articulated consistently throughout his career, and his oeuvre emerges as a result of this. However, as the Bugwriter tells Lee, in *Naked Lunch*, 'All agents defect ... and all resistors sell out. That's the sad truth, Bill' (Cronenberg, 1991). What does this mean, in relation to Cronenberg? The figure of the agent occurs in many guises through his work, but Cronenberg's 'agents' are never so neatly in control of their fates as the label 'agent' might suggest. Regardless of the ultimate site of agency, the agent – as this figure occurs in Cronenberg's films – has been positioned by and represents a specific discursive position (be it political or, in Lee's case, libidinal); the agent is subject to the disciplines inherent in their discursive orientation as an agent, and is therefore defined by them. To defect, which the Bugwriter indicates is depressingly inevitable, may very well involve moving one's discursive position as one attempts to meet the often contradictory or impossibly demanding disciplinary requirements of the hegemony, but defection is never to be understood as escape. Hence the movement, for Lee (for example), from New York to Interzone (which is his movement through the various demands of his ideological landscape) finishes with his full recuperation into Annexia.

What *Videodrome* demonstrates is the apogee of perversity in Cronenberg's work as he continues to utilize what Žižek identifies as pre-ontological material to trouble interpretation and to lead the audience member towards the Real of interpretive impossibility. As I have noted, from *Video-drome* forwards there seems to be a series of general trends in Cronen-berg's work that, again while not strictly teleological, do indicate a kind of cumulative movement in his focus and in the 'Cronenberg project'. Chief among these is the gradual reduction of the spectacularly disruptive role played by the 'flesh' in his films: the fleshy irruptions that typify *Video-drome*, where the flesh explodes out from the pre-ontological, gradually shifts into films such as *The Fly*, where the flesh (still in enormous quan-tities) is now firmly located in the ontological realm of the diegesis. How-ever, with every reduction in the utilization of pre-ontological material comes an increase in the effects of the Real as the limit-sum of interpret-ation, as the site towards which the narrative leads and at which point it must necessarily cease. At the same time, we find a shift in the variety of formal mechanisms designed to structure perverse viewing conditions (through the arrangement or alignment of the spectator with a variety of 'gazes of the other'), moving from a site of fundamental importance in *Videodrome* to an absence of perversity in *A History of Violence*. So, over the course of Cronenberg's career, what has changed that might explain these changes in style, content and technique, if we assume that his ori-ginal intention (to 'show the unshowable') remains in place?

The answer comes with the solidification of Cronenberg's position as auteur, with all the concomitant (disciplinary) responsibilities borne by that position. As Cronenberg's career progresses and his films come to demonstrate a consistency of form, technique and content, it is clear that his films – all involved in critiquing a series of disciplinary structures – come themselves to function in a disciplinary fashion. In effect, Cronenberg's films train us in the art of reading Cronenberg's films. The trajectory of perversity has made him recognize the fact that audiences come to expect perverse spectatorial conditions from their encounters with his texts, which is why A *History of Violence* contains no such perverse positioning. Instead, it works – through its very conventionality – to undermine that perverse expectation (or, rather, expectation of perversity). However, does this necessarily mean that, to quote the Bugwriter, Cronenberg has 'sold out'?

From the outset, this document has worked to explore Cronenberg's intention to 'show the unshowable', demonstrating how this intention refers both to the inclusion of material that pushes up against a variety of disciplinary boundaries (that which *should* not be shown) and to that material that crosses into, or at least indicates, the very limits of intelligibility towards the 'politics of insects' (that which *can* not be shown, which *can* not be represented). This final chapter demonstrates that while Cronenberg's techniques might change, the intention to 'show the unshowable' remains firmly in place. What is missing from any accusation is the Bugwriter's own admission that 'selling out' is inevitable. After all, the point is not just that agents defect, but that *all* agents defect. This allows us to conclude two things. The first refers us back to Althusser and the manner with which any response to the call of interpellation demonstrates that one is always already a subject and, hence, an agent insofar as one claims agency, and insofar as having responded to the interpellative call, one is in the service of a higher authority. The second conclusion is that the inevitability of defection occurs because of the impossibility of ever entirely fulfilling every disciplinary demand one is subject to. It is this impossibility that makes heresy possible at all, in that utterly fulfilling one set of ideological demands reveals their inconsistencies and logical absurdities.

What Cronenberg demonstrates, over the course of his career, is that the interpellative call continues to come, must continually be answered, and never emerges from the same site continuously: the context of the call shifts and changes, and so too do the situations in which one responds. Max, in *Videodrome*, demonstrates the possibility of such agency. Indeed, Max is, if anything, an agent without agency, responding viscerally to the interpellative call (at Convex's request, Max literally 'opens up'). Similarly, Tom Stall is the interpellated subject (Joey Cusack) seeking (re-) interpellation (as Tom), while Nikolai stands as the doubly interpellated subject who, till the film's end, appears to be lost in 'the zone', the place where no choice (to be a policeman or a gangster alone) is possible, for either one compromises the performance of the agent as a whole. Thus Cronenberg's shifting trajectory of perversity in response to his own solidified position of disciplinary authority demonstrates the way in which the critic of discipline will respond to his own disciplinary status in order to draw attention to the interpellative call as a necessary frame.

Certainly, 'selling out' occurs, but here what is sold out is a position, a site of resistance that, through the process of becoming a disciplinary structure in its own right, is recuperated by the hegemony it once threatened and can therefore no longer be critical. Hence Cronenberg, the 'resistor', has sold out a site of resistance that has become exhausted, denuded of its ability to effect critical awareness. This is, after all, what happens to the flesh in Cronenberg's cinema. The function of the pre-ontological is to force a shift in an audience's ability to understand and contain the text it is working to interpret. Yet when that flesh, whose function is to collapse and problematize the invisible primacy of the Cartesian dialectic, becomes merely another characteristic of an auteur's work, the ability of the pre-ontological to rupture disciplinary structures has ended. This is the reason his cinema moves to, in effect, leave the meat behind. Instead Cronenberg's films increasingly explore the boundaries of the Real, illustrating it as a place of possibility that is horrifying in that it illustrates what lies beyond our ability to signify. This means that, across his career, the 'politics of insects' remains both an articulation of disciplinary resistance and a site for meaning-making and signification beyond our ability to recognize and decipher. Necessarily, the specific articulation of this insect politics changes as the films themselves respond to and critique their own altering hegemonic contexts. Nevertheless, Cronenberg's cinema appears committed to continuing this project and, as his work moves into what appears to be a third stage of disciplinary criticism, his attempts to extend discourse and representation into the utterly alien are as fiercely motivated as ever.

Notes

Chapter 1

[1] Cf. Baudry (1999), Comolli and Narboni (1999), de Lauretis, Heath and Wees (1980), among others.

[2] 'The political apparatus [functions] by subjecting individuals to the political State ideology, the "indirect" (parliamentary) or "direct" (plebiscitary or Fascist) "democratic" ideology. The communications apparatus by cramming every "citizen" with daily doses of nationalism, chauvinism, liberalism, moralism, etc., by means of the press, the radio and television. The same goes for the cultural apparatus . . .' (Althusser, 1994, 117).

[3] Althusser's discussion regarding the manner in which individuals respond to the clarion call of ideology finds an excellent Žižekian companion in the work of Klaus Theweleit who, in volume 2 of *Male Fantasies, Male Bodies: Psychoanalyzing the White Terror*, details at length the indoctrination processes at work in the German Officer Schools of the 1930s. Here we see demonstrated what Žižek would refer to as the (necessary) obscene underside to the interpellative process wherein the interpellated subject must work and suffer in order to be rewarded with the prize of visible interpellation, rather than simply respond to an ideological agency that, in order to function effectively, must remain effaced. Cf. Theweleit (1989, 143–64).

[4] 'With regards to the photographic image, Jean-Marie Schaeffer (1987) has clearly shown that a photograph's power to convince, often regarded as the power to portray a fragment of reality itself, rests on the implicit or explicit knowledge that a spectator has about the genesis of that image . . .' (Aumont, 1997, 81).

[5] Shaviro usefully defines the cinematic spectator, as distinct from other spectatorial formulations, as 'the form of subjectivity that not only experiences but is in large measure produced by cinematic affect' (Shaviro, 1993, 23–4). Thus we have an introductory movement towards the consideration of the cinematic spectator as emerging as a result of the cinematic experience and thus, carrying the results of this exercise into other spectatorial, and therefore subjective, experiences.

[6] Here the comparison is between Shaviro's unashamedly Foucaultian analysis and a more dogmatic psychoanalytic exploration which might view cinema as 'haunted since its inception by the spectre of a loss or absence at the centre of

cinematic production, a loss which both threatens and secures the viewing subject' (Silverman, 1988, 2). Thus, drawing on the work of Lacan, Silverman posits cinema as a site of lack (perhaps the pre-eminent example in the con temporary experience), where lack is to be understood as being of 'the absent real and the foreclosed site of production' (ibid.). Cinema, therefore, is lacking because images are false and the articulations of the cinematic apparatus is negative, always a reduction of the fantasized plenitude of actual experience.

[7] Indeed, part of this study's purpose is to return continuously to the concept of 'the Cronenberg project' and its attempts to 'show the unshowable' in order to explore how this project may be conceived of as offering different ways of understanding the films and their specific imperatives.

[8] Robert Fulford's criticism of *Shivers* concluded that the film '. . . did not warrant attention due to the numerous failures with its conventions' (Allinson, 2002), thereby punishing the director for his attempt to revise a genre with his specifically personal concerns.

[9] In the director's commentary track on the DVD reissue of *Fast Company*, Cronenberg notes that, having not seen this film for some twenty five years, it pleases him to think that it will now be publicly available and, perhaps, better understood.

[10] Cronenberg's film, I think, asks us to look beyond the standard ideas surrounding an exploitative text-audience relationship in order to think, also, of the ways in which certain actors, perhaps of a professional caliber distinguishable from their A-list colleagues, might sustain careers inside these kinds of genres and narratives. Indeed, one is drawn to consider the ways in which the B-movie / A-movie binary, in all of its forms, has increasingly collapsed in many contemporary genres.

[11] With Phil Savath and Courtney Smith, from an original story by Alan Treen.

[12] Cronenberg notes that his own familiarity with the racing community meant that the world of drag racing made sense to him: 'I got the drag racers' particular version, which is very much a beer-drinking, wet T-shirt thing. They even had T-shirts that said "Suck my pipes": a great phrase. I made sure I got that in' (Rodley, 1997, 73).

[13] 'I was doing a bit of documentary making with that movie. I was reading those Hot Rod magazines and was ready to build myself a hot Camaro. So I wouldn't disown one frame' (Rodley, 1997).

[14] The movement of the vehicles from right to left is maintained throughout the film and continues the trope of on-screen movement developed by the Western – the impetus to 'go West, young man', thereby locating the genre in geographic and gender terms.

[15] By which I make reference to the amount, and type, of machinery in the opening sequence, coupled with the now-execrable rock ballad that accompanies the big rigs on-screen.

[16] The point may be made that the Steadicam is utilized in order to provide the access of a hand-held camera with the same effacing of form that occurs with conventional camera use. In this manner, the Steadicam offers the possibility that the gaze of the camera is even more penetrative than previously imagined. The hand-held camera, in comparison, cannot help but draw attention to the fact of its presence, so marked is its image by the presence of the fallible operator.

[17] One of the few crane shots in the film. Cronenberg notes, with some relish, how the tight budget meant that the use of a crane, at all, was a luxury whose enjoyment he can still remember fondly, some twenty-five years later.

[18] It's telling, then, that there are moments when diegetic conversation is overwhelmed by the noise of the cars, but this engine noise never overcomes other sounds that might help us better understand the cars themselves.

[19] We shift our spectatorial position during the race so that we are with the cars as they begin their race, panning up the track (from right to left) to follow their progress, and then cut to rejoin them at the end of the track, matching the pan in the previous shot and panning to follow the cars over the finish line and past it.

[20] Our hero's car is closer to us than the villain's, thereby indicating that Billy has lost the race to Gary Black and intimating that, because his car is closer, he will have greater narrative significance. This moment prefigures the film's final conflict and gives us, also, an underdog upon which we can hang our allegiance.

Chapter 2

[1] Annabelle's youth is highlighted as one of the indications of Hobbes' 'dangerous' desires. As Linsky explains to St. Luc,

> . . . he [Hobbes] met her when he was lecturing at some private girls' school. They caught him examining her little tits for 'breast cancer' in the faculty lounge. She was twelve. Don't ask. It was craziness, believe me. (Cronenberg, 1976)

[2] It is worth comparing this statement with William Burroughs' oft-quoted paraphrase of Hassan I Sabbah, the Old Man of the Mountains: 'Nothing is true, everything is permitted.'

[3] Cf. Beard (1983, 23–31), Beard (2001, 49–50), Miller (1999), and Scheib (1993).

[4] Cronenberg's 'morphogenetically neutral tissue' is a clear homage to the 'undifferentiated tissue' that forms the centrepiece of the great William S. Burroughs routine, 'The Man Who Taught His Asshole to Talk' – which, in turn, would become a pivotal moment in Cronenberg's film *Naked Lunch*.

[5] In the *Rabid* screenplay Cronenberg refers to them as 'crazies' (2002a, 195).

[6] It is worth noting that the scientist figure at the centre of Cronenberg's 'breakthrough' independent feature *Crimes of the Future* is never seen at all, 'appearing' at the film's conclusion reincarnated as a small girl.

[7] Ira Livingston is less convinced of Keloid's altruism, noting that

> Keloid's reluctance . . . [to franchise the clinic] is only skin deep; in order to pursue his medical ambitions, he will leave the financial and managerial entrepreneurship to his partners. When news of the accident interrupts the meeting, he quickly acquiesces to the plan, and rushes off to attend the victim. (Livingston, 1993)

[8] It is worth comparing the figure of Rose with that of Carrie in Brian De Palma's 1976 film of the same name. Carrie, like Rose, occupies a liminal position as both victim and agent of destruction (however unwitting). Interestingly, Sissy Spacek was Cronenberg's first choice for the role of Rose.

[9] In his review of the film, Rhett Miller notes that

> Cronenberg has always had a distrust for medical authority, and his preoccupation is more than relevant in a nation where health care remains controlled entirely by the state. While *Shivers* also hinted at this scrutiny . . . *Rabid* is a much more elaborate staging of a similar concept, but this time the effect hits much closer to home. Montreal . . . is thrown into anarchy as the threat of medical malpractice and social unrest suddenly becomes very real – and very Canadian. (Miller, 1999)

[10] This is a problematic point because the very devices that make *The Fly* articulate and sustained – clearly defined protagonists and antagonists, character development and emotions arcs, clearly defined resolution – are the same devices that threaten to contain and, therefore, recuperate the heretical potential of this film. Not surprisingly, all of these devices are absent from *Videodrome*.

[11] Susan Sontag, in *Illness as Metaphor*, notes that '[c]ancer could be described as a triumphant mutation, and mutation is now mainly an image for cancer' (Sontag, 2002, 69). Thus Cronenberg's utilization of both the cancer metaphor to discuss his various 'diseases with purposes', and the manner with which he leads these irruptions of other-agency with import continues a long-standing tradition of referring to disease (and specifically cancer) in this manner.

[12] Cronenberg has a co-writing credit for *The Fly*, shared with Charles Edward Pogue.

[13] It could conceivably be suggested that Cronenberg's version of Body Horror marks a shift in that sub-genre's elaboration. Part of the horror implicit in the visceral destruction witnessed in the cinema of Romero, Hooper and Carpenter, is the schism between the body that suffers and the mind that remains able to experience that suffering in order to report it more effectively to the films' audiences. Cronenberg's elaboration on this theme forces us to helplessly witness a body that alters in response to some alien directive, and a mind that becomes increasingly *unable* to comprehend or represent those changes. The difference is that where the standard Body Horror film enables the audience in discursive relation to the protagonist, Cronenberg's disables them even as the protagonist is disabled.

Chapter 3

[1] This point, and its disciplinary implications, is considered in far greater detail in Chapter 6.

[2] Of course, as was noted in the first chapter, among the contexts elided in the process of viewing the cinematic texts is the context of production.

[3] As Cronenberg notes, '[b]ecause its imagery is rather innocuous, it's more palatable. It's certainly the least offensive film I've made; the only one where

grannies come out crying about the tragic love affair at the end. It's more gentle. Possibly that's one of the reasons I wanted to make it.' (Rodley, 1997, 114)

4 While, at this early stage of the narrative *The Dead Zone* has yet to formally confirm its genre, an audience lured to the film by Cronenberg's name would certainly be expecting 'something' to happen. Similarly, the film's tagline ('In his mind, he has the power to see the future. In his hands, he has the power to change it') leads us to expect the film to shift gears at an appropriate moment. As this document will go on to explore, that spectatorial expectation of what a director might or might not do, does come to function as a disciplinary structure in its own right. What Cronenberg does to counter or subvert those expectations is explored in Chapter 6.

5 It is interesting to note then that, despite the fact that they are both adults and schoolteachers, the presence of their date's time (after school) and place (an amusement park) gives notice to Smith's particularly infantilized (and infantilizing) performance of adulthood.

6 Smith's desire for isolation occurs both because his power – the visions – marks him as different, and because he is powerless to control those visions. It is interesting to consider how different *The Dead Zone* would have been had Smith been able to control, and productively utilize, his visions. Indeed, one might consider Smith's powerlessness in the face of a power that clearly influences his life, without reason or permission, as an allegory for the Althusserian interpellated subject.

7 Here, as with Brundle, is the negotiation of the flesh with the intellect – the arms of his lover reminds Smith of a greater social obligation and thus he is pulled from one side of the Cartesian binary towards a coherent centre. For the Cronenbergian protagonist, this movement to alter the terms of the mind/body dichotomy in any way is a sure indicator of disaster looming.

8 It is no surprise that all of Cronenberg's early films occur in winter – this corresponds with the closing of the Canadian tax year, meaning that while the Tax Shelter program was in operation, investment would come in a rush in October as '. . . potential investors panicked and looked around for film productions in which to invest their profits' (Rodley, 1997, 69).

9 Cf. Chambers (2000), Crane (2000, 56–7), Hogan (1983–4) and Strick (1984), among many others.

10 Peter Morris notes that while *The Dead Zone* was Cronenberg's '. . . most naturalistic and palatable film for a mainstream audience, . . . box-office receipts were modest' (Morris, 1994, 100).

11 Her first name is never given, a point made clear when, as part of the 'making of' featurettes that flesh out the DVD release, all concerned continue to refer to her as Mrs Cleg.

12 At this point in the film, the role of Mrs Wilkinson is played by Miranda Richardson as well.

13 Importantly, *Spider* does not have any point-of-view shots and, indeed, it could be argued that *Spider* marks one man's attempts to find a fixed and normal point of view.

14 Despite the fact that *Spider* is intended not as 'a clinical study of schizophrenia . . .[but rather] is a study of the human condition when it's pushed to a

particular extreme . . .' (Cronenberg, 2002b, director's commentary), Spider's notebook and particular style of writing, both inventions of Cronenberg's, find their real-life corollary in the work of Hans Prinzhorn who, in his *Artistry of the Mentally Ill* (1922) notes that 'Even the simplest scribble . . . is, as a manifestation of expressive gestures, the bearer of psychic components, and the whole sphere of psychic life lies as if in perspective behind the most insignificant form element' (Prinzhorn, quoted in Rhodes, 2000).

[15] Named in the credits as Flashing Yvonne.

[16] Even those shots that seem the least connected to Dennis' construction of his past bear the traces of his interpretive presence. Thus those incidental shots of Spider walking the streets of London are emptied of all life, leading Cronenberg to comment that 'we were really making an expressionist movie – that is to say that everything you see in the move is really expressing Spider's inner state of mind' (Cronenberg, 2002b, director's commentary)

[17] Cronenberg: Do you think there could ever be a computer game that could truly be art? Rushdie: No. (Cronenberg, 1995, 12)

[18] 'As a card-carrying existentialist I think all reality is virtual. It's all invented. It's collaborative, so you need friends to help you create a reality' (Rodley, 1999).

[19] At a crucial moment in *eXistenZ*, as Pikul and Geller prepare to move from the (apparently) primary diegesis of the game and into a sub-game, Pikul experiences a moment of anxiety:

> I'm very worried about my body. . . . Where are our real bodies? Are they alright? What if they're hungry? What if there's danger? . . . I feel really vulnerable . . . disembodied. (Cronenberg, 1999)

This moment occurs as he and Geller, who have downloaded new (sub-)identities to supplement their game identities (which, presumably, are supplements themselves), are experiencing a very bodily exchange that is part of the game's narrative impulse. At every moment, then, Cronenberg works to remind us that the body *will* not be forgotten. Indeed, multiplying the nested diegetic (sub-)identities only seems to increase the manner and force with which the body's own imperatives return.

[20] As Chris Rodley notes, 'This move away from the [techno-]city comes out of a decision . . . to remove from this world everything people would expect from a sci-fi movie about game playing. There are no computers, computer screens, televisions, sneakers, watches, clocks, jewellery or suits' (Rodley, 1999).

[21] As well as *The Matrix* (and sequels), one immediately thinks of *Dark City* (Alex Proyas, 1998), *The Thirteenth Floor* (Josef Rusnak, 1998), *Johnny Mnemonic* (Robert Longo, 1995), *Lawnmower Man* (Brett Leonard, 1992) and so on.

Chapter 4

[1] Although with significant qualifications. See Chapter 6 for an examination of the responses generated by *A History of Violence*.

[2] Cf. Beard (2001) and Rodley (1997).

[3] Cf. Beard (2001, 339).

4 See also Beard (2001, 338–43, 345–7) and Rodley (1997, 172–4).

5 Some of these 'sayings', which Beard refers to as a 'cloud of mysterious-Orient hokum' (Beard, 2001, 370), include the following: 'China is a country whose soul is firmly rooted 2000 years in the past. What I do, even pouring the tea for you now, it has implications' (Cronenberg, 1993); 'René. Please, let me keep my clothes on. It all frightens me. Modesty is so important to the Chinese' (ibid.); 'The Chinese are an ancient people. We cling to the old ways of life, and love. Though inexperienced, I am not ignorant. They teach us things, our mothers . . . about pleasing a man' (ibid.).

6 Richard Corliss, for example, complains that the film is defeated by a combination of poor performance and '. . . unlikely plot points; the diplomat daubs himself as Madam Butterfly before a rapt audience – of French convicts! Cronenberg is unlikely to find other spectators as gullible as they' (Corliss, 1993).

7 Both *mirror* and *marvel* derive from the same Latin root, *mirare* – 'to look at'.

8 The presence of externally oriented measurements of success are supported by the fact that Elliot appears to watch *Lifestyles of the Rich and Famous* obsessively.

9 It is Elliot, during his consultation and initial examination of Claire, who comments that he has often thought that there should be beauty contests for the insides of people's bodies.

10 Cf. Shaw and especially Jacobowitz and Lippe (1989, 67) and Creed (1990), among others. Interestingly, even Jeremy Irons found the twins relationship to be '. . . fundamentally homosexual, but Platonic' (Irons, quoted in Rodley, 1997). See Gittings (2001, 278–80) for a comprehensive overview of these readings.

11 Cf. Barker, Arthurs, and Harindranath (2001), Kuhn (1999), Petley (1997) and S. A. Wilson (2001).

12 In the introduction to the 1974 French edition of *Crash*, later amended in subsequent English-language editions (and reprinted again in the Vale/Juno collection *J. G. Ballard* [1984]), Ballard comments that

> Over our lives preside the great twin leitmotifs of the twentieth century – sex and paranoia. . . . Voyeurism, self-disgust, the infantile basis of our dreams and longings – these diseases of the psyche have now culminated in the most terrifying casualty of the century: the death of affect. (Vale & Juno, 1984, 96)

13 Famously, Ballard's protagonist bears his name. As he comments in the interview,

> The story is told by a first person narrator. A large part takes place inside his own imagination. . . . And I thought, well, these are my ideas, the products of my imagination. I wanted to force the reader to face what I was laying out, and the best way to do that, I thought, was to be honest, not hide behind a mask . . . but to throw the mask away and say, look, this is me, these are my fantasies, my dreams. I hoped that would give the book a little more authority. (Ballard, 1996)

14 Vaughan's statement should be compared with an earlier explanation of his project, which is '. . . something we're all intimately involved in: the reshaping of the human body by modern technology' (Cronenberg, 1996b, 35). This first explanation is later revealed to be a '. . . crude sci-fi concept that floats on the surface and doesn't threaten anybody' (Cronenberg, 1996b, 42).

15 Toronto was chosen for exactly this 'anywhere/everywhere' sense of anonymity so that while Ballard's novel is quite specifically set in London, at a specific (if never entirely revealed) time, Cronenberg's film is more deliberately adrift in the late twentieth century. Again, this is part of his attempt to empty the film, and characters, of the kinds of specific details that work so well in *M. Butterfly* and *Dead Ringers*.

16 Matt Smith, responding to Ballard's assessment of the 'death of affect' (see Note 12 above), comments,

> What this invocation outlines is an attempt to comprehend the psychic aetiology of a particular epoch, one characterized by a fundamental tonal shift in the category of the emotions: namely that this age is dominated by a mutation in emotional sensibility toward a certain dampening of affective response, or a shattering of subjectivity that eventuates a 'death' of affectivity. (Smith, 2006)

Chapter 5

1 Cf. Rodley (1997, 75–9).

2 Here the Greek etymology is referenced and not the Vedic ritual intoxicant referred to by Huxley in *Brave New World* (1932).

3 For a more complete discussion of hysteric symptoms, the reader is directed towards Georges Didi-Huberman's *Invention of Hysteria: Charcot and the Photographic Iconography of the Salpêtrière* (Cambridge, MA: MIT Press, 2003).

4 Cf. Chapter 4's discussion of *eXistenZ*.

5 There is a crucial distinction between *Scanners* and *The Dead Zone* in that here we never experience Vale's 'scans' in the way we 'see' Smith's visions. Certainly the method of diegetically representing the process of scanning remains the same, but we are never rewarded with a glimpse of what it is that Vale apprehends while scanning. As will be explored below, scanning differs from Smith's prophetic sight in that scanning provides a physiological link with another individual while Smith's gaze remains at the surface – providing action, as it were, but no motive. What emerges from this consideration is the possibility that the scanning event is, by its very nature, unrepresentable.

6 This is demonstrated to be 'psychic' since no one appears to speak while the words are being uttered and, furthermore, the dialogue is treated with what sounds like a reverb so that each word sounds as though it is being uttered in a very large space. This treatment alone has become a clichéd way of representing 'interior or psychic speech'.

7 It may well be that these 'good' scanners represent a form of group therapy and that their scanning is designed to provide a state of health and well-being

for the participant members. Given their singular failure to achieve anything of note in the narrative, it is hard to avoid concluding that their presence is designed to serve some parodic function. At the very least, the fact that they are so torpid makes Revok's aggressive activity all the more attractive.

[8] It is this symptom that Ephemerol appears to block, which is why Ruth uses it as a scan suppressant.

[9] Given that Consec, as discussed, stands in for a range of hegemonic disciplinary structures. It is interesting to note that as a research and development company who specialize in issues of security and defence, Consec straddle the line between Althusser's ISA and RSA, working in one area to supply the material for the other.

[10] To be fair, after the yoga master collapses, we cut to Vale smiling and refusing Ruth's shot of Ephemerol, while the sound track contains sounds of a heart-rate monitor decreasing in speed, but this is, at the very least, inconclusive and Dieter Tautz is never mentioned again.

[11] Lack's performance as Vale has drawn near-unanimous censure. He is, for example, criticized for being '. . . utterly wooden and almost entirely absent as a personality on screen' (Scheib, 1999) and '. . . the flat reading of some his lines, particularly in the crucial sequence when he and the villain finally confront each other' (Brosnan, 27, 1981) has provoked laughter in audiences.

[12] Cronenberg notes, 'It's impossible to make a movie out of *Naked Lunch*. A literal translation wouldn't work. It would cost $400 million to make and would be banned in every country in the world – not an attractive proposition for a producer' (quoted in Emery and Silverberg, 1992, 57).

[13] Cf. Rodley (1997, 161–4).

[14] Lee was Burroughs' mother's maiden name and William Lee features as an alter ego in many Burroughs texts.

[15] Burroughs comments that

> I am forced to the appalling conclusion that I would never have become a writer but for Joan's death. . . . So the death of Joan brought me into contact with the invader, the Ugly Spirit, and manoeuvred me into a lifelong struggle in which I had no choice but to write my way out. (Burroughs, 1985, xxii)

[16] Although the book that Bill Lee is working towards compiling is never named, enough diegetic clues are provided to ensure we understand that this text will become *Naked Lunch*. However, in order to distinguish between Cronenberg's film and the book that Lee is diegetically constructing, the film title will always be italicized with the book title appearing in single quote marks.

Chapter 6

[1] Discussed in Chapter 2 and Chapter 4, respectively.

[2] Žižek, drawing on Lacan, would refer to these anchors as *points de caption* (points of capture), moments when, in interpreting the text, '. . . signifier and signified are knotted together' (Lacan, quoted in Evans, 1996). I suggest that the conventional narrative film-text has a number of these (e.g., the specific

interpretive intention behind the use of particular shots, angles, movements, etc.) and that part of Cronenberg's heretical process is to upset, trouble or remove these altogether. Crucially, Lacan comments that '. . . a certain minimum number of these points are "necessary for a person to be called normal", and "when they are not established, or when they give way" the result is psychosis' (ibid.).

3 Cf. Žižek (2001a, 208–13).

4 1953 is the year Lacan resigned from his presidency of the *Société psychanalytique de Paris* (SPP) and joined the newly formed *Société française de psychanalyse*, opening their inaugural meeting (on the eighth of July) with his lecture on 'the symbolic, the imaginary and the real'. Cf. Evans (1996, xxi).

5 It could conceivably be suggested that the characters who are killed on the Videodrome set and who later occur within Max's hallucinations (Nikki, for example) move from the ontological *into* the pre-ontological.

6 Doug Pratt, in his review of the DVD release of *Videodrome*, recounts Cronenberg's comments during production:

> Jimmy was complaining a lot about the difficulties of walking around with this 'stomach slit' prosthesis and what he had to do when his stomach is sort of opening and cassettes are being inserted, and he said to Debbie [Harry], 'You know, I've ceased being an actor, I'm now only just the bearer of the slit.' And Debbie said, 'Now you know what it's like.' (Cronenberg, quoted in Pratt, 2004)

7 Which begs the question – is the vaginal slit Max's own invention, thereby revealing much about his own psyche, or is it Convex's Videodrome-induced imposition on Max's body?

8 *Shivers* was released in 1976, *A History of Violence* in 2006. I am not considering the time spent prior to *Shivers* during which Cronenberg produced two short student films, *Transfer* (1966) and *From the Drain* (1967), and two longer independent features *Stereo* (1969) and *Crimes of the Future* (1970). While these films all evidence Cronenberg's concerns (as, of course, they should), they are not commercially produced texts and therefore circulate in an entirely different interpretive context to his commercial features.

9 It is worth mentioning, however tangentially, that it falls to a Canadian director to provide such a comprehensive non-ironic representation of the contemporary American small town. Certainly Lynch's and Cronenberg's work have long been popularly confused but it is here that Cronenberg proves how utterly different the two directors actually are. Indeed, to paraphrase Song in *M. Butterfly* 'Only a Canadian knows how an American small town *should* be represented'.

10 With the arguable exception of *Fast Company*.

11 It should be noted that Cronenberg's *A History of Violence* is a fundamentally different text than Wagner and Locke's graphic novel, upon which it is based. The novel answers every question raised about Tom (McKenna in the novel), provides full justification for all of his actions and has Tom solving his difficulties

with Edie midway through, after which she is a full supporter in his actions of violence and retribution. Cf. Wagner and Locke (1997).

12 It should be noted that this appraisal of *A History of Violence* occurs within the academy also. Thus the recent call for papers for the 2008 Film and History Conference notes that this film is his 'most mass audience–accessible to date' (Yates, 2007).

13 Here one is led to consider Vaughan's ritualistic tattoos in *Crash*, which offer a prescient suggestion of the violence these bodies are yet to suffer in their relationships with the automobiles that fascinate them.

14 Which should in no way be taken as a criticism, for the film is entirely effective both in terms of the ability of the formal techniques to efface themselves (as they are required by Western narrative convention) and in their ability to deliver a narrative that appears all the more 'natural' for that effacing.

Bibliography

Adria, M. (2001). 'So Close to the State/s: The Emergence of Canadian Feature Film Policy' (review). *Labour/Le Travail*, 236.

Allinson, A. (2002). *David Cronenberg*. Retrieved 18 April 2011 from http://www.sensesofcinema.com/2002/great-directors/cronenberg/?ref=ARKADASBUL.NET.

Althusser, L. (1994). 'Ideology and Ideological State Apparatuses (Notes Towards an Investigation)', in S. Žižek (ed.), *Mapping Ideology*. London: Verso, pp. 100–40.

Anderson, J. D. (1996). *The Reality of Illusion: An Ecological Approach to Cognitive Film Theory*. Carbondale and Edwardsville: Southern Illinois University Press.

Andrejevic, M. (2004). *Reality TV: The Work of Being Watched*. Lanham, MD: Rowman and Littlefield.

Ansen, D. (1993, 18 October). 'Much Stranger than Fiction'. *Newsweek*, 122.

Aumont, J. (1997). *The Image* (C. Pajackowska, trans.). London: British Film Institute.

Ballard, J. G. (1996). *Interview with J. G. Ballard*. Retrieved 25 March 2006 from http://www.jgballard.ca/interviews/fine_line_features_1997.html.

Barker, M., J. Arthurs and R. Harindranath (2001). *The 'Crash' Controversy: Censorship Campaigns and Film Reception*. London and New York: Wallflower Press.

Baudry, J.-L. (1999). 'Ideological Effects of the Basic Cinematographic Apparatus' (A. Williams, trans.), in L. Braudy and M. Cohen (eds), *Film Theory and Criticism: Introductory Readings* (5th edn). New York and Oxford: Oxford University Press, pp. 345–55.

Bazin, A. (2005). 'The Evolution of the Language of Cinema' (H. Gray, trans.), in *What Is Cinema?* (2nd edn). Berkeley: University of California Press, pp. 23–40.

Beard, W. (1983). 'The Visceral Mind', in P. Handling (ed.), *The Shape of Rage: The Films of David Cronenberg*. Toronto: Academy of Canadian Cinema, pp. 1–79.

—(2001). *The Artist as Monster: The Cinema of David Cronenberg* (1st edn). Toronto: University of Toronto Press.

Benedict, C. (2006). *Fast Company*. Retrieved 27 March 2006 from http://www.tranquility.net/~benedict/fastcompany.html.

Biocca, F. (1997, September). The Cyborg's Dilemma: Progressive Embodiment in Virtual Environments. Retrieved 1 November 2006 from http://jcmc.indiana.edu/vol3/issue2/biocca2.html.

Bokamper, J. (2000, 7 November). 'You'll Get More Than the "Shivers" Watching the Work of Cronenberg'. *Dallas Morning News*.

Breskin, D. (1992, 6 February). 'David Cronenberg: The Rolling Stone Interview'. *Rolling Stone*, 66–70, 96.

Brooker, P. (2002). *A Glossary of Cultural Theory* (2nd edn). London: Arnold.

Brosnan, J. (1981). '*Scanners*.' *Starburst*, 3, 24–7.

Burkart, G. S. '*Fast Company (1979)*'. Retrieved 25 March 2006 from http://www.monstersatplay.com/review/dvd/f/fastcompany.php.

Burroughs, W. S. (1985). *Queer*. New York: Viking Press.

—(1992). 'Introduction', in I. Silverberg (ed.), *Everything Is Permitted: The Making of Naked Lunch*. New York: Grove Weidenfeld.

Caldwell, T. (2002). '*Shivers*'. Retrieved 25 March 2006 from http://archive.sensesofcinema.com/contents/cteq/01/19/shivers.html.

Chambers, B. (2000). '*The Dead Zone (1983)*'. Retrieved 23 March 2006 from http://filmfreakcentral.net/dvdreviews/deadzone.htm.

Chaudhuri, S. (2001). 'Witnessing Death: Ballard's and Cronenberg's *Crash*'. *Strategies*, 14(1), 63–75.

Coe, J. (1997, 6 June). 'There Is No Paedophilia or Sexual Humiliation in *Crash*. Neither Is There Any Merit. But We Should Still Defend It from the Censors and Moralists'. *New Statesman*, 126.

Combs, R. (2002). '*Spider*'. *Film Comment*, 72.

Comolli, J.-L., and J. Narboni (1999). 'Cinema/Ideology/Criticism', in L. Braudy and M. Cohen (eds), *Film Theory and Criticism: Introductory Readings* (5th edn). Oxford: Oxford University Press, pp. 752–9.

Corliss, R. (1993, 4 October). 'Betrayal in Beijing'. *Time*, 142.

Crane, J. (2000). 'A Body Apart: Cronenberg and Genre', in M. Grant (ed.), *The Modern Fantastic: The Films of David Cronenberg*. Westport, CT: Praeger, pp. 50–68.

Crary, J. (1992). *Techniques of the Observer: On Vision and Modernity in the Nineteenth Century*. Cambridge, MA: MIT Press.

Creed, B. (1990). 'Phallic Panic: Male Hysteria and *Dead Ringers*'. *Screen*, 31(1), 125–46.

—(1993). *The Monstrous-Feminine: Film, Feminism, Psychoanalysis*. London: Routledge.

Cronenberg, D. (director) (1976). *Shivers* [35 mm]. I. Reitman, J. Dunning and A. Link (producers). Canada: Cinépix Film Properties Inc.

—(1977). *Rabid* [35 mm]. I. Reitman, J. Dunning and A. Link (producers). Canada: New World Pictures.

—(1979a). *The Brood* [35 mm]. V. Solnicki and P. David (producers). Canada: New World Pictures.

—(1979b). *Fast Company* [35 mm]. P. O'Brian, Michael Lebowitz, P. Savath and Courtney Smith (producers). Canada: Quadrant Films.

—(1981). *Scanners* [35 mm]. C. Heroux (producer). Canada: Avco-Embassy Pictures.

—(1982). *Videodrome* [35 mm]. C. Heroux, P. David and V. Solnicki (producers). Canada: CDFC.

—(1983). *The Dead Zone* [35 mm]. D. Hill (producer). USA: Paramount Pictures.

—(1986). *The Fly* [35 mm]. S. Cornfeld (producer). USA: Twentieth Century Fox.

—(1988). *Dead Ringers* [35 mm]. D. Cronenberg and M. Boyman (producers). Canada: Telefilm Canada.

—(1991). *Naked Lunch* [35 mm]. J. Thomas and G. Martinelli (producers). USA: 20th Century Fox.

—(1993). *M. Butterfly*. G. Martinelli (producer). USA: Geffen Film.

—(1996a). *Crash* [35 mm]. D. Cronenberg, R. Lantos and J. Thomas (producers). Canada: Alliance Atlantis.

—(1999). *eXistenZ* [35 mm]. R. Lantos, A. Hamori and D. Cronenberg (producers). Alliance Atlantis: Canada.

—(2002b). *Spider* [35 mm]. D. Cronenberg, S. Hadida and C. Bailey (producers). Canada: Columbia Tristar.

—(2005). *A History of Violence* [35 mm]. C.Bender, J.C. Spink, T. Emmerich, K. Alterman, C. Boyter, J. Braun, J. Greene and R. Kass (producers). USA: New Line Productions.

—(2007). *Eastern Promises* [35mm]. R. Lantos, T. Seaward and P. Webster (producers). USA: Focus Features.

Cronenberg, D. (1995, June–July). 'Cronenberg Meets Rushdie'. *Shift*, 3.4. Retrieved 11 April 2010 from http://www.davidcronenberg.de/cr_rushd.htm.

—(1996b). *Crash* (screenplay) (1st edn). London: Faber and Faber.

—(2002a). *Collected Screenplays* (vol. 1). London: Faber and Faber.

Cronenberg, D., W. Beard and P. Handling (1983). 'The Interview', in P. Handling (ed.), *The Shape of Rage: The Films of David Cronenberg*. Toronto: Academy of Canadian Cinema, pp. 159–98.

Cronenberg, D., and D. Schwartz (1992). 'A Pinewood Dialogue with David Cronenberg'. New York: Museum of the Moving Image.

de Lauretis, Teresa, Stephen Heath and William C. Wees (1980). *The Cinematic Apparatus*. London: Macmillan.

Didi-Huberman, G. (2003). *Invention of Hysteria: Charcot and the Photographic Iconography of the Salpêtrière* (A. Hartz, trans.). Cambridge, MA: MIT Press.

Eggers, P. (2005). *A History of Violence*. Retrieved 10 April 2011 from http://replay.waybackmachine.org/20070702094010/http://www.hour.ca/film/movie.aspx?iIDFilm=8012.

Emery, P., and I. Silverberg (1992). 'Production History: Notes and Scenes from the Making of the Film', in I. Silverberg (ed.), *Everything Is Permitted: The Making of Naked Lunch*. New York: Grove Weidenfeld.

Emery, R. J. (writer) (1999). 'The Directors: David Cronenberg' [DVD], in R. J. Emery (producer), *The Directors: Profiles of Today's Most Acclaimed Hollywood Directors*. USA: American Film Institute.

Evans, D. (1996). *An Introductory Dictionary of Lacanian Psychoanalysis* (2nd edn). London and New York: Routledge.

Feher-Gurewich, J. (2003). 'A Lacanian Approach to the Logic of Perversion', in J.-M. Rabaté (ed.), *The Cambridge Companion to Lacan*. Cambridge, UK: Cambridge University Press, pp. 191–207.

Feng, P. X. (2002). 'False and Double Consciousness: Race, Virtual Reality and the Assimilation of Hong Kong Action Cinema in *The Matrix*', in Z. Sardar and S. Cubitt (eds), *Aliens R Us: The Other in Science Fiction Cinema*. London: Pluto Press.

Fisher, M. (2007, November) '*Eastern Promises*'. *Sight and Sound*, 57–8.

Foucault, M. (1980). *Power/Knowledge: Selected Interviews and Other Writings 1972–1977*. London: Harvester Press.

—(1983). 'The Subject and Power', in H. Dreyfus and P. Rabinow (eds), *Michel Foucault: Beyond Structuralism and Hermeneutics* (2nd edn). Chicago: University of Chicago Press, pp. 208–26.

—(1995). *Discipline and Punish: The Birth of the Prison* (A. Sheridan, trans.). New York: Vintage.

Freud, S. (1973). *Introductory Lectures on Psychoanalysis*. London: Penguin. First published 1916.

Gittings, C. E. (2001). *Canadian National Cinema: Ideology, Difference and Representation*. London and New York: Routledge.

Grant, M. (1997). *Dead Ringers*. Trowbridge, UK: Flicks Books.

—(2000). 'Introduction', in M. Grant (ed.), *The Modern Fantastic: The Films of David Cronenberg*. Westport, CT: Praeger, pp. 1–34.

Gregory, D. (director) (2004). *Shooting Cronenberg: Interview with Directory of Photography Mark Irwin*. W. Lustig (producer). USA: Blue Underground Productions.

Grunberg, S. (2006). *David Cronenberg: Interviews with Serge Grunberg*. London: Plexus.

Handling, P. (1983). 'A Canadian Cronenberg', in P. Handling (ed.), *The Shape of Rage*. Toronto: Academy of Canadian Cinema, pp. 98–114.

Hogan, D. J. (1983–4, December/January). 'King and Cronenberg: It's the Best of Both Worlds'. *Cinefantastique*, 14, 51.

Hoover, T. (2002). Spider. Retrieved 25 March 2006 from http://filmfreakcentral.net/screenreviews/spider.htm.

Hotchkiss, L. M. (2003). ' "Still in the Game": Cybertransformations of the "New Flesh" in David Cronenberg's *eXistenZ*. *The Velvet Light Trap* (52), 15–32.

Hwang, D. H. (1989). 'An Afterword by the Playwright', in *M. Butterfly*. New York: Penguin.

Jacobowitz, F., and R. Lippe (1989). '*Dead Ringers*: The Joke's on Us'. *CineAction!*, 64–8.

Johnson, B. D. (1999, 26 April). 'Virtual Director: David Cronenberg Returns to His Science-Fiction Roots'. *Maclean's*, 112, 62–3.

Kauffmann, S. (1993, 1 November). 'Transformations'. *New Republic*, 26–8.

Kay, S. (2003). *Žižek: A Critical Introduction*. Cambridge, UK: Polity.

Kermode, M. (1992, March). 'David Cronenberg'. *Sight and Sound*, 11–13.

Koehler, R. (2007, Fall) '*Eastern Promises*'. *Cinema Scope*, 76–7.

Krips, H. (2004). 'Couching Politics: Žižek's Rules for Radicals'. *Journal for the Psychoanalysis of Culture and Society*, 9, 126–41.

Kristeva, J. (1982). *Powers of Horror: An Essay on Abjection* (L. S. Roudies, trans.). New York: Columbia University Press.

Kuhn, A. (1999). '*Crash* and Film Censorship in the UK'. *Screen*, 40(4), 446–50.

Livingston, I. (1993). 'The Traffic in Leeches: David Cronenberg's *Rabid* and the Semiotics of Parasitism'. *American Imago*, 50(4), 515–33.

Lowenstein, A. (2004). *David Cronenberg and the "Face" of National Authorship*. Retrieved 28 February 2006 from http://www.kinokultura.com/articles/oct04-natcine-lowenstein.html.

Maher, J. (2002). '"We Don't Do Babies": Reproduction in David Cronenberg's *Dead Ringers*'. *Journal of Gender Studies*, 11(2), 119–28.

Mansfield, N. (2000). *Subjectivity: Theories of the Self from Freud to Haraway*. St Leonards, NSW: Allen and Unwin.

Maronie, S. (1981, February). 'David Cronenberg: Canada's King of Horror Enters the Science Fiction World with *Scanners*'. *Starlog*, 24–8.

Maslin, J. (1996, 20 May). 'Cannes Finally Gets a Noisy Controversy'. *New York Times*, section C, p. 11.

Mendik, X. (2000). 'Logic, Creativity and (Critical) Misinterpretations: An Interview with David Cronenberg', in M. Grant (ed.), *The Modern Fantastic: The Films of David Cronenberg*. Westport, CT: Praeger, pp. 168–85.

Miller, R. (1999). *Rabid*. Retrieved 3 August 2006 from http://www.canuxploitation.com/review/rabid.html.

Morris, P. (1994). *David Cronenberg: A Delicate Balance* (1st edn). Toronto: ECW Press.

Mottram, E. (1977). *William Burroughs: The Algebra of Need*. London: Marion Boyars.

Nayman, A. (2006, Fall). 'The Artful Violence of David Cronenberg'. *Montage*, 26–31.

—(2007). *Eastern Promises*. Retrieved 1 September 2009 from http://www.eyeweekly.com/print/article/21860.

Newman, K. (1988) *Nightmare Movies: A Critical History of the Horror Movie from 1968*. London: Bloomsbury.

Nixon, J. A. K. (2007). *A History of Violence* (DVD review). 2007 from http://www.amazon.co.uk/History-Violence-Viggo-Mortensen/dp/rentals/B000E6TVRS.

Petley, J. (1997). 'No Redress from the PCC'. *British Journalism Review*, 8(4), 1–8.

Pinsky, M. (2005). *Fast Company* (limited edn). Retrieved 25 March 2006 from http://www.dvdverdict.com/reviews/fastcompanyle.php.

PolarisDiB (internet pseudonym) (2005). 'Well Enough Done but Not Really Interesting . . .'. Retrieved 3 March 2007 from http://poll.imdb.com/title/tt0399146/usercomments?start=10.

Pratt, D. (2004, 9 February). 'Extras Corner'. *Rolling Stone*, 152.

Ramsey, C., and K. Wilson (1993/4). 'The Strange Object of Canada's Desire: Cronenberg Under Glass'. *POV*, 6–9.

Rhodes, C. (2000). *Outsider Art: Spontaneous Alternatives*. London: Thames and Hudson.

Ricci, N. P. (1991). 'The End/s of Woman', in A. Kroker and M. Kroker (eds), *Ideology and Power in the Age of Lenin in Ruins*. New York: Saint Martin's Press, pp. 301–17.

Roche, D. (2004). 'David Cronenberg's Having to Make the Word Be Flesh'. *Post/Script*.

Rodley, C. (1998). David Cronenberg's *Dead Ringers, The Criterion Collection Edition: David Cronenberg's Dead Ringers*. USA: Criterion Collection.

—(1999, April). 'Game Boy'. *Sight and Sound*, 9(4), 8–10.

Rodley, C. (ed.) (1997). *Cronenberg on Cronenberg* (3rd edn). London: Faber and Faber.

Rose, J. (2004). *On Not Being Able to Sleep: Psychoanalysis and the Modern World*. London: Vintage.

Sade, Marquis de (1987). *The 120 Days of Sodom and Other Writings*. New York: Grove Press. First published 1904.

Sanjek, D. (1996). 'Dr. Hobbes's Parasites: Victims, Victimization, and Gender in David Cronenberg's *Shivers*'. *Cinema Journal*, 36(1), 55–74.

Sargeant, J. (2001). *The Baying of Pigs: Reflections on the New American Horror Movie*. Retrieved 23 March 2006 from http://archive.sensesofcinema.com/contents/festivals/01/15/biff_nightmare.html.

Scheib, R. (1993). *Rabid*. Retrieved 27 March 2006 from http://www.moria.co.nz/horror/rabid.htm.

—(1999). *Scanners*. Retrieved 27 March 2006 from http://www.moria.co.nz/sf/scanners.htm.

Schwartz, V. R. (1995). 'Cinematic Spectatorship Before the Apparatus: The Public Taste for Reality in Fin-de-Siècle Paris', in L. Williams (ed.), *Viewing Positions: Ways of Seeing Film*. New Brunswick, NJ: Rutgers University Press, pp. 87–113.

Shaviro, S. (1993). *The Cinematic Body* (vol. 2). Minneapolis: University of Minnesota Press.

Shaw, D. (1996). 'Psychological Determinism in *Dead Ringers*'. *Film and Philosophy*, III, Winter.

Silverman, K. (1988). *The Acoustic Mirror: The Female Voice in Psychoanalysis and Cinema*. Bloomington: Indiana University Press.

Simon, A. (2001). 'The Existential Deal: An Interview with David Cronenberg'. *Critical Quarterly*, 43(3), 34–56.

Sirius, R. U. (1997). 'Sex Machine: David Cronenberg'. *Wired*, 184–5.

Smith, M. (2006). *The Work of Emotion: Ballard and the Death of Affect*. Retrieved 18 April, 2011 from http://www.jgballard.ca/criticism/death_of_affect.html.

Sontag, S. (2002). 'Illness as Metaphor', in *Illness as Metaphor and AIDS and Its Metaphors* (2nd edn). London: Penguin, pp. 1–87.

Stallybrass, P., and A. White (1986) *The Politics and Poetics of Transgression*. Ithaca: Cornell University Press.

Stam, R., R. Burgoyne and S. Flitterman-Lewis (1992). *New Vocabularies in Film Semiotics: Structuralism, Post-Structuralism and Beyond*. London: Routledge.

Strick, P. (1984, Spring). 'Uneasy Lies the Head: *Christine* and *The Dead Zone*'. *Sight and Sound*, 150.

Testa, B. (1995, Fall). 'Technology's Body: Cronenberg, Genre, and the Canadian Ethos'. *Post/Script*.

Theweleit, K. (1989). *Male Fantasies* (vol. 2). *Male Bodies: Psychoanalyzing the White Terror* (E. Carter, C. Turner and S. Conway, trans). Minneapolis: University of Minnesota Press.

Travers, P. (1993, 28 October). 'Sexual Butterflies'. *Rolling Stone*.

Turner, S. (2007). 'The Public Intellectual Is a Dog', in L. Simmons (ed.), *Speaking Truth to Power: Public Intellectuals Rethink New Zealand*. Auckland: Auckland University Press, pp. 85–101.

Vale, V., and A. Juno (eds) (1984). *J. G. Ballard.* San Francisco: Re/Search. Originally published as special editions of *Re/Search* 8 and 9.

Vatnsdal, C. (2004). *They Came from Within: A History of Canadian Horror Cinema.* Winnipeg: Arbeiter Ring.

Vernucci, A. (2006). *A History of Violence.* Retrieved 10 April 2011 from http://replay.waybackmachine.org/20070702094010/http://www.hour.ca/film/movie.aspx?iIDFilm=8012.

Wagner, J., and V. Locke (1997). *A History of Violence.* New York: Vertigo.

Westcott, B. (2006). *A History of Violence.* Retrieved 3 March 2007.

Wieczorek, M. (2000). 'The Ridiculous, Sublime Art of Slavoj Žižek', in M. A. E. Dementi (ed.), *The Art of the Ridiculous Sublime: On David Lynch's 'Lost Highway'.* Seattle: Walter Chapin Simpson Centre for the Humanities.

Wilson, S.A. (2001). 'Wounds, Vents, Openings: Resistance to Subject Formation Within the Twin Texts of "Crash"' (unpublished masters thesis, University of Auckland [NZ]).

Wilson, S. (2006). *A History of Violence.* Retrieved 3 March 2007 from http://hoopla.nu/films/ahistoryofviolence/ahistoryofviolence.html.

Yates, J. (2007). Call for Papers: The DAVID CRONENBERG Area. Retrieved 11 April 2011 from http://h-net.msu.edu/cgi-bin/logbrowse.pl?trx=vx&list=H-Amstdy&month=0706&week=b&msg=3hC8tGY0iX0MT%2BaRtCusBQ&user=&pw=.

Young, S. S.-F. (2002). 'Forget Baudrillard: The Horrors of "Pleasure" and the Pleasures of "Horror" in David Cronenberg's *Videodrome*', in E. P. Walz (ed.), *Canada's Best Features: Critical Essays on 15 Canadian Films.* Amsterdam and New York: Rodopi, pp. 146–72.

Žižek, S. (1992). *Looking Awry: An Introduction to Jacques Lacan Through Popular Culture.* Cambridge, MA: MIT Press.

—(1994). *The Metastases of Enjoyment: On Women and Causality.* London and New York: Verso.

—(2000a). *The Art of the Ridiculous Sublime: On David Lynch's 'Lost Highway'.* Seattle: Walter Chapin Simpson Centre for the Humanities.

—(2000b). *The Fragile Absolute – or, Why Is the Christian Legacy Worth Fighting For?* London and New York: Verso.

—(2001a). *Enjoy Your Symptom! Jacques Lacan in Hollywood and Out* (rev. 2nd edn). New York and London: Routledge.

—(2001b). *The Fright of Real Tears: Krzystof Kieslowski Between Theory and Post-Theory.* London: British Film Institute.

—(2001c). *On Belief.* London and New York: Routledge.

—(2006). 'Why Are Laibach and the *Neue Slowenische Kunst* not Fascists?' In R. Butler and S. Stephens (eds), *The Universal Exception: Selected Writings* (vol. 2). London and New York: Continuum.

Index